The Techniques of

Master Gem Polishing

A Comprehensive Overview of the Techniques, Tools and
Knowledge Required to Apply a Fine Polish on
All Types of Gemstones

By Gerald L. Wykoff CSM GG

Adamas Publishers
PO Box 1991
York, PA 17405

© 1994 Gerald L. Wykoff CSM GG

ALL RIGHTS RESERVED. PRINTED IN THE UNITED STATES OF AMERICA. NO PART OF THIS BOOK MAY BE REPRODUCED, STORED IN A RETRIEVAL SYSTEM OR TRANSMITTED, IN ANY FORM OR BY ANY MEANS, ELECTRONIC, MECHANICAL, OR BY PHOTO COPYING, RECORDING, OR OTHERWISE, WITHOUT THE PRIOR WRITTEN PERMISSION OF THE COPYRIGHT HOLDER.

Library of Congress, Cataloging-in-Publication Data

Wykoff, Gerald. 1930—
A comprehensive overview of the techniques, tools and knowledge required to apply a fine polish on all types of gemstones
p. 320 cm. 23x15
Bibliogrphy p.
Appendix
Includes index.
ISBN   Library of Congress Catalog Card Number:
0-9607892-9-4   93-74975
TT212.W95   1994
739.1274—dc20 $24.50

Introduction

Of all the craft challenges in lapidary, polishing remains the most vexing—albeit the most rewarding.

There are few project completing steps in any craft that can quite compare with the excitement and sense of inspired satisfaction prompted by a beautiful gemstone brought to its ultimate conclusion...a brilliant, well executed polish. It is not too surprising given its enormous importance, therefore, that this critical area of lapidary finds itself entangled in such a vast web of fact mixed with fiction.

For years, gemcutters labored under the mistaken impression that a theory based on a mysterious Beilby Layer explained why the surface of a gemstone abruptly assumed a smooth, glassy layer—presumably different from the rest of the mineral specimen—which reflected light so brilliantly. Later, so-called fact finders decided that a Scratch Theory, based on finer and finer particles of diamond grit, better explained the phenomenon. It explained a gem polish as scratches so fine and closely arranged that the human eye could no longer distinguish between them, hence a bright polish.

Inventors of these theories and supportive scientists claimed they had discovered "evidence" of the validity of these ideas. Today, we know better and both the Beilby Layer and Scratch Theories are in disrepute. Of course, polishing hasn't suffered. We pretty much know how to polish gems. That isn't the problem as this book reveals. We just don't yet have an acceptable answer of the "...how and the why..." and into the vacuum rush pulverization, burnishing, nanotribology, planing and a host of other suggestions. As for myself, I believe polish results from a covalent electrochemical process and am well on the way to proving it—if seventeen consecutive failures count for anything.

In the meantime, gemcutters are left, regardless of theory or proof, with the excitement of bringing gems to their most brilliant best... even if they don't quite understand what causes such magnificence. That's what this book is about: the practical aspects of polishing gems...and the hows and whys can come later...if ever.

—Gerald L. Wykoff CSM GG

TABLE OF CONTENTS

Gem Polishing Theory

An Overview of Gemstone Polishing 1
    cabochon polishing 1
    carving polishing 1
    faceter polishing 1
Thickness and Polish Ease 25
Almost All Laps Are Different 26
Amount of Polish Critical 41
Applying Polish 42
Polish Condition Theory 50
    the polishing act 60
Details on Gem Polishing Theory 63
    understanding polishes 64
    selection of polishes 66
    selection of proper carriers for polishing 68
    polishing felts are aggressive 70
Growing Trend In Polishing Practice 78
More Details On Flat Facets 82
Contemporary Polishing Theory 85
How to Interpret Polishing Imperfections 91
Understanding Luster 122
Understanding Polishing Marks 126
Glass Polishing Practice 151
    the how and why of polishing gems 151
    shaping comes first 152
    theories alike 153
    Carborundrum grinds faster 153
The Quality Of Reflectivity
    sheen is different 174
    what is the polishing relationship 175
    reflectance percentage table (*also listed in Tables*) 176
New Polishing Theory 235
New Theory on Mixing Polishing Powders 295

Polishes and Carriers

Cloth Type Polish Carriers 7
Polishing Criteria 9
Powder Or Paste 10
The Correct Polish Amount 12
Colloidal Polish 13
Wax Polishing Lappers 17
    for large slabs 18

wax lap for faceters	18
Colloidal Silica	23-83
Pellon Laps For Cabbers	28
Polish Paste Can Boost Polishing Ease	83
Colloidal Silica: An Outstanding Polish	104
Rouge Is Most Satisfactory	156
Making Up Effective Polishing Combinations	159
A Tip On Polishing	196
The 14,000 Lap	278
overlay laps	282

Polishing Techniques

To Score Or Not To Score	15
Using Thin Film Coated Polishing Disks	22
Managing Your Laps	27
Working With Acetate Films	29
Using Resin To Control Edges	38
Using The Right Lap	41
Lap Scoring Technique	47
Avoiding Orange Peel Effect	54
Polish Preparations	56
Some Polishing Principles	57
Techniques On Use Of Felt Buff	70
Develop Pressure Skills	72
Avoid Area Surface Touchups	104
Techniques On Using Colloidal Silica (CS) Polish	109
Additional Techniques With CS	111
Handling Pesky Polishing Problems	125
Dedicated Polishing Pads A Good Strategy	129
Methods For Managing Repeatability Problems	130
partial polish	131
Hand Lapping Skills	141
middle of flat polish problem	141
Equipment Needed For Hand Lapping	142
Polishing Extremely Thin Sections	161
Managing Light Is Vital To Good Polish	162
lighting is important	163
reflection important, too	165
magnifier use	166
options for improving sight	167
Techniques On Using Thin Polishing Films	221
available with adhesive back	226
must be handled cautiously	227
make your own thin laps	229
notes on edge rounding	230
options on using thin film polishers	231
an adhesion factor	231
applying wax to film	233

Polishing Thin Slabs 202
Proper Illumination 283
      shadowing technique 287

Self-making Equipment
Make Your Own Buffing Wheels 19
Make Your Own Diamond Paste 34
      diamond-olive oil solution 34
      special olive oil paste for diamond 34
      make your own olive oil paste 34
Pie Pan As A Polishing Bowl 71
Making Your Own Mini Wheels 75
      mini wheels for fantasy cutting 76
      shape buttons into profile 76
How To Make A Polariscope 96
Making Your Own Diamond Polishing Laps 100
You Can Make Your Own Copper Polishing Lap 137
      making polishing strips, too 139
      fine grits can be embedded with finger charging 139
Another Method To Make Your Own Diamond Polishing Paste 146
Thin Metal Polishing Films 266
      turning to metal 267
      why copper polishing films are superior 270
      options with metal film disks 271
      olive oil as adhesive 272
      applying wax to polishing surface 273

Stones
Stones That Are Difficult To Polish 15
      cabochons 16
      faceted 16
Stay Wet And Cool When Polishing Opal 71
The Way Top Polish Turquoise 73
Polishing The Feldspar 74
Tips On Corundum Polishing 149
      more on polishing corundum 149
Polishing Sapphire Cabochons 169
Polishing Rhodonite And Jade 169
Professional Secret For Polishing Jade 195
      polishing tips on jade 52
      polishing jade isn't that tough 90

Special Polishing Procedures
Polishing Extremely Thin Sections 39
      for curved surfaces 43
Making a Low pH Lubricant 69
Advanced Tips on Ceramic Lap Use 250
      opinions on coolant-lubricant liquids 251

finer prepolishing helpful? 252
Polishing With Wood Wheels 252

General

Cliff Jackson's Wax Lap 95
Potpourri on Polishing 96
Good Use For Ceramic Lap 146
Using Casting Resin to Control Edges 160
The Impact of Frictional Heat 170
Enhancing Tigereye 188
    heat treating tigereye 189
    bleaching tigereye 191
    heat treating bleached tigereye 194
    dyeing bleached tigereye 194
What About High Production Rates 207
    cuts six preforms 208
    make your own sander-polisher lap 210
Crystallographic Information 236
A Matter Of Safety 247
    cadmium is a problem, too 248
    safety using acids 249
Summary Of Polishing Problems 254
Wax Coating of Polishing Surfaces 273

Equipment and Tools

Special Polishing Laps 44
    Dyna laps 45
    Leeco Hypno Scored Lap 45
    pelletized laps 47
Willems Hollowed Out Cab Polishing Wheel 108
Superglue to Avoid Edge Rounding 134
    CA forms crust 136
Wire Diamond Polishing Tools 140
The Mehanite Lap 158
Phonograph Records Make Effective Polishing Laps 214
    place over prepolish disk 214
You Can Make Your Own Mirror 215
    mirror's best use 216
    equipment needed 218
    mirror technique for facet location 218
    cause of discrepancies 220
    polishing 221
Making Special Polishing Tools 253

Tables, Lists, Charts

Gemstone Specifications List 112
    major gemstone species and varieties 114
    transparent gemstones (for faceting) 116
    stones that require special care 116
    gemstones that are hard and durable 116
    fine grained, textured gemstones (for cabochons) 118
    stones that are difficult to polish 119
    stones with granular texture, coarse or uneven grain 120
    gemstones that polish swiftly with CS 121
    gemstones that polish well with colloidal oxide polish pastes... 121
Mohs Hardness Scale 154
Reflectivity Percentages Table 176
Recommended Polishes for Use with Various Gemstones.................... 178
    tin oxide 178
    chrome oxide 178
    aluminum oxide 179
    cerium oxide 179
    diamond 180
    tripoli 180
Comprehensive List of Buffs, Laps and Polishes
    cabochons 181
    faceting 183
Unique Characteristics of Polish Carriers 185
Polishing Combinations 236
Lap Materials Table 277
Lighting Method Table 293
Definitions for Lighting Terms 294

Appendix

Appendix 1 295
1—list of useful lapidary suppliers 295
2—rough gemstone supplies 296
3—general purpose lapidary supplies 296
4—Australian opal mines 297
5—cabochon equipment 297
6—gemcutting information 297
7—laps, wheels 297

Appendix 2 298
Descriptions of Materials Used in Polishing Gemstones............... 298-303

Appendix 3 303
Avoirdupois and Troy Weight Chart 303
Bibliography 305
Index 307

An Overview of Gemstone Polishing

The art—and the subjective considerations involved make it just that—of gemstone polishing represents the area that poses a true test of a gemcutter's skills.

It's the final step from a fashioned shape to a beautifully finished gemstone. If all the previous challenges involved in the grinding and sanding of the stone are performed properly, then the polishing phase should proceed smoothly. As any gemcutter knows, "if" is an immense prerequisite. Not only must the preceding operations be conducted properly and well, but the gemcutter faces a sometimes bewildering array of laps, wheels, polishes, conditions, etc. to assure that the polishing phase responds to the gemstone's needs.

Cabochon Polishing...

For the cabochon cutter, the options are wide but manageable. Cabbers usually don't encounter the task of flat-to-flat matches and repeatability challenges with which a faceter must constantly contend. Nor do most cabs pose uncommonly difficult angles, recesses, and complex surface plans that a carver or sculptor faces.

A cabber often deals primarily with either a rounded polishing surface from a wheel or a flat surface such as from a pad. The polishing carrier materials involve felt, leather, plastic, canvas, wood, metal and various types of cloth buffs. Most of these polishing carriers accommodate oxide chemical polishes as well as fine diamond with equal proficiency.

When a rounded cabochon top is involved, cabbers will often stretch a piece of leather or cloth over a bowl-like holder. This produces a certain amount of "give" in the polishing material which imparts an even, disciplined polish over the rounded stone surface. In any event, cabochon materials are often selected so the rounded mineral may be pushed or pressed into the polishing surface to achieve the same action ...even if the "rounding" is a bit more limited than with the bowl type polisher.

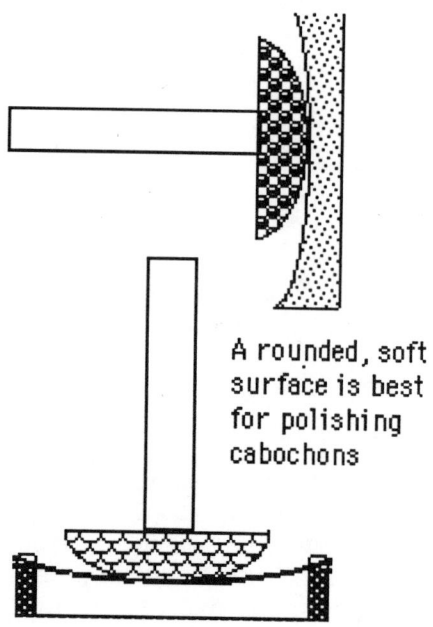

A rounded, soft surface is best for polishing cabochons

Carving Polishing...

For the carver—and the same principles pretty much hold true with the new fantasy type cuts—an approach similar to the cabochon cutter's is applicable.

Where the carver's challenge differs from the standard gem-cutting regimen lies in the need to polish small complex areas.

For this reason, a carver will opt for a wide variety of polishing tools and materials with which to carry the polish. Carvers often use small diamond polishing tools. Other polishers range from whittled wooden points to small felt or silicone wheels suitable for use with a Foredom or similar hand tool.

The edge of a hard felt pad or wheel also sometimes find considerable use as a polishing agent for carvings and sculpted work.

Faceter Polishing....

For the faceter, polishing technology offers a wide selection of materials. The first challenge that a faceter must overcome is selection of the most suitable lap for use on a specific type gem crystal.

In gemcutting, the general rule has always been: for harder

Master Gem Polishing

stones use a a harder polishing surface, and use softer polishing surfaces for softer stones.

More decision are involved concerning the type of polishing lap to use than just selection on the basis of appropriate hardness.

Here are some of those additional areas that must be considered in every faceting polish challenge:

- ◆ smooth surface—is the lap true running?
- ◆ porosity — do loose polishing grains have reservoirs or pockets to nest in so as to perform the best polishing job?
- ◆ hard surface — the stone preferably rides on a polishing medium, not on the lap. Is the lap surface hard enough to resist pressure and keep a layer of polish between it and the facet?
- ◆ flat surface — is the polishing surface flat? If not, you may have edge rounding, scratching or other problems.
- ◆ rpm speed — what is the best speed to maximize results between stone, polishing compound, and lap?
- ◆ retention capability — can the lap surface hold or retain the polish? This is especially important when using high viscosity or water soluble polishing materials.
- ◆ scratch potential—how likely are scratches to occur when using a particular type of lap? For example, ceramic tends to scratch softer stones which can be polished without scratches on copper or Lucite laps. Pelletized resin laps scratch very little, especially when used with oxide chemical polishing compounds.

The lap selection includes:

Ceramic —made of alumina oxide, the ceramic lap is the hardest lap in lapidary. Originally produced for the computer industry, the hard disks represent a conversion—especially so that they will contain some degree of surface porosity—for use in lapidary.

Mehanite (cast iron)—Mehanite is a registered trade name owned by General Electric. Like the ceramic lap, a Mehanite cast iron lap features desirable porosity and is flat and hard.

Type Metal—high in the scale of hardness, type metal is seldom used alone for lap making. Some gemcutters who pour their own laps often use pure type metal and these laps are quite responsive for middle range Mohs stones. Type metal, for the most part, finds most lap use as a combination with tin.

Tin—tin metal laps are next in the scale of hardness and are viewed by many faceters as the best all-around polishing lap. Used with chemical oxide polishes, they can be expected to impart an acceptable commercial polish with a minimum of fuss and difficulty.

Tin-Lead —slightly softer than a pure tin lap, the tin-lead lap was popularized by the late Henry B. Graves, founder of the Graves Company. He saw a tin-lead lap as the near universal lap when used with Linde A (alumina) polish. Although alumina works superbly in combination with tin/lead, lead is sometimes used alone. In recent years, the popularity of lead has dropped off because of its reputation as a carcinogenic.

Master Gem Polishing

Pelletized Resin Bonded Laps —best realized in Crystalite's Fast Lap or Raytech's Last Lap, these hard, tough, durable laps produce excellent polishing results. They are made by saturating an epoxy or polyurethane resin with metal pellets. Many gemcutters contend that pelletized resin bonded laps scratch much less than any

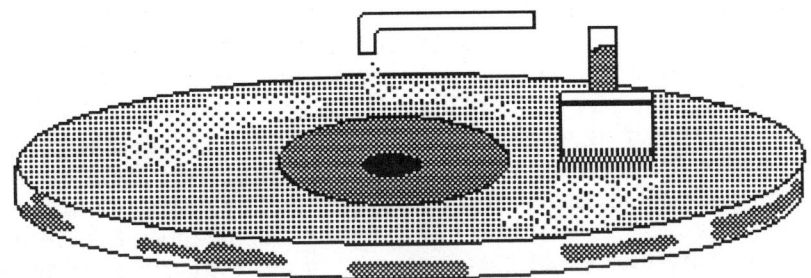

To place water, you can (1) use a brush; (2) turn on a drip control, and (3) apply with your fingers.

other type and are suitable for both diamond and oxide polishes.

Plastic —a number of plastic resins are used in producing plastic laps. They include phenolics, vinyl, epoxies, polyurethanes as well as Lucite and Plexiglass. Softer than metal or ceramic laps, plastic laps offer a microscopic amount of surface "give" so the facet may sink into the surface slightly. Old phonographic records also (grooves = scoring) make useful soft polishing laps for soft stones.

Some gemcutters criticize plastic laps, claiming they eventually age from water absorption and their softness encourages facet edge rounding or corner smothering. Others say such rounding is merely the result of excessive polishing or pressure. After extended use, plastic laps do tend to glaze over. This glazing can easily be removed by rubbing with a silicon carbide stone.

Mylar—Mylar (polyester film) is quite soft but encompasses its own category because of its uniqueness as a diamond and chemi-

Master Gem Polishing

cal oxide polish carrier. The techniques for coating diamond or metallic oxide abrasives on Mylar best known as Ultralap™ was developed originally by C. Allen Lindquist of Easton, PA, for the Phizer Company and is used primarily for the magnetic tape industry. Such thin laps are also useful as gemstone polishers—and their slight but uniform thickness helps reduce repeatability problems. Many gemcutters buy 6" diameter film laps or simply scissor out disks from coated square sheets, slip them over 6" or 8" prepolishing laps, apply a boost of diamond paste or colloidal polish to accelerate polishing, and use this one-lap setup for prepolish and polish. Thin acetate and vinyl film disks can also be prepared and used the same way.

    The best way to "boost" an Ultralap™ with colloidal paste consists in smearing a few dots of polish on the coated surface and then let dry. When it's time to polish, first spritz very lightly with vinegar and polish...no additional lubricant. The polish should come up very rapidly but keep in mind that these laps can kink or fold easily: A bit too much of careless pressure or working too near the pe-

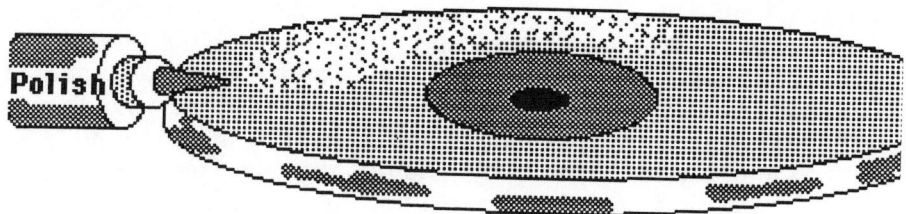

A small pinch or accordion bottle is very useful for dispensing a controlled amount of diamond-olive oil mix or metallic oxide polish paste on a turning lap. It's a good idea to have several such bottles, each with its own type.

riphery of the lap—and you may have a quick, expensive disaster. The lap jumps up, kinks or folds and is ruined for further use.

Thin Metal Films—Because commercial diamond coated Mylar films have proved so expensive and treacherously short lived, many gemcutters are turning to thin metal polishing films, especially copper and phosphor bronze. Copper's attraction lies in its hardness (3 Mohs for copper compared to 1.6 Mohs for Mylar) and its affinity for diamonds. When diamonds are rubbed over a copper surface, the metal quickly works hardens around the mineral, holding it firmly in place. As for Naval bronze, it is highly porous and these tiny reservoirs provide ready "seating places" for diamond particles so the latter may function so much better.

Not only can copper and bronze films—as well as tin, brass, steel and Titanium—be obtained in 3mil and 4mil thickness, the metal is easy to cut and charge with diamond or metallic oxide polishes. It's big benefit, though, lies in cost effectiveness. Commercial diamond coated Mylar disks cost $20-$30 each and it's a hefty loss when one kinks, folds or creases: it is ruined. A metal film can also suffer these damages—but you can iron them out and reuse them. Indeed, you can often repair a metal film disk by placing it between the pages of a thick book for a few days.

Cloth Type Polish Carriers...

In the category of cloth-type polishing surfaces, canvas, muslin, felt and leather should be included. Tightly woven canvas is a ready carrier for diamond paste polishes. For this reason it is often sold with an adhesive backing for attachment to a more firm master plate. Leather, too, generally requires a backing, either firm or sponge, and is used where felt may be considered too aggressive.

Felt—Yes, felt can be considered a cloth type polishing material. It's extensive and effective use as a separate material, especially for cabochons and carved work, deserves separate consideration. It will impart a fine polish on most gemstone materials but gemcutters should remain wary of its readiness to undercut as well as the expected tendency to round off edges quickly. For good reason, felt remains a polishing mainstay for cabochon cutters

Pellon—Pellon is a well known, albeit somewhat controversial, cloth-type polishing lap material . Lapidaries want to use the hard almost plastic like Pellon, not the softer cloth material that is

Master Gem Polishing

virtually useless. The soft surface can still contribute to edge rounding problems for gemcutters, particularly faceters. As a table polishing agent or a cabbing pad, it is effective because it retains high viscosity type polishes including the new colloidal silica. For this reason, many cabbers are turning to Pellon.

W*ood* —as a soft material that offers sufficient surface hardness, wood makes a useful polishing carrier. Harder wood is recommended for lapidary use. It should be soaked in molten wax to inhibit later water absorption. Most contemporary wood polishing is done on motor driven maple wood spools or star cutting devices

W*ax* —for exceptionally soft materials, wax is very often the polishing carrier of choice. Most gemcutters prefer to make their own wax laps, even using an old 45 or 78 rpm viny phonograph record in place of wax. The record can be very effective because the vinyl is sufficiently soft plus the narrow sound grooves provide outstanding ready made scoring lines which foster quick removal of debris. See page 17 for wax lappers.

A cabber uses considerable pressure when polishing on a diamond pad, a principle that's especially important when polishing jadeite or nephirte. Both jade types respond to speed, heat and pressure.

Master Gem Polishing

Polishing Criteria...

Earlier, it was suggested that polishing is more of an art than a mechanical process. When one considers all the subjective aspects that are involved in polishing a gemstone, art does seem an apt definition. These various aspects include hand pressure, position on the polishing lap, lap speed, lap type and surface condition, polish type and consistency, and stroke.

It is no great secret that some gem minerals can be polished with few problems while others pose the most vexing challenges. The crystals themselves with their peculiar grains, optical and mechanical properties, crystal structures and rough conditions demand ever changing profiles of talent, skill, patience and determination.

Also, polishing with diamond grit is far different than polishing with oxide chemicals. For one thing, much less pressure can be exerted with diamond grit. Heavy pressure is one thing. Excessive pressure is like asking for scratches to appear because the stone is forced down through the diamond grit onto the lap surface. If any oversized random diamond particles are available for rolling, they will tend to tear at and abrade the mineral's surface.

Use a relatively light stroke when polishing with diamond. **Note:** *The above admonition should be avoided when polishing jadeite or nephrite on a diamond Crystal pad: here you use plenty of pressure and don't worry about the heat.*

Diamond grit exerts both a burnishing action and a pulverizing action on a crystal surface that's being polishing. If you bear down, especially if you're using a relatively hard surface wheel or lap, you'll shift away from the smoothing action into a grinding mode—and that you may not want. With metal oxide polishes, you seek a damp-dry condition of the polish on the lap/wheel combined with modest pressure. Most experienced gemcutters also use a moderate lap speed when polishing with metal oxides.

It has been suggested, especially by Phil Bean of Seattle, WA, who invented the Fac-Ette faceting machine, that burnishing is the culprit that encourages heat. The heat, Phil contends, is a vital necessity in getting the surface of a material to "flow" in order to produce a polish. This reaffirmation of the debunked Beilby Layer theory may or may not be true, but there is strong evidence to show that some burnishing contributes to the polishing action.

Master Gem Polishing

Powder or Paste...

The question of whether to use a powder or colloidal paste in gemstone polishing involves a bit of word trickery.

Dry powders as such aren't used all that much in lapidary. A liquid to act both as coolant and lubricant will usually be added to any diamond grit or metal oxide polish. In traditional diamond polishing, the diamond particles are mixed with an special carrier even though some of the combinations represent the diamond cutter's own special secret mixture.

The same holds true with metal oxide powders. Used dry, they can scratch as readily as dry diamond particles. What each gem cutter seeks normally is a unique damp-dry texture. Water is most often the coolant-lubricant in colored stone cutting, applied with a drip control with a spray bottle or with your fingers.

What causes considerable difficulty among gemcutters arises from the failure to achieve a proper damp-dry condition. If the mixture becomes wetted too much, polishing action is inhibited. If too dry, scratching is a likely possibility. Obviously, the solution to effective polishing lies in achieving just the right amount of dampness. Some gemcutters, intermittently spritz the lap or wheel with a bit of

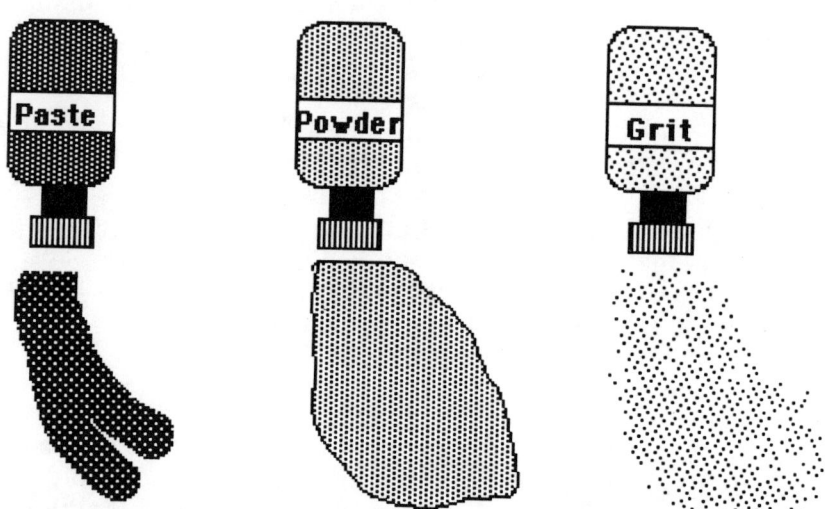

A paste is pre-wetted while powder must have water added to be effective. Grits or loose powders utilize coolants, too, but tend to roll more on polishing surfaces.

vinegar to achieve a gentle dampness—and, of course, to lower the pH which encourages more effective polishing action.

On a horizontal lap, some gemcutters run their drip system while others employ a brush or sponge or even finger application. A finger dipped in water then touched on a mound of metal oxide powder will lift enough polish for immediate transfer to a damp lap. It takes a few intermittent fingertips worth of water with no powder to keep the lap constantly wet. The foregoing is a simple but effective approach for many gemcutters who have worked out their own system with considerable consistency and effect.

Still, a system involving powder in just about any stage of the operation can be unacceptably dirty. Because too many faceters object to the messiness in common polish application, the American Society of Gemcutters in 1991 performed the necessary R&D to develop colloidal polishes.

Many gemcutters control the consistency of chemical oxide polish pastes by dipping their fingers into a water supply and using wet finger tips to pick up a small supply of polishing powder.

Colloidal is a chemical term that refers to the suspension of finely divided particles *e.g.*, metal oxide polish, into a continuous medium like a jelly or glue. By adding a surfactant and other harmless water thickening chemicals, ASG was able to produce tin oxide, aluminum oxide, cerium oxide and chrome oxide in colloidal form. Ownership of the polishes were subsequently turned over to Rick Ford, who operates mAgi, Box 426, Beavercreek, OR, 97004. Ford promptly refined the formulae even further and began formal marketing.

As presently constituted, these polishes exist in a liquid-like form, ready-to-use without water. Furthermore, the powder particles will not settle to the bottom but rather remain in suspension in the liquid water carrier. mAgi now recommends that a bit of vinegar or diluted muriatic acid be added to the wet polish—and the results are rather exceptional. What this means to gemcutters is that they have permanent suspension of polishes transformed into liquid form, ca-

Master Gem Polishing

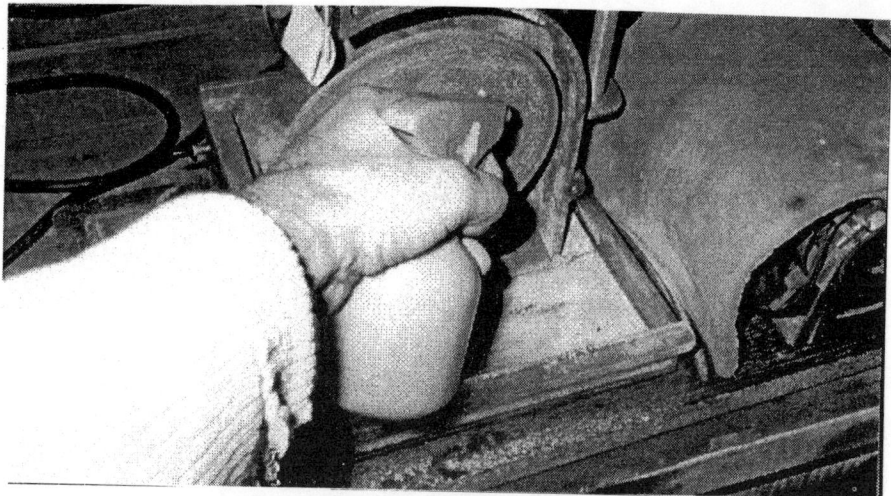

Colloidal silica is convenient to apply. Because of its high alkalinity, it's probably best to apply it to a wheel or lap with a squeeze or trigger bottle.

pable of accommodating an acid "boost," and ready for immediate use with the ultimate goal of establishing and maintaining the desired "nearly dry" polishing condition.

Because the polishes are in a thick watery paste form, they can be applied through the nozzle of the containers or with a finger tip. As a result, the polish dispensing phase is clean, quick and predictable . . . with a minimum of contamination difficulties.

The Correct Polish Amount...

In lapidary polishing, the accepted rule is: less is best. The first mistake that a beginner will invariably make involves applying too much polish to a pad, wheel or lap. A polishing surface should be kept barely wet with a thin polish slurry. During those moments when the polish is just about ready to "dry out" the chemical polishing action will usually be at its maximum.

Not surprisingly, the same "less is best" also rule holds for diamond polishing.

Among experienced faceters, it is common to clean a ceramic or Meehanite lap, apply a couple of 2-second long spritzes of diamond spray—and then wipe off the surface of the lap with a clean tissue.

Why do they wipe the lap off with a tissue? The answer is: they want to remove excess diamonds particles. The fewer diamond particles on the lap the better the polishing action.

When using metal oxide polishes or diamond grit, keep the "less is best" rule firmly in mind for faceting and cabbing. If you think there's about the right amount, chances are you may have too much. Thin slurry means: you should be able to look through a metal oxide polish slurry and see wide expanses of the carrier itself.

Note: *If you're using a bit of vinegar (ascetic acid) or diluted oxalic or muriatic acid with the polish (and this is highly recommended with all metal polishing laps) you need not worry about the stone riding on the lap itself. The acid sets up a thin oxide film on the metal and it's this additional polish encouraging agent that accelerates a fast polishing action. That's why acid is often added to polish—both diamond and particularly metal oxides.*

Colloidal Silica...

Throughout this book you will see a number of references to the utilization of colloidal silica as a gem polishing agent.

Colloidal silica is a highly viscous liquid that is mildly caustic (with a pH about that of Fels Naphtha Soap). It has been used for years in the computer and electronic industry to polish silicon wafers. Colloidal silica's introduction to lapidary came from faceter Clint Fruitman, residing in Tucson, AZ, and doing mineralogical graduate studies at the University of Arizona. He observed the chemical's extraordinary and swift ability to polish gem crystals, including hard corundum. ASG conducted a series of studies to pave the way for colloidal silica and it has become popular with many gemcutters of all disciplines. It's advantages are speed and ease.

The drawbacks are mostly due to its high viscosity and cost and to it's constant effort to crystallize upon contact with the air. The chemical is thinner than plain water so not much centrifugal force is required to sling it away—and colloidal silica is too expensive for that.

When it appears that the CS on the lap or wheel is crystallizing, give it a quick vinegar spritz. This will re-invigorate the polish. If CS becomes dry on the lap, it will often scratch.

Master Gem Polishing

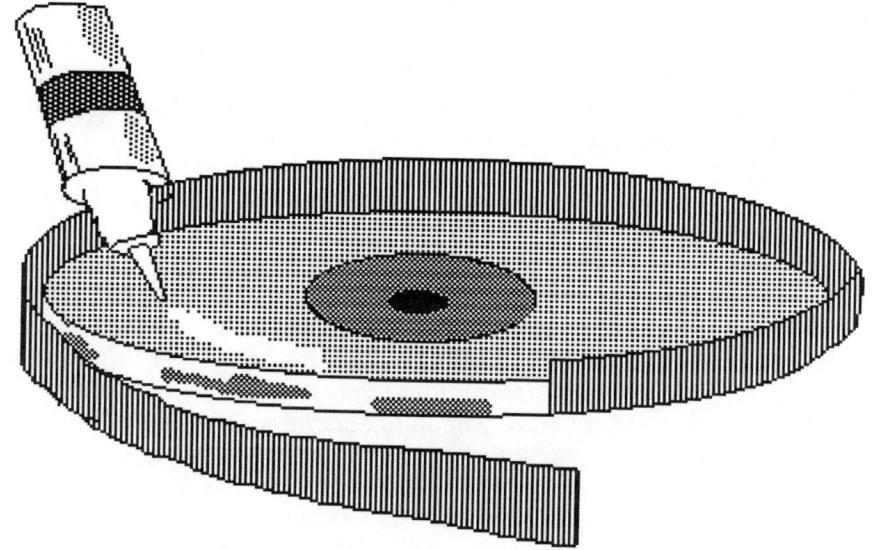

Colloidal silica poses a few more problems to work with than standard polishes. Thinner than water, it slings away easily unless steps are taken to control its loss. Cloth or textured laps work well to hold the liquid and a coffer dam to keep it on the flat lap works even better.

Some of the other options that gemcutters use with CS are:
✔ use it with Pellon cloth. The colloidal silica will soak into the cloth material and remain there. Be careful about edge rounding, though, if you use Pellon for faceting.
✔ used or new Ultralaps or thin acetate (frosted side up) make good carriers. The textured surfaces provide a good "grip" on the liquid and holds it better than a high polish surface. Use only a drop or two of colloidal silica at a time.
✔ with masking tape, dam up the outer edges of a standard polishing lap so the colloidal silica can be retained.
Because of the mild caustic nature and the readiness to crystallize, always use eye protection *e.g.*, safety glasses. You'll not soon forget the pain if you get some splash in your eyes and it crystallizes. Which is what it will do!
If you get some on the skin and it crystallizes in your pores it may cause a slight itching. In both cases—eyes and skin—wash

Master Gem Polishing

it may cause a slight itching. In both cases—eyes and skin—wash with water. Use water alone on the eyes and soap and water on the skin. It's a good idea to keep a special eye-cup First Aid unit handy when using colloidal silica—or any other polishing powder.

To summarize, don't allow the above admonitions to scare you away from this remarkable polish. Used with care, CS is a magical polishing product. For expansive cab surfaces or other large flats or for faceters who elect to cut and polish the table first (to get this often difficult faceting task out of the way at the beginning) colloidal silica can be an effective polish. It can't be all things to all gemcutters, but used with care and attention to its qualities few polishes can match it for response to virtually all gem mineral types.

To Score or Not to Score...

Scoring a lap means to use a razor blade or a section of hacksaw blade to cut a series of grooves into a lap surface. Theoretically, these grooves provide a reservoir for polish and debris. It's reasoned that the combination inhibits scratching and promotes better, faster polishing. The numerous, parallel grooves means that the full impact of hard, rolling-on-the-surface particles will be reduced so the stone's surface exposure to polish will be more uniform.

All it does, say some faceters, is provide an interruption in the lap surface and dissipate frictional forces which are vital to a burnishing action "flow" inducement. Regardless, continued testing confirms that scoring does indeed provide some values. There is less scratching on a metal lap that has been scored. As a result of scoring, a metallic oxide polish also works faster with better coverage of the lap. Some recommendations on how to score will be given later on pages 47-49.

Stones Sometimes Difficult to Polish

Regardless of your experience, gemological and lapidary knowledge and your sensitive hands, you may still expect to confront stones that will cause trouble. On the next few pages are the gem types that can be most troublesome—and which will often challenge you to extemporize your polishing strategy.

Master Gem Polishing

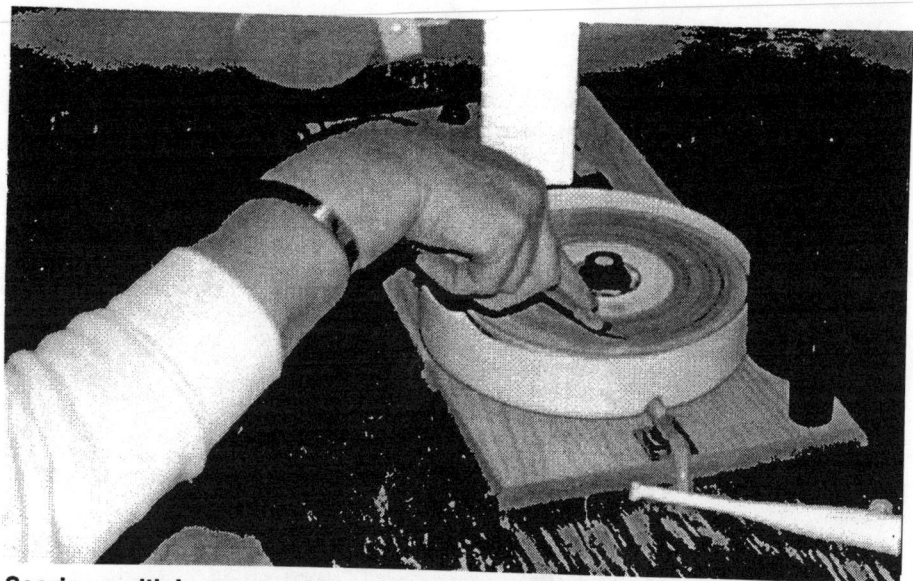

Scoring multiple grooves in a polishing lap with a razor or hacksaw blade, is a controversial tactic in gem polishing. It's supporters claim the tiny grooves in the lap surface carry away residue and inhibit aggregation.

Cabochons

Cat'e eye (unpredictable)
Cinnebar (clogs readily)
Labradorite (scales)
Nevada Opal (flakes)
Pyrite (crumbles)
Smithsonite (heat sensitive)
Malachite (undercutting)

Cassiterite (slow)
Hematite (debris)
Ledidolite (undercuts)
Ruby (spotting)
Sapphire (spotting)
Serpentine (slow)
Rhodochrosite (shock prone)

Faceted

Andalusite (orientation)
Apatite (variable)
Benitoite (unpredictable)
Cassiterite (slow polish)
Chrysoberyl (slow polish)

Alexandrite (slow, difficult)
Augelite (brittleness)
Brazilianite (edge crumbling)
Calcite (heat sensitivity)
Crocoite (heat sensitive)

Master Gem Polishing

Smithsonite (heat)
Diamond (grain direction)
Euclase (cleavage)
Hematite (slow, difficult)
Peridot (unpredictable
Ruby (patchy)
Sphalerite (cleavages)
Euclase (cleavage)
Hematite (slow, difficult)
Kunzite (cleavage)
Topaz (cleavage)
Cat'e eye (slow)
Labradorite (furrowing)
Nevada Opal (heat sensitive)
Epidote (brittleness)
Phenacite (slow)

Demantoid (impurities)
Dioptase (brittleness)
Fluorite (cleavage)
Kyanite (cleavage)
Pyrite (crumbling)
Sapphire (patchy)
Sphene (furrowing)
Fluorite (cleavage)
Hiddenite (cleavage)
Spinel (unpredictable)
Zircon (very variable)
Obsidian (heat sensitive)
Ledidolite (undercutting)
Quartz (scratching)
Diopside (scratches easily)
Scheelite (scratching)

Wax Polishing Lappers...

Every so often, a cabber encounters a polishing challenge posed by a large cabochon or agate slab. When confronted with this kind of situation, the usual alternative consists in reaching for a flat surface polisher.

That's not so easy for most cabbers. They simply don't have such a tool in their workshop inventory. The only response then is to make one—and it's often a good idea to make a wax lapper so you'll have it when needed.

For polishing relatively soft minerals, the selection of wax can be critical. The choice becomes irrelevant, though, is you choose ordinary pink casting wax which is sold is rectangular sections. You can buy a box at a time of 16 gauge wax in sheets about 3.5 inches square.

Get a base about 8-12 inches square. The base material shouldn't warp when wet *e.g.*, glass, micarta, Formica, thick plastic. Take about four squares of the wax pieces and glue them to the base with a spray-on adhesive or contact cement. Butt the edges as tightly together as possible. Work out any bubbles in the wax with a pin prick. Lay a flat weight over the wax to weight them down evenly and firmly.

Master Gem Polishing

Once the cement has set, use a V-shaped chisel or linoleum carving tool (you can buy one at an art shop) and cut a series of deep grooves in the wax about 1/2-inch apart so they form squares.

Before using, you'll want to assure flatness in the wax surface. To do this, lay a warm piece of plate glass over the wax which has been well coated with liquid detergent. Weigh the warm glass down with a brick or two for a few minutes. Then—and this is important—slide the warm glass off: don't lift it.

To polish on your new wax slab polisher, the surface of the stone must be lapped flat with a finish of 1000 or finer. Use a thick slurry of cerium oxide for most materials. Using plenty of pressure and a figure-8 motion, rub the slab the full length of the lapper.

For Large Slabs...

For truly large slabs you have to change the procedure. They're often just too big and create too much friction to be slid around by hand on the lapper.

To do big work, get a block of steel or lead of convenient size. Attach the sheet wax as before to the metal's flat face and dress the wax. Now for the different approach: you finish a large slab with the lapper placed on top of the slab.

Wax Lap For Faceters...

For faceters, wax laps are just as easy to make. Use a rounded metal or plastic base with the center hole already cut out, and attach the pink wax sheets carefully against each other so no spaces exist between them. Trim away any excess on the outer rim and cut out the center. A sharp knife or an Exacto blade will do the job nicely.

Don't groove the faceting polishing wax lap. This lap you'll want to true. The trueing task can be done with a cutting tool. Made out of a metal dop, nail or short length of $1/4$-inch round steel rod. Place the tool in the dop arm of your faceting machine, using a 45 degree adaptor so it will hold a good vertical position. With the lap spinning, use light pressure and make light machining cuts to the surface of the wax until it is perfectly true.

The above technique is the easiest way to make wax laps. You can almost as easily melt the pink wax and cast your laps to any

Master Gem Polishing

thickness you want. For the flat wax slab polisher, cut out a ring about $1/8$"-$1/4$" wide from heavy paper, or the edge of a belt. Cement this to a flat base in a centered circle. Pour in a small amount of melted wax around the rim so it first seals the corners. Then pour in the rest up to the level of the rim. Be sure the rest of the wax isn't too hot so it doesn't melt the corner seals and run out.

For pouring a faceting lap, make a paper or tape coffer dam around the periphery of the rounded base lap. Hold this in place with cement and a rubber band. Allow enough of the paper or tape to extend at least $1/8$" above the base. Plug the center hole with a wooden dowel or some rolled up paper. Use a bubble level to make certain the base lap is level. Next pour in the molten wax to the top of the paper or tape. Strip off the coffer dam material after the wax has hardened and machine the surface flat with the same tool mentioned earlier. Why is a cast or poured lap preferable? Well, a cast lap can be refaced many, many times. And wax laps of any type become disfigured rather quickly even with proper use.

Make Your Own Buffing Wheels...

Buffing wheels come in all sorts of materials...chamois, cloth,

Master Gem Polishing

muslin, felt. And they're getting more and more expensive.

You can make your own buffing wheel easily enough, too. The materials are available in any auto or hardware store at a fraction of their finished retail lapidary cost.

To make your own synthetic chamois buffer, for example, go to an auto store and buy one of the chamois towels used to dry off the family car. These towels are usually about 18x27 which is enough to trace a half dozen 6-inch circles. Using a 6-inch grinding wheel from your shop, trace six circles in the material. Be sure you trace the arbor hole dead center.

Now trace the edges of the arbor hole which will hold and support the buffing wheel. Halfway between the outer edge and the flange outer edge, draw a third circle. You can draw this circle with a compass or find a can or bottle about the right size. This circle is the stitching circle.

Important: mark two of your circles with these three rings. That will give you a guide on each side of the finished wheel.

Cut out the disks with a pair of scissors. You might find that curved-blade scissors works best for cutting the circles. If you don't have one, any scissors will work all right because after stitching, you'll trim up the outer periphery anyway.

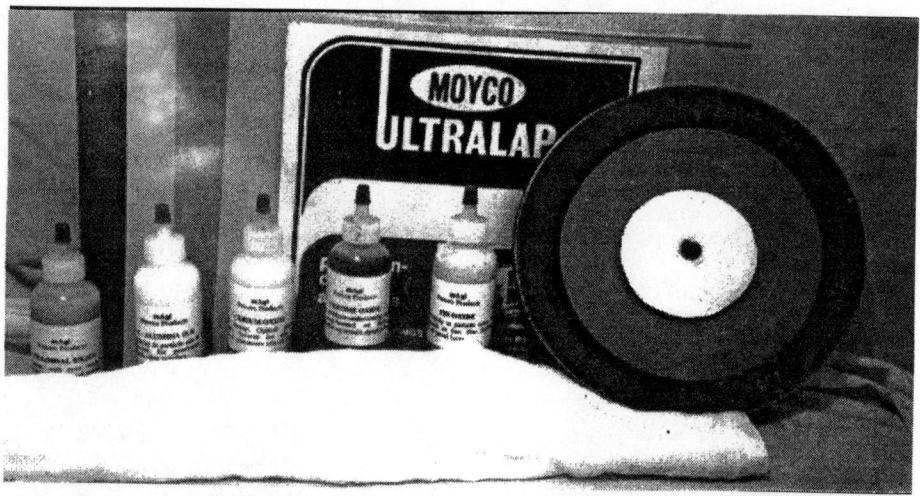

New colloidal oxide polishes, like diamond polishing products, help organize your workshop and avoid the mess often associated with polishing.

Master Gem Polishing

To cut the shaft or arbor hole, fold the material through the middle of the circle and cut out the hole paper-doll fashion. Use a canvas or strong needle for stitching the six circles together. Any strong thread will do but waxed cotton twine is best because it is strong and durable. Stack the circles together, push a wooden dowel through the arbor hole to keep everything in registration and start stitching the works together.

Note: Some buffing wheel manufacturers use rubber cement in the area covered by the flange to hold the circles together. This is a good idea and just about any good glue suitable for cloth will perform well. If you decide to add glue, do it before you begin stitching. When stitching, use a small piece of metal, a thimble or a flat file to push the needle through the thick material. Half-inch stitches will do nicely. You'll have a decidedly sore thumb if you don't use a pusher.

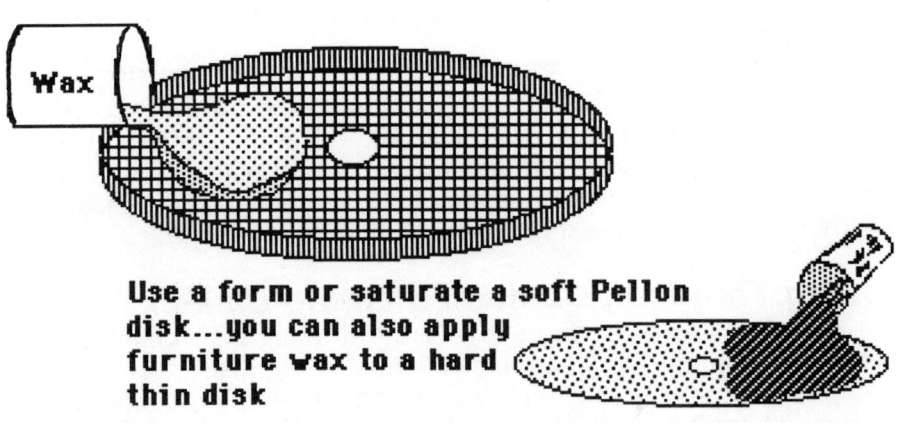

Use a form or saturate a soft Pellon disk...you can also apply furniture wax to a hard thin disk

To make a wax polishing lap, melt up Kerr carving wax and pour it into a self-made form. A canvas pad embedded in the wax near the polishing surface lends additional, important strength. As options, glue a Pellon lap to a hard surface then saturate it with either Kerr or ordinary beeswax. This makes a highly efficient wax lap because the surface can be planed flat on a flat lapping machine with a sharp edged cutting tool. Rectangular Kerr pads glue applied to a lap and then torch heated to a homogenous flow works, too.

Master Gem Polishing

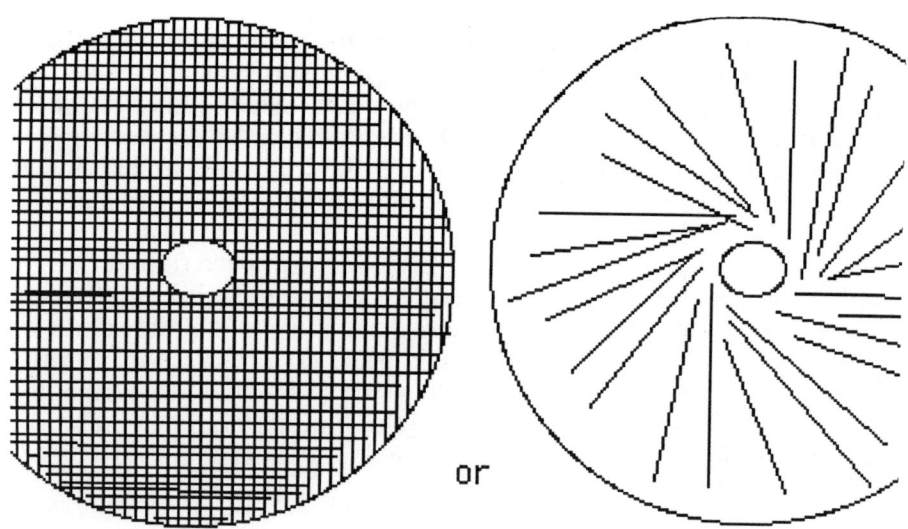

Scoring in the square mode can be a very effective for most polishing laps, especially wax laps. It takes longer to do but the results are often superior in speed and final finish.

When you've finished stitching and have tied off the end thread, slip your new buff wheel onto the arbor. Turn on the motor at slow speed and trim the outer periphery of the wheel with a file. When you've got your wheel running smoothly with no loose ends, you're ready to apply polish—and polish gemstones.

Using Thin Film Coated Polishing Disks...

More and more gemcutters are following the technology trends of paste polishes on thin coated polishing disks.

Time was when faceters solved the bulk of polishing requirements by reaching for some Linde A powder and a tin/lead lap. Since it was introduced, this combination seldom failed to produce beneficial results with nearly any type of stone...with the obvious exception of the very hard ones..

Today, though, a growing number of faceters want to avoid repeatability and cheating problems so they polish a tier of facets as soon as the tier has been pre-polished. With older polishing technologies this polishing strategy wasn't practical. Polishing usually involved a complete change of laps which invariably introduced serious repeatability challenges. Most polishing laps usually differ from the thickness of the prepolishing lap just used. Historically, that's meant the machine mast height setup changed accordingly so subsequent facets would lay flat-to-flat on the new surface. Today, faceters prefer a thin, smaller diameter tin, copper, Mylar or acetate lap atop the larger prepolishing lap. That way, the prepolish and the polish functions can be conducted with a convenient up or down click or two on the cheater. For more details, see page 221.

Not just faceters are changing their methods. Many cabbers have moved away from traditional, messy polishing powders in favor of Bruce Bars and colloidal suspensions. In other words, loose powders introduce just too much dirt to suit their needs. The new paste-like polishing formulations have the additional additives which contribute to faster, superior polishes.

New colloidal oxide polishes, like diamond polishing products, help organize your workshop and avoid the mess often associated with polishing.

Much of the desire for more efficient chemical polishing paste no doubt arises from the popularity of diamond grinding and polishing products. These various diamond grits are available in a paste compound and come nicely packaged in hospital-type syringes. They can be applied easily and neatly in measured amounts. Further, they can be spread effectively over the polishing surface.

Colloidal Silica . . .

Awaiting only a minor technological improvement or two to make it a nearly universal lapidary polish, colloidal silica provides remarkable polishing capabilities.

As stated before, this remarkable new polish was introduced to lapidary by the American Society of Gemcutters after a series of intensive laboratory examinations at the University of Arizona. A fast acting polish that is especially useful for materials over 7 Mohs hardness, colloidal silica's major deficiencies are its high viscosity and dependance on cloth-like polishing pads.

Master Gem Polishing

Buffing wheels can be made by 1) tracing the diameter on the cloth; 2) marking the arbor flange ring; 3) cutting out the circles with a pair of curved nose scissors; 4) stitching the cloth pieces to give the buff strength.

Buehler Ltd, a major producer of colloidal silica, even sells special perforated polishing pads for use with its CS. Faceters certainly won't find these pads to their liking, but cabbers probably will. Small facets not only drop through the perforations but the cloth-like material promotes unacceptable facet edge rounding. For cabbers, though, the characteristics of the cloth pads are not only acceptable but desirable. The cloth tends to follow the rounding of the cab surface and can build a superior polish.

Still, the disadvantage for both cabbers and faceters remains with the high viscosity of the polish. Fling from centrifugal action of swiftly turning laps and wheels contributes to excessive loss of the silica. A gemcutter must keep supplying polish to the wheel—at least until the supply is exhausted.

Recognizing this drawback, ASG is continuing its research, with various chemical additives and formulations under test. Some of the new permanently suspended solutions appear promising.

In the meantime, gemcutters have innovated their own response to the CS problem, largely because the polish does such a fine job. These innovations include using colloidal silica on thin plastic films (the CS tends to remain a bit longer on the soft matte

Master Gem Polishing

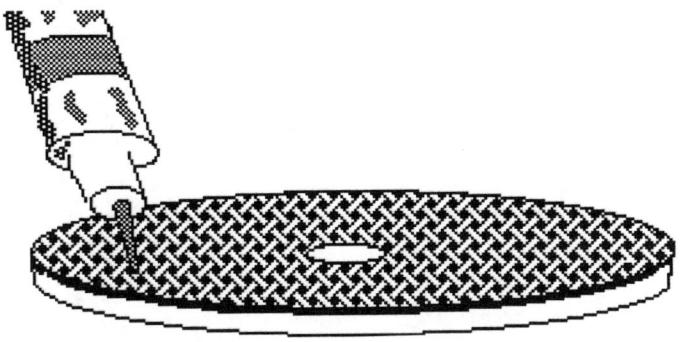

The Mastermet polishing pad, used with colloidal silica, makes a marvelous polishing combination for nearly all cabochons.

finish of Mylar or acetate thin films).
    To cut down on fling loss, other gemcutters use masking tape to build a sort of coffer dam on the outer edge of a thick polishing plate. With this paper barrier up, the centrifugal force hurls the silica against the barrier where the gemcutter can swing the stone into the outer edge and work the polish back onto the lap.
    The dam idea has been especially popular among gemcutters because colloidal silica actually improves in polishing action after being used a number of times. Some gemcutters report they have re-used colloidal silica up to a dozen times. The swarf? It's apparently the agent that improves the silica's polishing action.
    It would behoove any gemcutter to give this remarkable polish a try. The results may prove worthwhile. Too many gemcutters are of the incorrect opinion that colloidal silica applies only to faceting. This isn't true. It's an excellent polish, useful for cabbers and carvers, too, who aren't limited to flat surfaces.

Thickness vs. Polishing Ease...

    Most sanding and polishing difficulties encountered by faceters arise from repeatability.

Master Gem Polishing

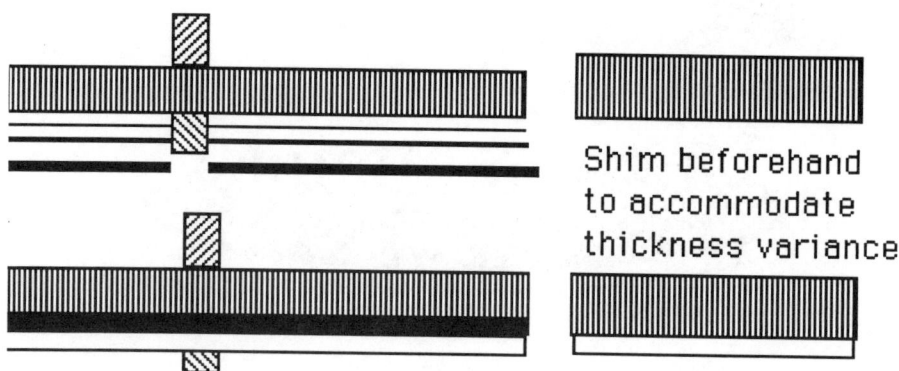

Because virtually all laps differ in thickness, a good strategy consists in prepping—by shimmying—so all your laps will be of uniform height.

Repeatability isn't a problem that plagues cabochon cutters. Because cabbers work by hand, instinct and experience guides them in making any adjustment between the various wheels and grits. Only when the cutting process involves flat areas does a cabber begin to feel the need to accommodate for differences. Even when polishing the flat base of a cab, most cabbers are comfortable about the polishing—and can afford to be relaxed. The base often has little to do with the excellence of the gem. Most even do it by hand because a dopstick would often just get in the way. Things are different for the faceter, whose every move is influenced by machine controls. It's not entirely unfair to say that faceters don't cut gemstones as cabbers do: they mill them with a machine.

Nothing will give a faceter more difficulty that lap thickness...or rather the need to change laps that are different in thickness.

Almost All Laps Are Different...

This represents a way of saying that utilization of different laps usually introduces different thickness values. Almost all laps are different. Manufacturers even today obey no standard industry lap thickness criteria. Consequently, each maker's product line differs markedly from the others. Should a faceter switch from a grinding

Master Gem Polishing

lap to a prepolishing lap in the normal conduct of faceting, the change will probably involve a change in lap thickness, too.

It doesn't matter either if a faceter uses the same manufacturers' laps: they often also differ in thickness. When lap thickness changes, then the mast head likewise needs a height correction.

It is this continuing obligation to correct all the time that slows faceting...and, worse, introduces fatigue and error. Faceters constantly encounter difficulty maintaining the vital flat-to-flat orientation between facets and lap. Repeatability obviously isn't a great nuisance in the step between grinding and prepolishing: after grinding you must smooth and tune facets with a finer lap anyway. The real difficulty arrives between prepolishing and polishing where consistent, accurate flat-to-flat orientation between facet and lap is vital.

It goes without saying that all laps are different, even ones made by the same manufacturer. Therefore, the faceter must accommodate this condition by effective lap management...and pre-planning.

Managing Your Laps...

Even with a wide array of fine commercial products, gemcutters continue to innovate with polishing technology.

I have long recommended to faceters that they spend an evening measuring carefully the thickness of their entire lap inventory. If all laps are indeed different, then the faceter can accommodate this condition only by effective lap management. Knowing the thickness of each lap represents the first vital step in lap management.

Using paper, thin plastic, thin metal, you should shim your laps so they are of identical thickness—or as close to identical as you can get. Thus, when you must change laps from grinding to prepolishing to polishing, you will not encounter the need to make radical changes in your machine setup. It doesn't take long to prepare your laps. And, believe me, the dividends are worthwhile.

Yes, it's true that some of the fine faceting machines on the market like the Facetron, Poly Metric and the new MDR units are amazing demonstrations of accuracy. But they don't adjust automati-

Master Gem Polishing

cally to a thickness change. They must be manipulated—and using laps of the same thickness will minimize this nagging obligation.

Before you start a faceting session, pull out the laps you'll be using and measure them. Is any shimmying required so the grinding and prepolish lap are alike in thickness? How about polishing? Will you use a separate polishing lap...or a base lap with a thin film polishing disk mounted on it...or will you simply mount a thin film slip disks on the prepolishing lap.

The key to effective polishing of faceted stones lies in heading off unnecessary difficulties before they arise. Make your plan... chances are you've done it many times before...and then work the plan. Know how you will handle the polishing operation. Once you've addressed a problem and taken steps to resolve it, the actual performance represents little more than simply carrying through.

Pellon Laps For Cabbers...

It's true. Cabbers who avoid quartz probably don't use Pellon all that much. As a matter of fact, most cabbers aren't even familiar with this fine polishing material...that's the hard plastic-like mat erial now, and not the soft Pellon.

Pellon is available in a range of porosity and soft to hard types. Make certain you obtain the hard, firm, smooth Pellon, not the soft cloth kind used by clothiers. The latter type is useless for lapidary purposes. Pellon finds best use in faceting, cabbing, and flat polishing when glued to a stiff backing like a metal disk and is then charged with either a chemical-water mix or a Bruce Bar. Diamond use is touchy. Standard lapidary cement will hold it to a lap.

For lapidary purposes, be sure to use the hard, firm type...not the soft cloth sold to clothiers (this kind is useless in gemcutting).

Before cementing to a master disk, iron the Pellon to remove wrinkles. To avoid bubbles, apply the cement evenly. If you do get bubbles, work them out with your fingers toward the edge.

John Sinkankas reports that Pellon Laps are especially efficient for quartz and chalcedony flats. Use cerium oxide and Linde A

Master Gem Polishing

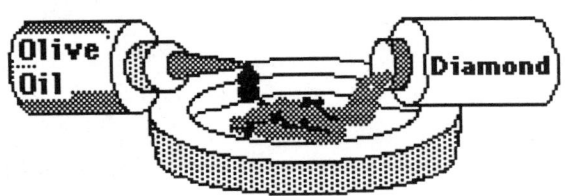

When making your own diamond paste with olive oil, use only a drop or two of oil per carat. The old rule "less is best" holds true in diamond.

for best results. You're better off using shaped or smoothed stones on Pellon. It's not too good with rough edges so stay on guard against sharp edges or shards in the stone material: these can catch the Pellon material and rip.

Working With Acetate Film...

Faceters who have worked with acetate film insist that a couple of easy-to-follow rules will produce acceptable results:

First, get the extra heavy matte acetate sold to blueprint shops. This is much thicker than the usual commercial coated polishing films. The thicker material is much less likely to tear, fold, or rip when exposed to heavy polishing pressures.

Even if the blue print has lettering and writing on it from previous use, the plastic is still usable. Graffiti can be removed with soap and water—or by polishing action which will remove it in record time. Use a standard 6" or 8" lap as a template and outline the round shape and $1/2$" arbor hole with a felt tipped pen. A pen writes best, of course, on the side with the textured finish. Use this textured side for polishing...or for waxing.

For polishing,

Master Gem Polishing

a thick acetate lap is used the same as thin tin, copper, or Mylar. As with virtually every thin film, just make certain you have plenty of water or olive oil on the base lap to assure good suction *i. e.*, adhesion between the polishing lap and the base lap. Always use the roughened side a plastic film if you want polishisng pastes to stick well. Diamond paste achieves much less of a "grip" on the smooth side—although it has worked very well on those occasions I worked it on the smooth side..

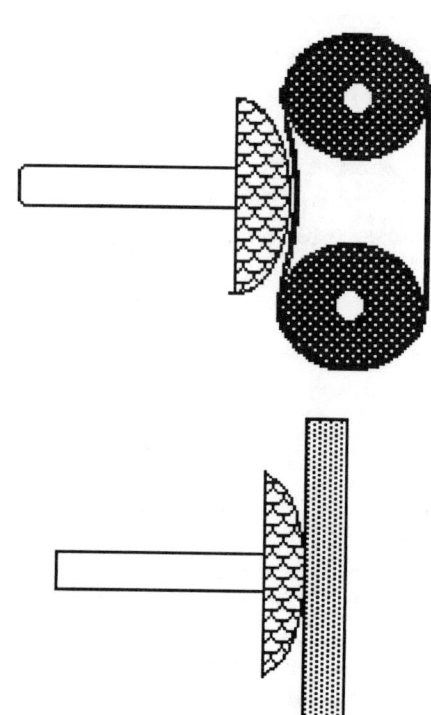

In polishing, whether with diamond or oxides, strive to avoid a lap condition that introduces or accommodates polish lumping. Lumps often pose an open invitation to scratches.

Here are a couple of tips for applying polish. A paste—whether diamond or chemical oxide—adheres well to a thin lap. If working with dry oxide polishing powders, you must take extra precautions to avoid any lumping. Upon introduction of unwetted lumps to a spinning lap, most will be crushed by the pressure of the stone bearing down on the lap. Not all the lumps are crushed, though. It takes only an instant for such an aggregation causing gremlin to slide under the stone's surface...and a scratching condition occurs. With a paste or colloidal polish, the polish is already

Master Gem Polishing

wetted and the texture of the compound is controlled. As a result, the colloidal polishes work efficiently for this kind of application. You can easily control the amount and the application. In the absence of a permanently suspended polishing paste, mix up a thick slurry of oxide and water beforehand. Once the lap is turning and you have a reasonable and slow water drip flow you can even apply the oxide-water paste with your finger tips, smearing it on near the spindle and finger working the polish out toward the lap's outer edges.

With diamond paste, you can makeg a double-mesh polishing lap. Use a grease pencil while the lap is turning to mark a ring about two inches in from the edge on an 8" lap and one inch in on a 6" lap. Stop the machine and apply a couple squirts of 1200 mesh diamond paste on the line, dragging your finger through the small diamond paste mounds and smearing it around the outer ring.

Use light pressure with wet and dry sanding paper for both sanding out and polishing...the abrasive particles really "bite in" under heavy pressure.

Use the same procedure with 14,000 or 50,000 mesh diamond paste on the inside near the hub. Make sure your fingers have been cleaned from the previous operation: you certainly don't want contamination problems. Also, remind yourself to wipe off a stone or facet before proceeding to the inner 14,000 diamond mesh area after having used it in the 1200 ring. These pastes stick well.

Profit Opportunity...

Here's a "real sleeper" profit opportunity for gemcutters who are up on their polishing technique.

Almost all cities and communities have an underground water/sewage piping system. These systems eat up a lot of money for regular maintenance authorities. One of the methods used in maintenance work calls for a special camera that is fed into the pipes where it can snap internal photographs of pipe conditions.

These cameras are invaluable for cost effective maintenance because they allow crews to inspect the pipes without the exorbitant

Master Gem Polishing

cost of digging up. The cameras aren't cheap either and, unfortunately, the cameras' lens invariably sustain severe scratching after prolonged use and exposure to the elements in the pipes.

It costs upwards of $700 to $1000 for an authority to purchase a new lens each time. That's what was happening in North Carolina until Certified Master Gemcutter James Gray of Asheville found out about it. The authority brought James the lens and for $75 he polished it, using standard lapidary procedures. When he'd finished, James handed back the clear lens. It was promptly slapped back into the camera and worked just fine. The authority said, "thanks" to James—and said they'd see him soon again for the next repolishing. The result? A nice new and profitable market for James Gray—plus a happy water authority who'd found a way to save money and still get excellent results.

What was involved? "Not much at all," says James. He was contending only with scratches, where hard particles and debris were

To make your own diamond and olive oil paste, use a mortar and pestle to crush up some garlic into a paste which is then mixed with olive oil and stirred until a thick paste is formed. Introduce diamond grit, and you have an effective diamond polishing paste. Lemon extract will kill the garlic smell.

Master Gem Polishing

contained in the water swishing past the camera in the pipe. James' approach was to hand polish the convex lens. By first sanding very lightly on a wet, new 400-600 grit belt sander, he removed the heavy scratches (" . . . the scratches were heavy enough to see with an unaided eye and it was obvious the camera would take no worthwhile pictures with such a lens"). The key to success at this phase of the operation was light hand pressure.

Once the heavy scratches were out, he used a two-step pre-polish approach. He very lightly sanded the lens surface on a new wet 600 belt sander and then switched to a worn, wet 600 belt. This removed 80% of the scratches: the ones left were so deep that it would have meant destroying the lens to get them out.

For polish, James went to cerium oxide on leather. Again, a light touch was used because the last thing he wanted to do was alter the spherical discipline of the lens itself. He made certain the leather had a soft backing so the polishing surface would conform to the rounded lens. Belts have a lot of give and will follow the curve.

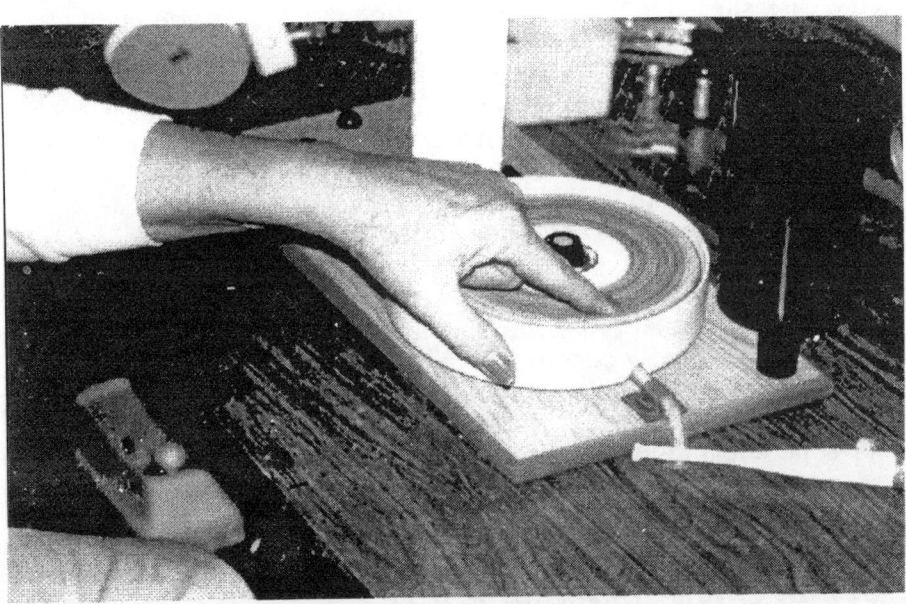

When applying gemstone polishing pastes, a good technique is to dip a finger tip into the paste and then apply it to the turning lap with the fingertip. The fluid chemical will keep the lap wetted sufficiently.

Master Gem Polishing

When he reviewed the lens at the completion of his efforts, the North Carolina gemcutter had a well polished lens ready to go back to work in the camera. The deep, severe scratches were still there but they'd been reduced. The proof was in the shooting: the lens worked like new again. This is just one more example of imagination in utilizing your lapidary skills. Other opportunities abound...if you wish to produce income from gemcutting.

Make Your Own Diamond Paste...

You can easily make your own diamond paste. Here are two approaches and each will produce quick, inexpensive results. The commercial syringes containing diamond mixed with a water soluble paste are expensive. No doubt about it.

Diamond -Olive Oil Solution...

The first method for making your own diamond concoction is the easiest. Go to the grocery store and purchase some plain old olive oil. Mix it with diamond powder which can be purchased quite cheaply in 100 carat vials.

Mix the two elements in a plastic teaspoon. The best mix contains 5 carats of diamond powder in the spoon with 8-10 drops of olive oil. You can mix with your finger into a very thick slurry and then apply the diamond to the lap wheel in dabs with your finger, rubbing the solution over the entire surface. It takes only a few seconds to recharge it after a stone or two. For convenience, place the surplus in a small cosmetic jar with a wide mouth. This way, you can stick a small brush into the diamond bearing olive oil. Your finger tip will usually contain enough diamond to recharge a couple of polishing rings. A copper paddle (page 43) works well, too.

While the olive oil-diamond mixture is suitable for finger or copper paddle application, you may be looking for a way to reload one of your exhausted syringes. For that, you'll want to make your own paste. Here are a couple ways of doing this.

Special Olive Oil Paste For Diamond. .

The first way of making your own diamond paste—olive oil and diamond powder—might prove the easiest because a second method involves commercial olive oil paste. Suppliers of olive oil paste are difficult to find.

This product, the result of an industrial product utilizing high pressure and heat, has a consistency somewhat like lard or Crisco. It's not all that well-known to the lapidary community because its principle use has been in the cosmetic industry. You'll need to obtain the paste from a cosmetic industry supplier and these can be found in the Yellow Pages or from an industrial index catalog.

Olive oil paste rubs into the fingers just like hand lotion, doesn't splatter easily, doesn't get rancid or give off an odor, is virtually colorless and not greasy, and possesses a high melting point—just the characteristics desired in a diamond grit carrier.

Furthermore, olive oil paste is easily stirred with a popsicle stick which can be used to transfer controlled amounts of the mixture to a syringe or directly to a lap or belt. Again, a small cosmetic jar is perfect as a holder for surplus paste because the wide open mouth allows you to remove and return material. The thick paste is

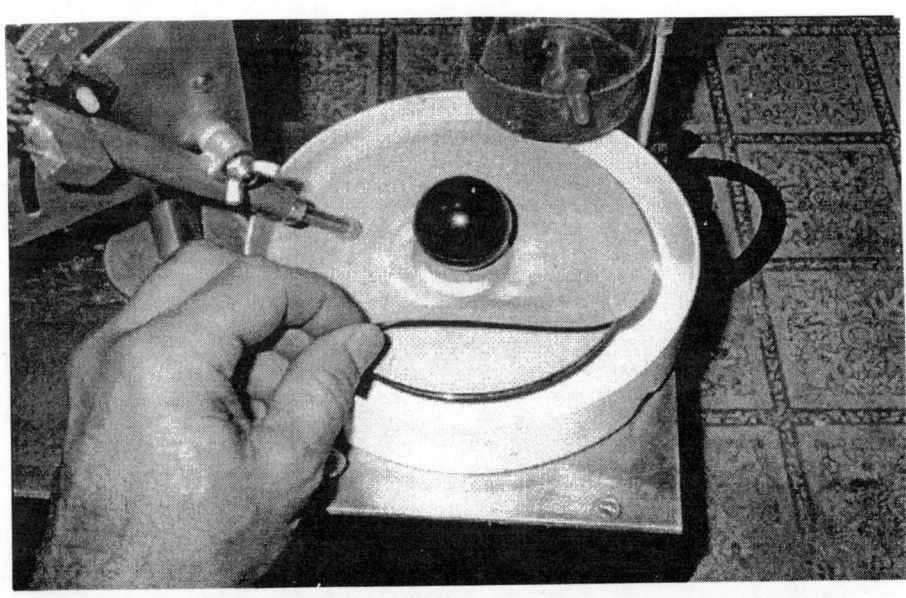

Water or olive oil provides the necessary suction for holding a metal or plastic thin disk a base lap. Wet the base lap, lower the wetted thin disk to the surface and press out bubbles and excess.

Master Gem Polishing

perfect for filling up old diamond syringes. You don't need to clean the syringe out: just use the same diamond mesh as before and you'll have no trouble.

The mix formula calls for about 2 carats of diamond powder for each 5 grams of olive oil paste. Seldom will there be justification for exceeding this ratio: additional diamond won't produce significant results so any add-on is pretty much wasted.

Place half of the olive oil paste in the bottom of a small bowl or cup and then pour the diamond dust on top. Add the rest of the oil paste and stir and stir. The finer the grit the more stirring you should perform to assure that no diamond lumps remain and that the diamond is evenly dispersed throughout the compound.

If you intend to mix more than one batch with the same bowl or cup—and it's strongly advised that you use a different mixing bowl with each different mesh size to avoid contamination—it's obviously best to start with the fine mesh size and work up to the more coarse material. When you're finished stirring, the stick can serve as a spatula for picking up the compound from the mixing

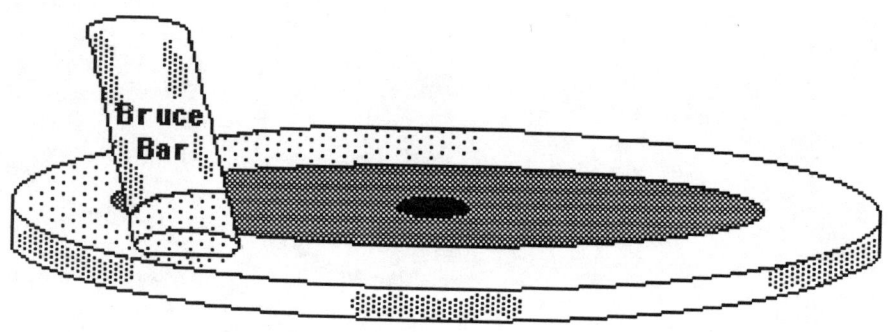

Diamond paste and Bruce Bars can be used to make two-tone finishing laps. Use coarse grits on the outside and finer ones on the inside..you can even mix the types of polish on the same lap.

bowl and transferring it to the cosmetic jar. Each grit jar should be plainly marked and labeled. Of course, you can transfer the paste to a lap with your finger. If you can't locate a source for olive oil paste, below is an alternative method.

Make Your Own Olive Oil Paste...

You don't need to buy expensive diamond paste . . .even when finding a supplier of commercial olive oil paste proves impossible. You can make your own—and it's just as good as the commercial brands.

You may not know it but olive oil paste is an ancient product. It is preferred by Spanish peasantry as a marvelous alternative to butter which melts in the Spanish summer. Besides its resistance to melting in higher temperatures, olive oil paste possesses numerous other benefits. It doesn't splatter, won't melt at high temperatures, doesn't get rancid, is virtually odorless and isn't greasy.

Small wonder that Spaniards developed their own formula for olive oil paste. You can follow the ancient formula with supplies purchased at the corner grocery store. The way to make olive oil paste is to use a mortar and pestle to rub into a paste one ounce of peeled garlic (don't worry about the odor: there's a way to handle that). Next mix this paste with 3-4 ounces of olive oil. Continue with constant rubbing up with the pestle and the oil-garlic will convert itself to a pasty mass, similar to the consistency of soft butter.

Keep in mind that garlic is a member of the Lilium tribe of flowers, called the *genus allium*. The chemicals in the olive oil combine with the garlic to form the paste compound. Any other of the flowers in the Lilium tribe can be used but they are not quite so easy to obtain as plain garlic. To control the garlic odor, according to Holly Shimzu, top botanist at the U. S. Botanical Gardens in Washington DC, just add some lemon juice.

Lemon juice is renowned for removing garlic smells from the hands. You can also introduce a drop or two of perfume into the paste. Either chemical will remove the objectionable odor and do nothing to impair the basic chemistry at work. If you wish to elevate the temperature tolerance just add a small bit of mutton fat from your butcher. Mix the fat into the paste and a substance known as stearin in the fat will do its magical work.

Once you have a nice paste consistency, go ahead and mix

Master Gem Polishing

about 2 carats of diamond to each 5 grams of olive oil paste. You'll find that this mixture works just as well, perhaps even a little better, than commercial diamond pastes. Water won't wash the olive oil paste away quite as quickly as it will commercial pastes either

Using Resin to Control Edges . . .

If a faceted stone is already completed and you wish to polish the table with colloidal silica on a Buehler's Mastermet™ or a Pellon Lap you'll find that a resin crust around the table's edges can serve your purposes well...especially with large tables.

Place some Vaseline on a section of glass. Then make a small clay coffer dam around the Vaseline treated areas. Next, place the table flat down on the treated area. Next, pour some polyester casting resin around the gemstone so that it fills in around the table. The reasoning behind this preparation is that the cast resin around the stone's table will absorb any curvature tendency. When you bring the table down flat on the polishing surface the table will polish out flat while the resin will protect the facet edges from

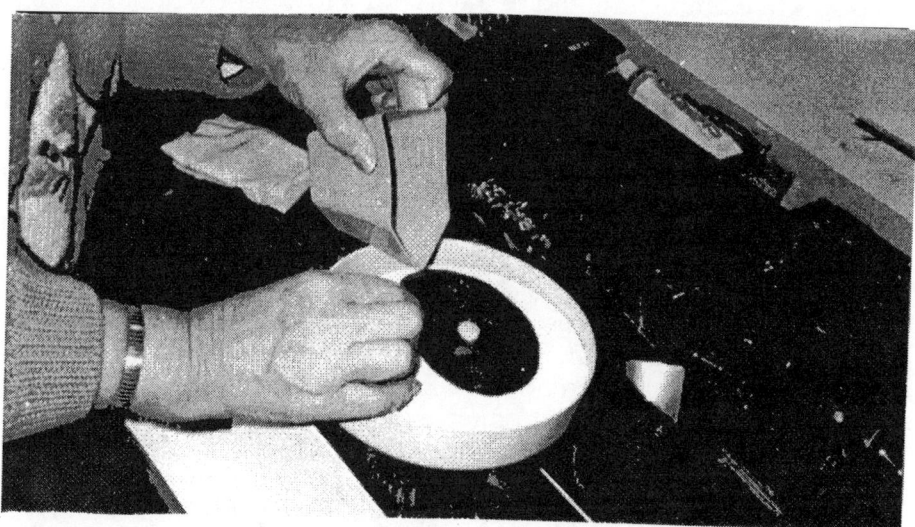

Keep those old ceramic laps to be used as master or base laps for polishing. A hard ceramic lap works beautifully with thin metal or plastic polishing films and even Pellon.

Master Gem Polishing

rounding. This same effect, incidentally, can be achieved using baking soda and cyanoacrylate glue. Pack the baking soda around the table and then apply superglue. The resulting crust will protect the table.

As for cabs, you can use felt or Pellon on a rubber pad or fixed to Lucite. The most fundamental approach, of course, involves the traditional use of a leather or felt pad or a cloth pad on rubber. All of the materials will hold the moisture well, a vital necessity with colloidal silica. Oxide polishes, as emphasized earlier, work best when they are damp-dry, even on cloth polish carriers.

Polishing Extremely Thin Sections . . .

Trying to cut and polish extremely thin sections of gem material isn't the simplest challenge that a gemcutter will face.

It isn't all that difficult, though, given the judicious use of some two-faced tape. You need something to grip when working on thin slabs or pieces. By holding on—or dopping to—a larger section you have much better control over the thin section. A larger rock or block of wood can be held easier in the hand.

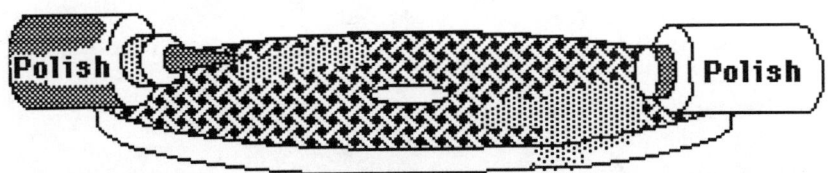

With squirt/squeegee type dispensers, you have better control of liquid polish application than with an open mouthed bottle.

The easiest and best way to apply a wet polish is with an accordion type bottle, or a pressure pump. It's easier to apply controlled bursts this way.

Master Gem Polishing

So, sand a piece of hard wood to a smooth surface. The wood section should be larger than the thin slab to be polished. Use industrial tape with adhesive on both sides (regular commercial two-way tapes sometimes lose their strength in the presence of wood AND water).

Cut the tape lengths to about 1" longer than the wood block so you can tack or staple the ends onto the block for extra holding strength. Then press the slab onto the tape. It won't come off despite any misgiving you might feel. You may find that plate glass and chemical oxide polishes work best with thin, large sections.

When the slab is finished, heat it slightly and it will separate nicely from the tape. Slide the slab to remove it rather than pry. Prying can cause the slab to break. If you're dealing with a heat sensitive stone, use a sharp Exacto knife to cut the stone away. Acetone will remove the tape stick-um quickly.

Can one-sided tape be used in a pinch? Of course it can. Drop some superglue on the non-adhesive side of the tape and press it around the wooden block. Staple or tack the ends so the tape remains taut. Allow the assembly to dry and in a few moments it will be ready to accept a slab. During use, pressure will keep the slab in place.

Master Gem Polishing

Polish Critical...

It bears repeating that of all the phases in gemcutting, polishing remains the most remarkable—and unpredictable.

For a gemcutter who has been working for hours on a complicated cut, the polishing operation represents the final barrier between his or her efforts and the realization of a beautiful gemstone.

Yet, polishing can be the toughest obstacle of all. So many variables enter into a successful polish that it sometimes seems more a matter of luck and pluck than practiced discipline. Over the long run, luck has rather little to do with effective polishing. A sound knowledge of the materials and of your equipment will prepare you for most gem polishing challenges. That's where experience comes in. The beginner relies on luck to achieve the proper polishing combination. A certified gem cutter, one who knows lapidary equipment and tools, depends on experience and the ability to make meaningful calculations as to what is needed in any given situation.

Using The Right Combination...

Polishing, for most cutters, resolves down to a matter of using the right belt, wheel or lap, polishing compound, water drip and pressure. All will vary with the stone, and the gemcutter simply must find the convoluted combination that will produce the kind of polish that is desired.

Current research focuses on the part that water, with its tiny molecules, plays in a polish. It apparently accelerates the rate of fracture growth in glass because it can penetrate the tiniest opening. So the question now is: does it do the same thing to gem crystals?

A key issue in polishing seems to be the amount of polishing compound. In this area, there is little controversy: less is best. It is an axiom that is consistently violated by beginning gemcutters and constantly practiced by award winning cutters. Only in rare circumstances will a thick polish application be warranted. Despite warnings to the contrary, they believe—until experience finally proves otherwise—that a bit more polish on the lap will drive the gremlins away.

With diamonds or chemical polishes, only a small amount consistently outperforms a heavy dose. Cutters using ceramic laps actually wipe off the lap with a towel before using. Thin, damp slurries have long been preferred—and the results show it—for gaining

Master Gem Polishing

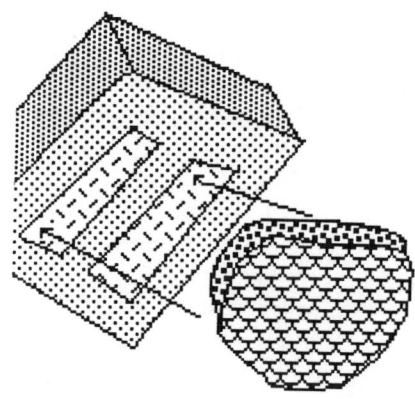
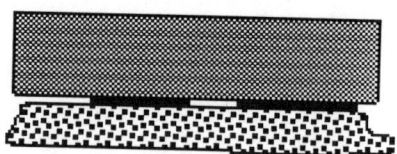

Extremely thin mineral slabs can be smoothed down easily if you first adhesively attach a wood block or two or to the surface of the slab so as to provide a firm hand grip.

quick polishing results—or have been experiencing scratching—check on your use of compound. You may be using too much or allowing it to get too dry. A little less polish and more dampness may be in order. You can easily get yourself into a lively discussion over possible winning combinations for polishing. As to the amount of polish—not too much!—there is seldom argument.

The expression, "lighten up!" should indeed be reserved exclusively for gemcutters. There's another benefit to be derived from "less is best." That is, heavy amounts of polish—along with excessive hand pressure—are the principal culprits in edge rounding. The polish sometimes builds up in front of the leading edge of the stone and this causes rounding. When the loose polish rolls up and hardens, it can cause scratching as well.

Applying Polish...

Applying a chemical polish can sometimes be a messy affair. One reliable technique for making polishing application easy and disciplined is this:

Obtain an "accordion type" plastic bottle or a squeeze type

bottle used for squirting window polish. Fill the bottle with a thin slurry of the polish. When you need to apply polish just squeeze the bottle and spritz a small amount on the polish carrier. Usually the bottles can be adjusted so they either squirt or spray. I prefer spray.

In the absence of a squirt bottle, obtain a flexible bottle and puncture the cap or lid with small holes...using a needle or brad nail.

For Curved Surfaces...

The polishing rule for flat and curved surfaces is: flat polishing surfaces for flats or facets and spongy or rounded polishing surfaces for rounded stone surfaces.

A good principle to follow for complicated surfaces is to try and match the configuration of the stone's surface with the polish carrier. Curved tools for curved surfaces; flat ones for flat surfaces.

Don't allow yourself to get trapped into an effort to impart a good polish on a rounded surface *e.g.*, rounded cabochon top, with a

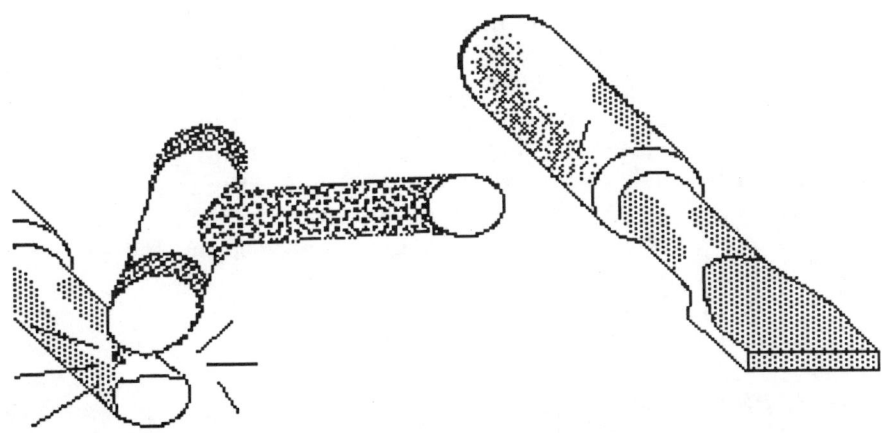

Because copper wire is malleable, insert a section of wire into a wooden handle, then hammer out the copper tip flat. A paddle serves nicely to pick up small amounts of diamond-olive oil mix for transfer to a lap or wheel.

Master Gem Polishing

hard or firm flat pad or lap. When polishing rounded surfaces, use something that will "give" to your pressure or is rounded...so the polishing pad conforms to the stone's rounded shape. Remember: flat surfaces impart flat finishes.

Note: The above warning, of course, is invalid not only for curved facets cut by Poly Metric Company's new OMF curved faceting machines but also for a regular coned surface made by revolving a stone against a flat sanding lap. These are disciplined one-dimensional curves and as such are best polished with the same form of flat polishing surface that was used in cutting the curves.

The best polishing tool for rounded stone surfaces is a dish polisher. This consists of a bowl-like device over which leather or chamois has been stretched and fastened down tight like a drum head. Thus, when a rounded stone is pushed into the polishing cloth it will give slightly and allow contact to be made around and over the curve of the stone. By adjusting the orientation of the stone, you impart a neat, disciplined polish over the entire surface.

Some gemcutters insist that they can sufficiently force the rounded crown of a cabochon into a felt polishing pad or a rubber backed pad. Perhaps they can. But a dished out polishing wheel over which has been stretched a 6" or 8" span of leather or chamois saves a lot of time and anxiety. That's because you know the stone is in contact with the polishing agent and no unwanted flats are likely to show up later when you inspect your work.

You can buy or make a cavity lap. With a compass, draw a 6" or 8" circle on a piece of 1/2" thick white pine (it's soft and easy to work with but should be waterproofed or dipped in wax. Saw out a ring of the same diameter that's about 1/2" wide and glue this to the periphery of the disk. Now cut a center arbor hole in the center of the disk and tighten a nut against the bottom of the disk.

You'd be well advised to cut out a groove about 1/8" deep around the outer perimeter of the disk. The groove allows you to cinch a cord snugly around the leather or chamois, keeping the latter in place when you exert pressure against it.

Special Polishing Laps...

A number of special polishing laps are available from manufacturers.

These laps include the resin polishing laps produced by

Master Gem Polishing

Dyna Ltd of Boise, ID; Hypno Lap made by Leeco Company of Valencia, CA; the Fast Lap and Last Lap, both of which are pelletized metal resin bonded laps, made respectively by Crystalite Corporation of Westerville, OH, and Raytech.

In the next few pages, an extensive discussion of each type lap is provided.

Dyna Laps...

Some of Dyna's polishing laps for faceting are an offshoot of the company's Glass Lap technology. The laps are permanently bonded rechargeable polishing laps which feature a resin surface. The resin creates a useful "drag" against the face of the stone causing the polish to work harder and more efficiently. Available in both 6" and 8" diameter the laps work with both cerium oxide and tin oxide. These polishing oxides are bonded into the lap's resin surface. The company also offers 8-ounce re-charge chemical units for boosting or re-charging the laps when the original charge polishes out.

Once the lap surface becomes glazed from use, it is time to re-charge. This is performed quickly and easily with a 1" fan-type paint brush. After an application, the gemcutter should wait a minute for the liquid to dry and then polishing can be resumed.

Polishing pressure and action will burnish the chemical into the lap surface, Dyna claims. The lap is kept cool with the usual slow water drip.

Dyna claims the cerium lap is excellent for quartz, apatite, benitoite, beryl, dioptase, feldspar, opal, obsidian, scapolite, smithsonite, sodalite, sugelite and spodumene.

The synthetic tin lap works well with garnet, peridot, topaz, chrysoberyl, andalusite, apatite, danburite, diopside, enstatite, epidote, euclase, sphene, spinel and tourmaline.

Leeco Hypno Scored Lap...

The Hypno Scored Lap made by Leeco consist of a Lucite lap that features a spiraled scoring pattern.

This particular scoring, says Darrell Lee, Leeco President, makes polishing quartz and other Lucite-responsive stones a cinch. While most lap scoring is performed so the lap surface contains a

Master Gem Polishing

For polishing gemstones, the axiom "less is best" holds true. Less polish on the wheel or lap will usually outperform a thick application of polish—with much less danger of scratching caused by lumping or aggregation.

complete array of concentric circles, Lee approaches the polishing task from a whirlpool preference.

With special tooling, he cuts a neat, precise, squared off channel which spirals from a start at the arbor hole and proceeds ultimately to the edge of the lap. The whole concept of this kind of proprietary scoring is anti-aggregate. Having someplace for the debris to gather—out of the way of the facet surface—is quite important. You don't want swarf scratching your nice clean surface. But too much scoring tilts only to debris control.

An accordion or squeeze type dispensing bottle makes a fine polish applicator. With controlled squeezes you can learn to apply just the right amount each time.

You have other needs for the scoring function such as a polish carrier, a reservoir for swarf and water. The spiral scoring on a Lucite lap means that the channel is moving constantly across the stone's surface, exposing it to the polish and coolant—even when the stone is held motionless.

Given this action, a good scrubbing works on quartz and similar type minerals. The scoring channels are deep enough to carry the proper amount of polish yet also carry off the debris. What the facet is contacting under these conditions is a pure, moving and constant polishing surface devoid of harmful contaminants.

Lee, incidentally, is critical of concentric circle scoring. If you take a standard knurling tool, he contends, and hold it to the moving lap surface you'll have a series of score marks—none of which truly allows an exit for the debris. It'll hold polish, yes, but it will also hold swarf which ultimately can combine and cause aggregation. That spells scratches.

Thus the advice is to avoid concentric scoring. If you score a lap, extend all the lines from the arbor hole to the outer edge. The straight lines should be angled ahead slightly...not extending in a perpendicular direction. By angling the lines you minimize the amount of sling or materials you'll lose due to centrifugal force.

A scoring channel, to be long lasting, should be about .05" deep, Lee says, because any less fails to provide the ability to hold polish and debris. A light scoring will scratch the surface and perform some polishing assistance. Eventually, though, heat and pressure will soon burnish light surface deformations away and you'll be left with a surface that needs scored again.

Pelletized Laps...

The Fast Lap and Last Lap are resin bonded with tiny metal pellets to give strength. What makes these laps so useful is their ability to plane a surface extremely flat and their readiness to go to work with either a diamond or an oxide polish.

The other benefit is: they can be used as either a prepolishing lap or as a polishing lap.

Lap Scoring Technique...

Scoring a lap involves considerable controversy. Practiced mostly by faceters but also done for cabochon polishing, the practice involves cutting, scratching, or gouging a pattern of grooves in

Master Gem Polishing

the face of a polishing carrier as a means of improving the latter's polishing efficiency.

As indicated earlier, the theory behind the process claims that the grooves provide a reservoir for polish and for debris. By removing the debris from the surface of the lap, aggregation has less chance to rip into a facet. Actual practice does show that polishing action usually improves with a scored lap.

A razor blade makes a fine tool for scoring even though the resulting channels are a bit narrow. Use a steel ruler or some similar straight metal piece and lay it across the lap. Move the ruler about 1/8" to 3/16" at a time and drag —with heavy pressure—along the rule to assure a straight line. Let up slightly on the pressure as you near the outer edge of the lap: this dimming effect will reduce sling, and keep you from running the blade off the edge with a "thump" which can be a bit threatening.

Working with a razor blade will leave a somewhat rough

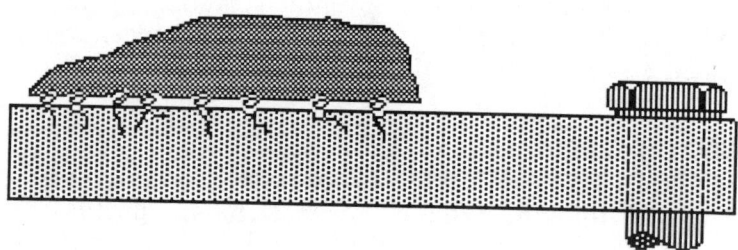

Abrasive particles press into the surface of a mineral, chipping out small conchoidal chunks. These must be removed—including sub-surface fractures—before the stone will accept a good polish.

Master Gem Polishing

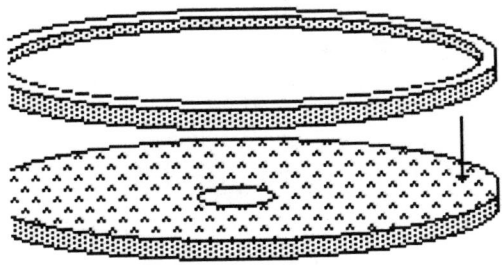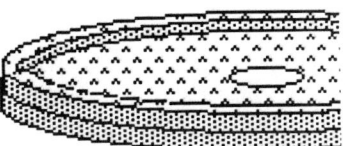

To make a dished polishing wheel, saw or cut out a series of rings. Waterproof the wood and glue it into a bowl like shape. You don't need a real deep cavity to achieve good polishing results.

surface but the ridges can be easily burnished down with a piece of agate or corundum. In smoothing down, it isn't necessary to use a lot of pressure for an extended period. You want those channels open. By lightly burnishing down the channels they have a shorter life—or no life at all even before you start polishing.

The very slight bumpy effect you feel the first time you use a metal polishing lap that's just been scored isn't all that dangerous.

How about a hacksaw for scoring? Yes. They duplicate the scoring tool. The difficulty with a hacksaw blade is in getting strong enough pressure which can be equalized over the entire section of blade you're using. For that reason, I don't recommend a piece of hacksaw blade that is too long. Get a blade about $1^1/_2$-inches long MAXIMUM. That's plenty. Cut a channel in a piece of hard wood which can serve as a handle and then epoxy the blade into the wood. You can get a good, easy grip and control with the handle and this results in better, deeper scoring. The best direction for hacksaw scoring should be identical with the razor blade, out from the arbor hole at a

Master Gem Polishing

slightly inclined angle.

Scoring as a valuable aid to polishing has been demonstrated enough that there should be no reluctance on the part of any gemcutter to cut into his/her favorite metal or plastic polishing lap. The epitome of scored polishing laps came a number of years ago when Herb Karray of the original MDR Company, took a radial saw and scored a tin lap in a criss-cross pattern.

The lap performed exceedingly well for polishing many stones, but for some reason it never quite caught on with gemcutters. Say those who tried it, the lap was marvelous, well scored, and the scoring would have lasted for a long time. MDR just couldn't sell it...apparently too expensive. Admittedly, it did give a bit of a rough run but the polishing action was superb.

Polish Condition Theory...

Why should a polishing surface be "damp-dry?"

A reasonable answer might be: polishing is a slightly abrasive action, too. If the polish is too thick or too wet the stone's surface does more sliding than it does abrading.

The key to polishing is to gain some slide but with only

By combining a diamond impregnated resin with reject computer memory disks, Dyna manufactures a popular, low priced, lap line. The laps measure $5^{1}/_{4}$" in diameter and require a special adapter to fit the standard $^{1}/_{2}$" arbor.

Master Gem Polishing

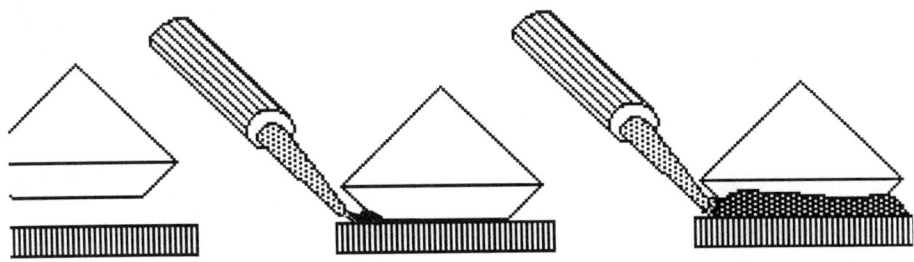

Use epoxy and polyester casting resin to form a crust around a table facet, then polish on a cloth polishing surface. The resin will keep the edges of the table from rounding.

slight abrasive action. If your polish is wet, the facet will slide: if it's too dry the abrasive action is too harsh and the facet might scratch. By keeping the polishing surface in a constant damp-dry condition you gain the slide plus the abrasive action. Consequently, the facet passing over this damp-dry polishing compound will polish because there is just enough abrasive action to induce polishing. Now you know why modern polishing theory holds that what takes place on the surface of the facet might involve both Beilby Theory (chemical action) and diamond polish (scratch action).

For years, gem polishing was explained as either a product of the Beilby layer or a diamond scratch layer. Research has moved the polishing mystery up a notch, confident now that neither theory truly explains why a gem surface polishes. What happens, scientists say, is what people thought prior to Beilby: that the irregular surface of the mineral is reduced somehow to a near flat condition so that light rays reflect and refract with rigid parallel and uniform discipline.

Dop up a practice stone—either cabbing or faceting—and practice with different polishing laps and materials...working to get

Master Gem Polishing

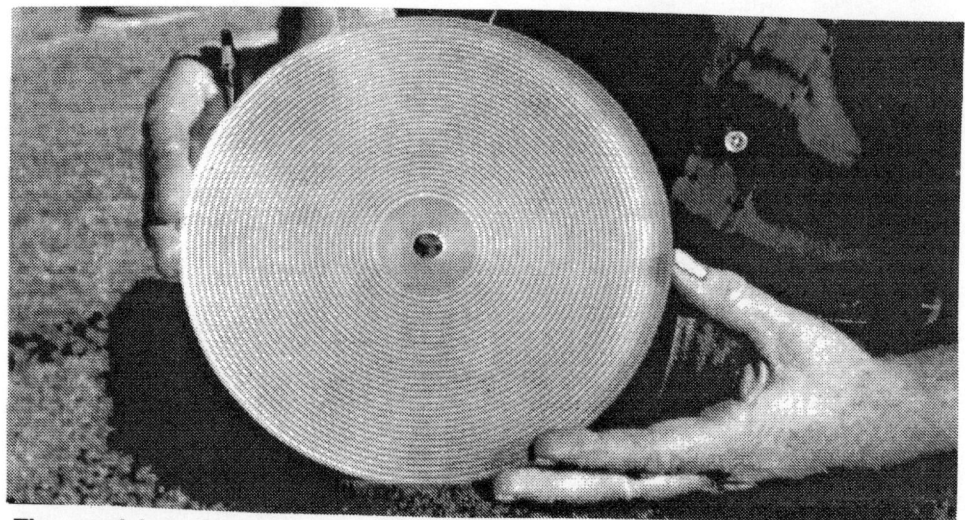

The special scoring in the face of a plastic lap gives the Hypno lap its special personality. Remember that for proper scoring there must be an exit path for the debris to remove itself from the polishing surface. In the Hypno lap, the scoring channel is a spiral.

the damp-dry condition that works best for you. The practice will greatly expand your polishing talents.

Polishing Tips on Jade...

Not all that many cabochon cutters do it but keep in mind that jade can be polished without special polishing compounds and buffs. The trick is this: use 4/0 flint sandpaper. That's it!

Attach the paper to a regular sanding disk which contains a sponge rubber cushion. For the rounded cabochon you want a soft, spongy polishing surface to assure maximum contact between the stone and the sandpaper. Also, break in the flint paper until the abrasive becomes powdery with a hard stone before polishing.

Run the disk about 250 rpm for best results.

Talk to a half dozen jade specialists and, chances are, you'll receive half a dozen recommendations on the type of buff which works best with jade. Truth is, they all work and that includes 1) leather; 2) muslin; 3) velvet; 4) hard felt; 5) wood laps; and 6) diamond impregnated canvas. About the only uniform rule you'll hear is that pre-polish—with ALL scratches removed—is critical.

Master Gem Polishing

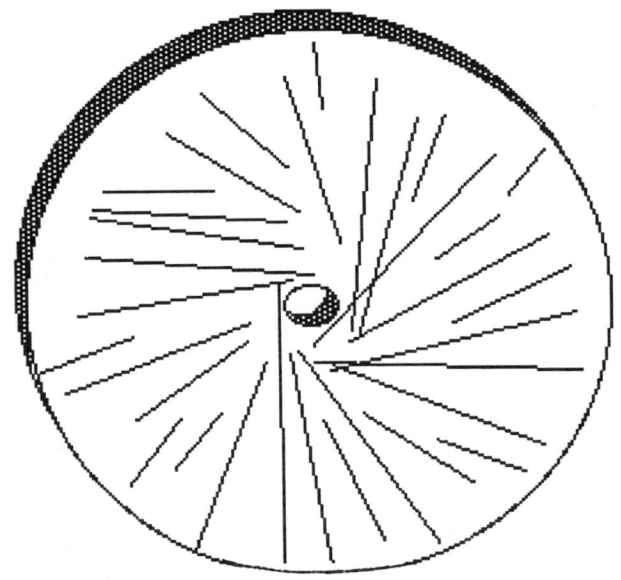

The best scoring direction is slightly advanced radial lines. This helps keep the polish from being slung away by centrifugal force. Some gemcutters use an Xacto blade to score narrow deep ridges.

Diamond leather pads and leather with aluminum oxide or chrome oxide are the preferred polishing combinations. Diamond polishing techniques call for "stepping up" to progressively finer particles until the maximum polish has been achieved. With the oxide polishes, mix the powder with a half-half combination of water and vinegar.

Some gemcutters even mix 1 part aluminum oxide with 9 parts chrome oxide. This is the mix used by many professional jade cutters as a replacement for the old—but very effective—Jade Luster Powder. Such cutters are known not only to use but actually prefer the use of tin oxide on leather, muslin and hard felt buffs. For the usual oxide polishing approach, the jade will need to be applied with considerable pressure to the pad. This high pressure tactic will generate plenty of heat, enough that dopping waxes turn molten. The benefits supposedly realized by allowing jadeite or nephrite to heat up during polishing is still debatable. Most tests, though, tend to verify the virtue of heating the jade even though (as you'll read in the

Master Gem Polishing

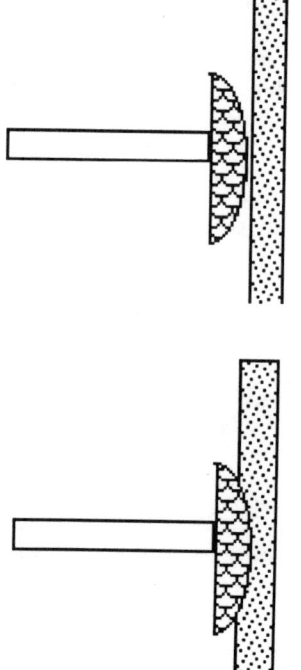

For rounded cab domes and spheres, a softer felt or leather allows some "give" to the stone's surface so as to impart a more even finish.

next couple of paragraphs) some evidence shows that heat causes the fibers to pull out.

If you plan to try the professional approach of using tin or cerium oxide, here's a tip that will improve your chances of realizing a fine polish. After grinding the jade piece to shape and smoothing it with 600 wet sanding cloth, smear the outside $1\frac{1}{2}$ inches of a leather polishing lap with No. 1200 metal lapping compound. Work the stone on the compound charged leather at high speed. This action will produce a semi polish that can be easily finished off to a fine polish with tin or cerium oxide. You can obtain metal lapping compound (it's really only carborundum in grease: so it's easy to make!) at an auto supply house or a machine shop.

Avoiding Orange Peel Effect...

The greatest challenge in working with jade has always been this: how can you avoid the pitted or orange peel effect when grinding or sanding this high fiber mineral?

The words "...high fiber mineral..." is the key to most of the pitting problems with jade. So-called holes you'll find in a finely sanded jade are actually the left over from having the fibers pulled out during the harsh cutting process. In a process described by Ted Purkheiser for *Rock & Gem Magazine*, the approach is to use wet

Master Gem Polishing

grinding and sanding to keep the jade cool. From the grinding wheel, he recommends that the jade be brought through progressively finer wet sanding papers...150 to 225 to 400 to 600.

Allowing the 600 paper to dry, the procedure then is to touch the jade to the dry paper in quick rolling motion bursts to avoid heat. Gradually, the jade will develop a fine gloss. Once the gloss is achieved, the piece is ready for polishing with Jade Luster Polish or its equivalent (one part aluminum oxide and 9 parts Chrome Oxide in water). Paint a slightly thickened polish on a smooth leather buff running at about 800 rpm and polish to a fine sheen. What happens is that the luster polish also cuts slightly while it smooths the surface. Keep the jade against the leather surface until the compound is completely dry. That's when you'll note a high polish developing. Heat at this juncture, Ted says, is very important and valuable. Don't be the least reluctant to allow the heat to build up when polishing jade. It's contributions is highly beneficial as increased temperatures have little or no effect whatsoever on the mineral.

This same polishing approach, incidentally, will also prove extremely useful for

A felt polishing pad or disk tends to undercut, but it does represent a superior polish carrier, particularly for rounded or complex shaped stones.

agate and other hard-to-polish stones—as long as you remember that most of these other stones don't take all that well to high temperatures. It's well known, of course, that many minerals can take the heat. Even then, it's best to bring them up to heat slowly: thermal shock isn't good for most stones.

Polish Preparations...

Many gemcutters don't spend a lot of time philosophizing over chemical oxide polishes. They buy a supply of powders from their favorite vendor and go ahead and use it.

Truth is, this simplified approach works well more than it causes problems.

Sometimes, though, a special preparation procedure can produce results for a difficult situation. For example, adding a pinch or two of non-suds producing detergent powder to a polish will help keep the surface of a metal polishing lap wet. **Note:** *Use a powder detergent if you expect to store the polish for a time before using it. If you intend to use the polish right away, use a liquid detergent. The detergent acts as a wetting agent, actually making the polish more slippery. This is important with softer stones. When the facet of a stone of 6 Mohs or softer hits a dry spot on a metal lap it can easily get scratched.*

Other times, adding some vinegar to cerium oxide will dramatically reduce scratching when polishing quartz.

In the past couple of years, much publicity has been extended in behalf of colloidal or permanently suspended oxide powder polishes. It's easier to buy a commercial mix of colloidal polish, but you can easily enough make your own. You need only a surfactant and these can often be purchased at the local drug store. B. F. Goodrich also makes a commercial water thickener called Carbopol™, an acrylic acid polymer with pseudoplastic properties. The product comes in an extremely fine micronized powder (Carbopol 676) or in a liquid (Carbopol 681).

Carbopol is one of the agents used by the American Society of Gemcutters when it researched and developed an entire line of colloidal polishes. The trick to introducing Carbopol to a water-oxide solution is to sprinkle the fine powder slowly while stirring vigorously. If you put the chemical in haphazardly it will clump up

Master Gem Polishing

because the powder particles wet out swiftly. An electrical kitchen mixer will do the job rather well. You don't need much Carbopol to thicken the water and produce a good suspension of polish. Mix the Carbopol at about 1:10 by volume with the polish.

The result of the mix—water plus Carbopol plus oxide powder—will produce a relatively permanent suspension of the powder in the water. Still, there will no doubt be times when the polish will need to be given a good shake to disperse the particles. Some settling does take place over time.

Also, get the tough part out of the way first: mix the water and Carbopol first, then add the powder.

Some Polishing Principles...

It goes without saying that in order to produce a fine polished finish on a gem crystal it is first necessary to remove all scratches, pits, and other imperfections on the surface. This means the surface

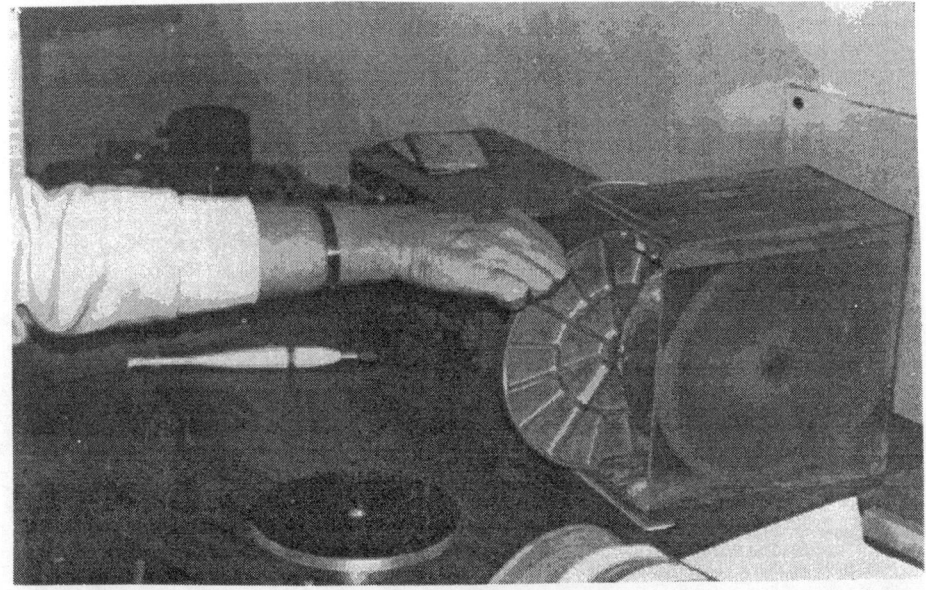

It would be nice if a truly universal polishing agent-carrier combination existed, but gemstone personalities are just too variable. Any good gemcutting shop will need to have a selection of polishes and laps.

Master Gem Polishing

should possess a perfect plane so the light rays may be reflected in a uniform, parallel manner without interference.

According to Hugh Leiper FGA, a crystal may also have been subjected during abrasive activities to microscopic pitting *i.e.*, the formation of sub-surface incomplete conchoidal fractures. Such fractures penetrate the surface of a material but do not cause a conchoidal chip to be formed.

The key to effective polishing then is somewhat of a planing action. First and foremost in any polishing decision involves achieving the most effective way to hone the surface down uniformly to an average level of the tops of the myriad of tiny pits, scratches, and depressions. This is done by "stepping through the grits" or progressively reducing the size and height of the depression-rims through the use of finer and finer abrasive grits.

A gemcutter could start a cab or facet at 225 grit then move to 600 grit and then to a finer grit or even a polish. To assure that the mineral surface is progressively worn down, many cabbers insist on

The key to effective gemstone polishing lies in the proper address of the stone's surface to the polishing powder particles. An effective carrier encourages an appropriate address that works.

Master Gem Polishing

working wet. Once upon a time—and still occasionally for specific reasons—gemcutters work cabs with dry sanding paper.

After initial grinding and sanding, the final abrasive step involves pre-polish. This is the step where all of the tiny depressions have been reduced in size until they are no longer eye visible. Nonetheless, there may still be the sub-surface partially-started conchoidal fractures to be dealt with. Removing these nuisances is what pre-polish is all about. Pre-polishing continues until these sub-surface fractures have been removed also...and a smooth matt remains.

Here is where experienced eyes and a magnifier come in so handy. When the sub-surface fractures have been removed, the surface of the stone should take on a plush, velvet-like appearance. It will no longer have any dullness (the residual dull appearance is caused by light interference from the sub-surface fractures).

When sub-surface fractures have been removed, the surface of the stone should take on a plush, velvet-like appearance. It will no longer have any dullness (the residual dull appearance is caused by light interference from the sub-surface fractures).

In the case of cabochons, many cutters prefer a wet 600 sanding cloth for pre-polish. The 1200 grit lap is preferred in most cases by faceters. Regardless of the type of gemcutting, though, the step through procedures are the same. Effective polishing involves a recognition of the cause of pits and scratching during the abrasive work and then the removal—or planing down—of the depression rims. Once a uniform surface has been achieved, and this will be visibly apparent, the stone is ready for polish.

Inspection with a magnifier will show the changing personality of pits and scratches on the surface. A magnifer used after coarse grinding will reveal many fine parallel sanding marks. After sanding a cab with a wet 600 cloth, magnified inspection should reveal no visible scratches. Be wary at this prepolishing point. Many gem types give false signals. They appear almost polished but tiny scratches re-

Master Gem Polishing

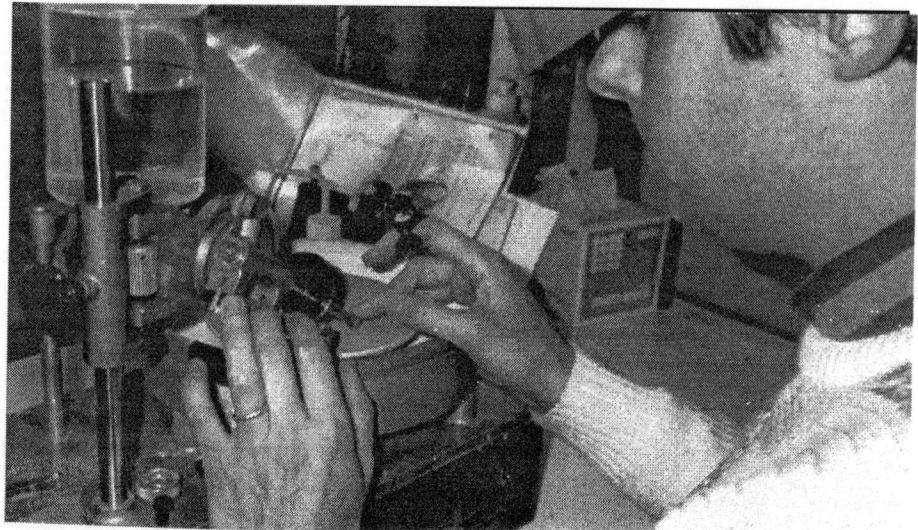

The selection of a proper carrier for polishes is a key to successful lapidary polishing. For general all-purpose polishing, many cabbers prefer leather and felt, while the majority of faceters seem to prefer metal laps.

main partially hidden by the surface gleam. Black jade or obsidian is a good example. Says experienced gemcutters, you should live long enough to polish a scratch out of obsidian or jade.

Inspect very, very carefully. If anything even resembling the possibility of a scratch remains, go back to prepolishing. If the scratch is deep enough, you may have to return to one of the sanding grits. The scratch or pit MUST be removed: polishing won't get it out. And don't think that because you're using diamond polish you can indeed remove deep scratches. You can't—without damage.

The Polishing Act...

The polishing act itself involves bringing the gemstone into contact with a suitable carrier for a wet of damp-dry slurry of a polishing compound which has a *high melting point.* For many polishing tasks, it's sufficient to coarse grind, sand, pre-polish and then touch the cabochon to a leather or felt buff that's been saturated with oxide polish. Faceters go through the same sequence and often turn

Master Gem Polishing

to Linde A on a tin-lead lap.

Sometimes, though, a different combination is required. Here is where some knowledge and experience with different polishes and carriers is valuable. The following offers a discussion of various polishing carriers and the polishes that work best.

Wood—used for centuries in Europe, wood wheels and laps are generally a close-grained hardwood. In the past, the polish of choice was "Rottenstone." Rottenstone is similar to tripoli, now used extensively for polishing metals. In lapidary, the preference was for "Air-Float tripoli," the finest grade because coarse particles are removed through a process of collecting only the dust particles that will float in the air. Today, wax impregnated wood laps are often used with diamond polishes and thick oxide pastes. If you have only diamond powder, smear some lipstick (contains fine carnauba and other waxes) on the wood: it's a fine holder for diamond particles.

Metal—lead or type metal give excellent results, as does tin-

In facet polishing, a thin, damp-dry polishing slurry on a lap will generally be revealed by the "readable" trail following the facet as the lap surface turns rapidly underneath.

Master Gem Polishing

lead. Most of the soft metal wheels and laps are used with fine alumina, but harder alloys are introduced to make them suitable for diamond use. A Pellon lap secured to a metal lap for use with Linde A makes a good polishing lap for both cabs and faceting.

Felt—although it tends to undercut, hard compressed felt is almost universal both with amateur and professional cutters. It will wear for years if properly cared for. Two elements of caution should be noted when using felt: first, its readiness to undercut leads many lapidaries to expect that felt and an oxide polish will remove scratches (it will but the results aren't good!), and second, felt builds heat quickly even to dangerous levels so plenty of water should be used. It's true that excess water removes the polish more quickly but the slight loss is worth it to keep heat under control.

Cloth—ordinary canvas (made of cotton) used with diamond as the polishing agent is a favorite for polishing jade. Sometimes the canvas is soaked in paraffin so the polishing compounds will stick. Pellon used loose or adhesively attached to a firm base lap makes an

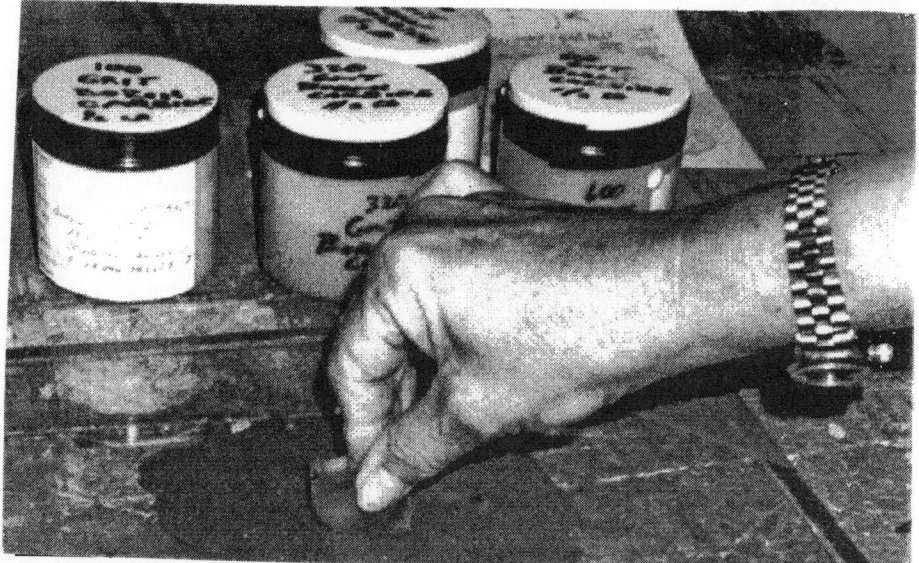

Flat cutting specialists and cabbers often use loose silicon carbide grit for an efficient pre-polish...before proceeding to polish.

exceptionally effective polishing carrier. It is often used with the new colloidal silica for polishing stones as hard as corundum. Don't overlook the effectiveness of wool carpeting as a carrier, particularly when you have a difficult jade polishing job ahead.

Leather—this material has a great many applications and has long been a favorite of cabochon cutters. Stretched over a curved or bowl-like backing, it will conform readily to the profile of virtually any cabochon shape. The most prevalent type is so-called "elk hide" or chrome-tanned leather with the rough side out. For final finishing, though, the hair side should be turned out and run very wet. Cowhide is very efficient also.

One popular application calls for a 12" diameter by $1/8$" thickness leather disk attached at the center only on a metal base lap upon which a sponge rubber backing pad has been adhesively attached. When run at high rpm, the unattached section of leather becomes flexible and it extremely effective with diamond and lipstick for applying a final, brilliant touch up polish on almost any material, especially hard minerals such as corundum, chrysoberyl, spinel.

Details on Gem Polishing Theory...

As indicated earlier, a final and brilliant polish will appear when a mineral surface has been smoothed flat with no dimples, pits, scratches or other imperfections are present on the surface or the subsurface. This happy state of conditions can be realized by introducing the stone's properly prepared surface to a carrier of metal or cloth-like material containing fine diamond particles or micronized metal oxide powders, the latter usually in a damp-dry state.

The diamond scratch and Beilby layer theories for explaining polishing action no longer are accepted as valid explanations for what happens to create a polished surface. Probably what does happens, theorists now feel, is that the polish is carried across the face or surface to be polished. This swift movement of a polishing agent creates an atomic disturbance in the surface of the mineral. The chemical interaction of the polish, water lubricant (recent studies have shown that water has a slaking action on crystals) and mineral acts in combination to alter the immediate surface somewhat.

Master Gem Polishing

The subsequent friction generates considerable heat at the point of contact between the stone surface and high temperature polishing powder particles (a polish should always be selected that possesses a higher melting temperature than the stone being polished). This allows the polish to effect a wiping-away action at a microscopic level of the atoms from the top surface of the stone or crystal.

Understanding Polishes...

To come to a true understanding of gemstone polishing, it is important to have a thorough understanding of the polishes used for cabbing and faceting. To understand the underlying principles involved in their appropriate use is also important.

Some cutters try to differentiate between polishing powders and diamond grit as to which is most effective in contributing to a smoothing-planing of a mineral's surface. Despite an apparent lack of significant difference, such a distinction may be helpful. Certainly,

A selection of hard Pellon laps belongs in every gemcutter's workshop because of its versatility and readiness to work with almost all polishes.

the hard diamond powders can make directly for a finely honed surface polish that leaves little residue of surface or sub-surface imperfections. Metal oxide powders, though, perform the same function but use a chemical combination that theoretically leaches the surface while using heat-friction to shift or plane down a microscopic layer of mineral surface. Lest a doubter think that diamond particles don't generate heat, too, an invitation is extended to watch a diamond facet being cut—and observe the flying sparks.

It's well known that Linde A is a tradename for micronized aluminum oxide. Linde A consists of a 70,000 mesh of crushed, accurately sized synthetic corundum. Such a powder is fully capable of planing any mineral surface save diamond. In the past, observations

such as the relative sizes and hardness of alumina and powder made many theorists wonder if the distinction drawn between a scratch theory and a Beilby layer theory was truly grounded in fact. Research since has shown that neither theory explains fully why a mineral surface takes a fine polish.

One probable modern answer lies with a pulverizing theory. Microscopic abrasive particles pulverize and thus reposition surface and sub-surface imperfections until the surface has been flattened. Thus light rays will encounter little interference in reflecting.

All abrasive activity creates pits or a slaking off of elements in the mineral surface. Hard stones can take considerable abuse and give up a lesser amount of their surface—and in tinier chunks—to the polishing action. Softer stones slake off easier and in bigger chunks...which is why softer polishing carriers and polishes are used with softer stones. The ac-

Master Gem Polishing

tion wanted is surface redistribution..repositioning various elements ... of the pit rims, not creating microscopic ravines in the surface.

Selection of Polishes...

With respect to the above theorizing, gemcutters must select polishing powders and carriers that will perform the polishing action without excessive gouging. For any polish, two considerations are vital: temperature melting point of the polish itself and lap hardness. Almost any polishing agent will produce a polish on some stones under a given set of circumstances. The catch is this: polishing agents to work efficiently require a higher melting point than the stone due to the higher temperatures generated at the point of contact between the stone and the polishing wheel...thereby inducing a chemical or molecular interaction between the stone and the polish alike.

This explains why a whitish polishing agent invariably turns color—to a dirty grey—during polishing use and why a relatively soft polishing powder such as cerium oxide can produce a polish on a harder material like quartz. Cerium melts at 2600° C. while quartz melts at 1600° C. Its 2050° C. melting point keeps alumina well

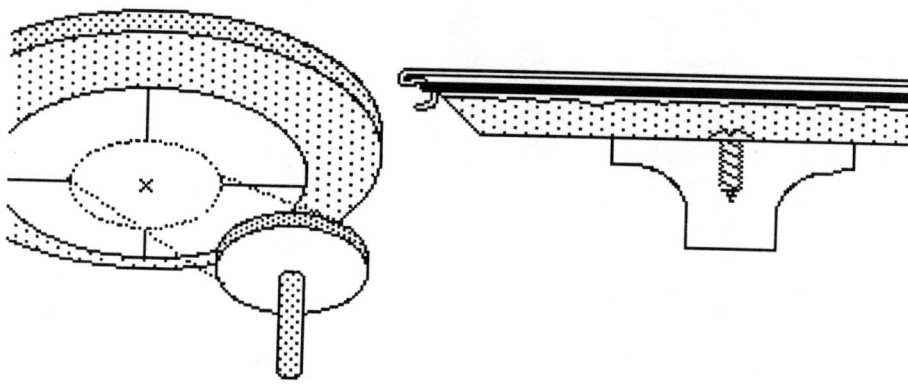

It takes only a few moments to attach a flange to the center of a metal pie pan—and PRESTO! you have a bowl for leather polishing.

Master Gem Polishing

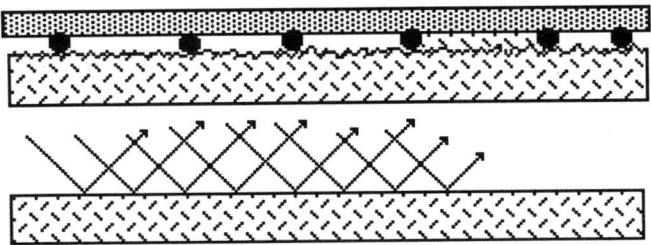

To reflect light properly, a surface must be optically flat so light rays are disciplined

Modern polishing theory suggests a pulverizing-redistribution effect in which surface and subsurface imperfections are removed to provide for a smoother, more even surface for reflecting light.

above the melting temperature of most commercial gemstone materials—and explains why the old Linde A was and remains such a stalwart gem polishing agent.

There's another rule to observe, too. The higher the temperature differential the easier—and faster— the stone will polish. Inasmuch as the hardest glass melts at only 800 degrees or so, you can readily understand why even tin oxide (melting point 1130° C.) will give it a quick, fine polish. Cerium oxide (also known as ceric oxide and cerium) with a MP of 2600° C. does better, and is the most plentiful of the rare earth metals. It can be messy to work with. On Lucite, it makes a superb polishing agent for quartz and beryl, too.

Other useful polishing powders that have declined somewhat in usage include natural aluminum oxide and silicon dioxide. Silicon dioxide is usually encountered in the form of Tripoli and is mostly now used in metal polishing—rarely for gem polishing. Aluminum oxide, known to most people in the lapidary industry as Linde A, has actually been a proven polishing agent since pre-Roman times. Then it was crushed natural corundum and today is still sometimes referred to by such names as sapphire powder, ruby dust, ruby powder, diamontine, Damascus powder, alumina, and levigated alumina.

Master Gem Polishing

Selection of Proper Carriers For Polishing...

The selection of an appropriate wheel, lap, pad, or belt for polishing is not all that difficult because, unlike cutting, the carrier surface itself has relatively little to do with the actual polishing action. A carrier's primary function is to allow the stone to be brought to a proper address to the polishing powder so the wiping action may function. A polishing lap or wheel functions primarily as a temporary but necessary carrier for the polishing agent with considerable pains taken to eliminate or reduce contact between the stone surface and the carrier surface itself.

It has been tested and confirmed that lap hardness appears to exert some influence when using oxide type polishes. Soft stones polish more readily on soft carriers and the harder ones tend to produce superior results in harder stones. This tendency has been explained as a justification for the wiping theory. The hardness of the carrier is needed to perform the holding function while reducing any

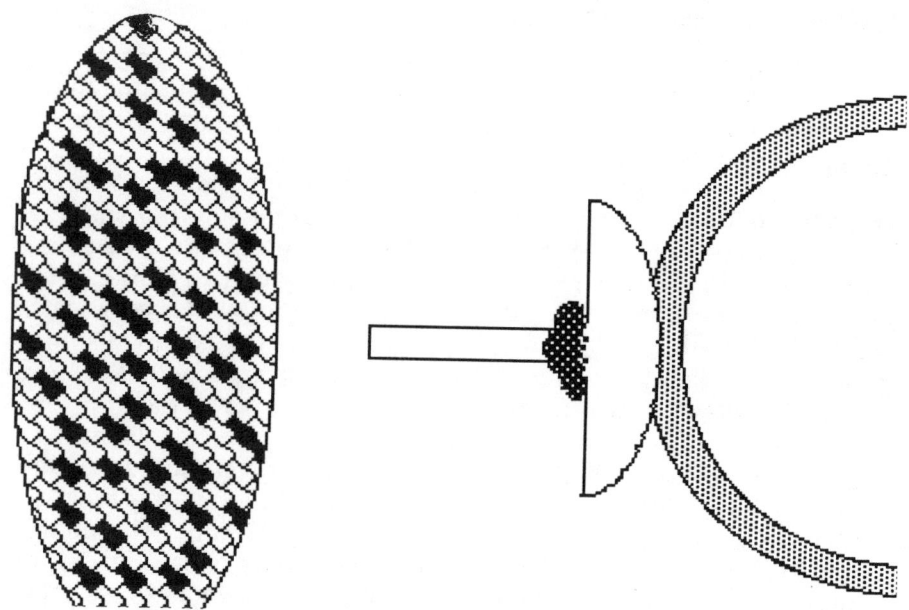

When polishing with a hard felt wheel, remember that felt tends to accentuate undercutting difficulties and heat buildup. Be careful how you manage felt.

excessive pulverization of the mineral's surface. Softer laps will plane down pit rims but won't be so apt to wipe away or slake off too much of the stone's surface. In similar fashion, hard laps are vital to the planing action because the harder mineral surface can better resists pulverization that causes large chips.

Consequently, copper, steel, zinc, ceramic make excellent carriers for polishing corundum (Mohs 9), chrysoberyl, spinel, and cubic zirconia (Mohs 8). Tin/lead, tin, and zinc come into effective use for stones of moderate hardness, while the more esoteric types—wood, wax, plastic, lead—are reserved for the softer stones. The cloths—canvas, muslin, Pellon—and leather, felt, and wood are excellent for textured cabochon minerals whose hardness usually falls in the moderate range. **Note:** *Don't allow the above observation to slide over into your selection of polishes. Truth is, hard diamond polishes often do an excellent polishing job on soft stones—using a soft carrier.*

Both diamond and metallic oxide polishing powders are effective for altering a gem surface so that both surface and sub-surface imperfections are removed: this action helps produce a fine polish.

Elsewhere in this book you'll find a short discussion on "wetting the water" in making your own polishes. One of the benefits of adding a detergent, it is pointed out, is a wetting action of the water. A wetter water spreads out more, allows you to keep the surface of the carrier wet...so the stone's surface comes into minimal contact with the carrier. Less scratching is the reward. Diamond paste or diamond powder with extender represent the same objective...keep the stone off the carrier surface. A damp-dry condition on a felt pad, a wetted condition on leather are more of the same.

It goes without saying that acid added to a polish sets up a hard oxide film on a metal surface. This film keeps the stone away from the actual carrier surface, which is why acid is so useful in reducing quartz scratching.

Making a Low pH Lubricant...

Looking for a lubricant-carrier for loose diamond polishing grit? Try mixing a cup of vinegar with a package of Knox unflavored gelatin according to the package instructions.

You'll not only get the acidic action from the vinegar, but the thick viscosity gives you a thixotropic substance (it stays where you put it!) that keeps grit from being flung from the lap. If you like to polish with loose diamond, this idea, says Don Clark of Yreka, CA, cleans off the facets much easier than extender fluid or oil.

A thin metal or plastic film user can beef up the working efficiency of any thin lap by adding a bit of 14,000 diamond to the polishing surface. The gel-like substance will cling firmly to metal and plastic film as well as cloth-like wheels and laps. This also makes it a good polishing supplement for any cabochon cutter or carver.

The mixture dries slowly with considerably less odor than vinegar used alone. Experiment with this material a bit and you'll see as I did that it can be used with just about any dry polishing agent as well as loose diamond powders . It doesn't work very well with pre-mixed diamond compounds or colloidal polishes so stick to the dry powders.

Techniques on Use of Felt Buff...

Long a favorite among cabbers and carvers, the felt buff easily retains its popularity as a general polishing buff.

Most gemcutters use a hard felt either in wheel form or as a thin pad available for cementing to a hard metal or wooden backing disk. Some gemcutters have even been known to make their own felt buffs, cutting them from old felt hats (often this is soft felt) or from sheet felt.

Polishing Felts Are Aggressive...

Elsewhere in this book you will read that felt must be used judiciously. It attacks aggressively, builds heat up quickly when friction is introduced, and is infamous as a promoter of undercutting. For that reason, you'll find that felt is best used with stones that possess an even texture and are not especially heat sensitive. You can use felt on a heat sensitive stone, but only so long as you check frequently on the stone's temperature. The old "cheek method" comes in handy. Just touch the stone to your cheek every so often and this will give you a quick, honest report on the stone's temperature.

Felt is one of the few polish carriers where a gemcutter enjoys

Master Gem Polishing

a wide safety margin on the amount of polish that can be used. You can nearly saturate the surface of felt and it will polish efficiently. Obviously, felt works well with a wet surface or with the traditional "damp-dry" condition.

Some gemcuters who also possess gold smithing skills have been known to use a tripoli treated felt buff to polish up their gems and precious metals, too. It's rather convenient to polish a finished piece of jewelry on a felt buff, confident that the tripoli polish will perform well on stone and on the metal.

Stay Wet and Cool When Polishing Opal...

When polishing opal always remember that heat can destroy your stone. Keep the stone wet at all times, even when doing a quick touchup. Experienced opal cutters use a completely worn out 600 grit sandpaper WET for the final pre-polish sanding. A tin oxide on a canvas wheel generally represents the best polishing combination. Many opal cutters also report good results with cerium oxide on a Pellon or cloth pad. Of course, the standard combination for opal polishing remains alumina oxide or tin oxide in a thin slurry on the rough side of the leather (with the leather mounted with a cushion or foam back).

Opal tends to come up to polish quickly so keep the leather wet (for cooling) and check for results after only a short time on the pad. Don't apply a lot of pressure: it simply isn't necessary with the soft opal. Reflected light will give you the best viewing for flat spots, the bane of all opal cutters.

Most opal is cut with a rounded top. That's why you will want a soft rubber or sponge pad behind the canvas, leather or other polishing pad for cushioning. Opal doesn't like heat and it most definitely does not like shock. Keep the opal moving on the wheel and never let it stop moving. To check for heat buildup, touch the opal to your cheek. You'll notice any heat increase immediately with this technique. Canvas doesn't build up heat quickly but any friction is bound to introduce a certain amount of temperature elevation.

Pie Pan As a Polishing Bowl...

Need a bowl upon which to attach a piece of leather for cab polishing?

Go to the appliance department of the local hardware store

and purchase a small pie pan. It's a simple matter to attach a steel flange so the bowl can be fitted to a machine. The lip on the pan is just right for securing the leather with a piece of monofilament nylon cord, thread or a wide rubber band. Such a pan polishing tool works as well as the commercial ones, and changes are quick.

Develop "Pressure" Skills...

It isn't discussed in detail all that much but PRESSURE is an element of gemcutting practice that must be understood—and utilized with skill.

In lapping, the removal rate and character of the abraded surface depends directly on the type of abrasive in combination with the lap, belt, pad, disk, spool or wheel used and on the AMOUNT OF PRESSURE. Even when the abrading agent is a silicon carbide wheel, pressure plays a large role in the performance.

Most gemcutters apply greater pressure when polishing and they often do it by habit and not necessarily with regard to the condition of the polishing surface and abrasives.

After gaining some experience with gemcutting, most individuals react instinctively to the pressure element, automatically adapting to the task at hand without giving a second thought to the magic it plays. In grinding, when a gemcutter bears down with considerable pressure on a coarse wheel, the pressure from the abrasive particles on the surface of the mineral causes deep chips to fly out. Later, in final shaping, s/he will utilize a feather touch...and this feather touch will produce a finish that is almost as smooth as the next finer wheel.

Try to remain aware of the role that pressure plays when polishing. Most gemcutters apply greater pressure when polishing and they often do it by habit and not necessarily with regard to the condition of the polishing surface and abrasives. Don't forget that the more there is of diamond particles imbedding in the polishing surface the finer the finish...and the slower the polishing action. That's why a commercially precoated polishing material often appreciates a speed-up "boost" *e.g..*, particles can roll freely on the carrier's surface,

Master Gem Polishing

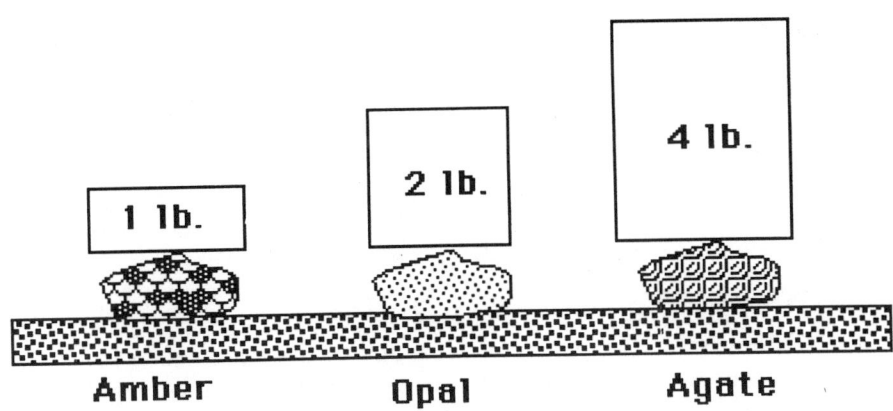

The application of hand pressure, whether polishing cabochons or faceted stones, should be the result of a conscious decision...not a demonstration of habit. Different stones require individualized attention.

helping to improve polishing action and thus polishing speed. The embedding principle accounts for the fact that different lap materials will give different performance with different compounds, varying with the amount of pressure.

A light touch during polish will invariably produce a finer finish even if the polishing time is a bit longer (and thus also a bit more exposure to edge rounding regardless of the polish, lap surface, speed or pressure). A good approach until you develop your own polishing technique is to start polishing with only moderate pressure then end with a feathered touch.

The Way to Polish Turquoise...

To many gemcutters, turquoise is a rather simple mineral and requires no special sanding or polishing techniques. For cutters who specialize in turquoise, such an attitude is a receipt for disaster.

Turquoise can be very challenging if the goal is to bring out as good a polish as possible. Because it is so soft, turquoise should be sanded on a fine grit diamond or silicon carbide wheel. Because of its tendency to absorb water, sanding with a dry clean, sharp sanding cloth is preferred at moderate speeds.

Leather or buckskin over a reasonably soft cushion backing—felt makes a suitable backing—using a lightly applied thin slurry of tin oxide paste represents the best polishing combination. Run the wheel almost damp-dry. When and if the polish starts sticking to the stone, wash if off the stone and start again.

Old turquoise cutters claim they get best results using light pressure on the center wet surface of the polishing pad and then gradually move to the drier, faster outer surfaces as the polish progresses.

Polishing the Feldspars...

Do feldspars really give you that much trouble in polishing? If so, try the usual: faceting—alumina on tin; cabbing—tin oxide on leather or hard felt. The popular Idaho and Oregon sunstones respond well to these polishing combinations, too.

Most cabbers apply a medium thick tin oxide or alumina slurry to a hard, damp felt wheel and apply considerable pressure. The preliminary step through procedure for feldspar cabbing material is to shape grind with a 220 wheel, and fine sand with 400 before prepolishing with a worn 600 belt. The finishing step for experienced feldspar cutters is to go a fast, hard polish. Feldspars, which aren't especially heat sensitive, generally don't offer all that much difficulty.

For the best success with feldspars, keep your cutting about 5°-7° off the cleavage plan...the same tactics that are used with topaz. When you attempt to fine sand or polish a feldspar too close to the cleavage plane you'll often experience slaking.

Faceters face most of the same challenges as cabbers when it comes to feldspars. All facet planes should be 5°-7° off the cleavage plane also. The major difference between faceted and cabbed feldspars is in the polishing combination.

Faceters consistently get better, faster results by using alumina on a tin lap. A feldspar cleavage won't open up all that easily so it's not too dangerous to employ a used scored lap where the scoring lines have been somewhat burnished over. This provides a considerably less bumpy ride for the stone than if you were to begin polishing on a freshly scored lap.

If you can't get a satisfactory polish with either tin oxide or alumina, try switching to cerium oxide (sometimes with an alumina booster). Cerium will often provide a nice polish on feldspar.

Making Your Own Mini Wheels...

Every gemcutter—regardless of discipline—should own a wide assortment of small wooden or plastic polishing wheels.

Gemcutters don't seriously consider making these small, handy polishing wheels, brushing off the idea with a curt, "I don't have the equipment or wood working skills for such things."

That attitude is a bit questionable. If you have a cabochon ma chine or faceting unit you have the equipment—and then some. If you can cut a gemstone, you certainly have the talent to work with wood or plastic.

Small wooden or plastic disks, with common nails as the mandrel, make great polishing tools for that particular job where special handling and treatment are required. Uniquely cut cabochons with deep recesses or channels or flutes are virtually impossible to polish with standard wheels, laps and buffs. A large faceted table can stubbornly resist even the most strenuous efforts to produce a smooth, even polish.

With a sharp edge on a small polishing wheel, though, any channel or flute will surrender to the polish. Large facets can be polished quickly and thus easily brought to a final polish with a carefully flattened mini wheel containing fine diamond.

If mini polishing wheels are so useful, why don't more gem cutters use them? Well, once the mental block of "no tools or talent" is removed, just finding the material and getting started can be a big hurdle. That obstacle is easy to overcome, too.

Small plastic polishing wheels? Button! Button! Who's got the button? Answer: the nearest sewing supply or craft store does.

Small wooden polishing wheels. Who's got them available commercially? Answer: the nearest craft shop where unfinished wooden parts are sold for people who like to make wood toys. The New England Wood Company produces an extensive line of such wooden parts and you'll find them in small plastic bags pinned in rows in the store's wood section. Be sure and check the type of wood. Some of these wheels are made with pine and other soft wood types and they just aren't satisfactory for lapidary use. You want hard woods, maple, ash, rosewood, etc.

The encouraging aspect about buttons and toy wood wheels is that they are all usually center marked and need only the addition of a regular mandrel or nail to complete. It's really that easy.

Mini Wheels For Fantasy Cutting...

If you'd like to do some Munsteiner or Fantasy cutting, mini wheels will make it possible. They can be quickly shaped into nearly any configuration you want. You can also make matching sanding and polishing pairs, using a sanding wheel to cut a channel or flute and then matching it up conveniently with the polishing wheel.

If you'd like to build up a small inventory of mini wheels and try your hand at some of the new cutting trends, just go to the nearest sewing (you can also buy wooden buttons in these shops) or craft shops and purchase some buttons with $1/2$-inch, $3/4$-inch and 1-inch diameters.

The buttons or wooden wheels can be centered on a small diameter wooden dowel stick or a nail about two inches long using a 5-Minute Epoxy.

Once the button or wheel is secure, place the mandrel in a $1/4$-inch hand drill and run the button over emery paper that's been attached to a hard, flat surface. With this setup, you can pretty much make any shape or configuration you want to apply on the button.

If you don't have a hand drill available, use your gemcutting machine. Make a shaper block (this consists of little more than a block of wood pierced with a hole that is the same size as your mandrel). To control depth of the preformer, set it atop a shim stack of ordinary playing cards and add or remove cards to get the desired height. You can cut out a disk of wood sanding paper and glue it to a firm base plate.

Shape Button into Profile...

Running the button on the sanding paper, form the profile that you want to use on the stone. Make at least three such buttons. You'll want at least one mini wheel for a 600 diamond, another with 3000 and one for 14,000 final polish. Some gemcutters may want a wheel with even finer grit. Because you'll no doubt be using water as a coolant-lubricant, the wooden wheels should be soaked in paraffin. Absent this, at least apply some carnauba wax-containing furniture wax to the wooden wheels. Keep in mind that not only does the wax protect the wood from water induced swelling but it also offers

Master Gem Polishing

a surface upon which the diamonds can embed.

It's all right to smooth the mini wheel surfaces, but not too much. A bit of a roughened finish provides "bite" for the diamond paste. In any event, working the tool against hard gem materials will eventually impose a completely appropriate surface on the mini wheel surface anyway. A couple of options exist for setting up to do hand polishing with a mini wheel. The one I recommend is a small electric motor containing a keyed chuck and bolted to a suitable platform for horizontal working. This is the setup that most professional cutters use because it offers maximum hand control and flexibility.

With a horizontal working arrangement you can keep the stone on the bottom of the wheel, maintain the use of both hands, and keep a sharp eye on polishing progress. Also, you can more easily introduce the coolant to the polishing area.

It is possible to use a hand held tool such as a Foredom but the difficulty of holding the work steady is greatly increased. For one thing, it takes one hand to hold the tool and the other to hold the stone. To keep the work cool, of course, you'll need to hold the work under the drip or pause for dips. It can be done with a Foredom, it's just that a stable polishing wheel is so easier to manage.

Once you're ready to go, smear a small amount of polish on the outer surface of the wheel. Coolant can be introduced with a small squeeze bottle or a drip arrangement. Also, most 1/4-inch drill motors are not water or shock proofed so put a barrier between the workpiece and the motor. You won't be using copious amounts of water so if you're careful the danger to the motor—and to you—is minimal. Just don't touch the motor while you're working with an electrical motor in a water wet environment.

Introduce the stone to the wheel slowly. Begin a slight polishing motion and then track the edge across the full face of one section of the area to be polished. Slowly move the stone back and forth until you've produced a satisfactory polish. Then move to the next section. The major problem with small wheel polishing is that a gemcutter tries to cover too large of an area at one time. Work small areas into polish and then blend them nicely.

Note: *Yes, a mini wheel will work nicely to give you a polish in difficult, complex areas. Don't overlook, though, the benefits of a mini felt wheel. They're easy to use, too, and they work just as fast and accurately—so long as the area to be polished it a bit larger.*

Growing Trend in Polishing . . .

More and more gemcutters are experimenting with the growing trend toward thin polishing laps and paste polishes.

Time was when every faceter solved the bulk of polishing requirements by reaching for some Linde A powder and a tin/lead lap. As a matter of fact, Linde A in combination with the tin/lead lap was heralded by the Graves Company as the best gemstone polishing combination. Graves still promotes it with good reason.

Today, though, a growing number of faceters want to avoid repeatability and cheating problems by polishing a tier of facets as soon as the tier has been pre-polished. With older technologies this alternative wasn't all that practical because it usually involved a change of laps. Even today, almost any lap change implies a significant repeatability challenge. Most polishing laps are often slightly different in thickness from grinding and sanding laps. To accommodate this lap thickness difference, the machine setup needs to be adjusted to accommodate the height—and sometimes the index, too—so the facet will lay flat-to-flat on the new surface.

The result? Faceters increasingly are turning to thin film laps that contain a "boost" application of diamond or oxide polishing paste by 1) dropping the thin film polishing disk over the pre-polishing lap and polishing up a row of facets, then removing the

Master Gem Polishing

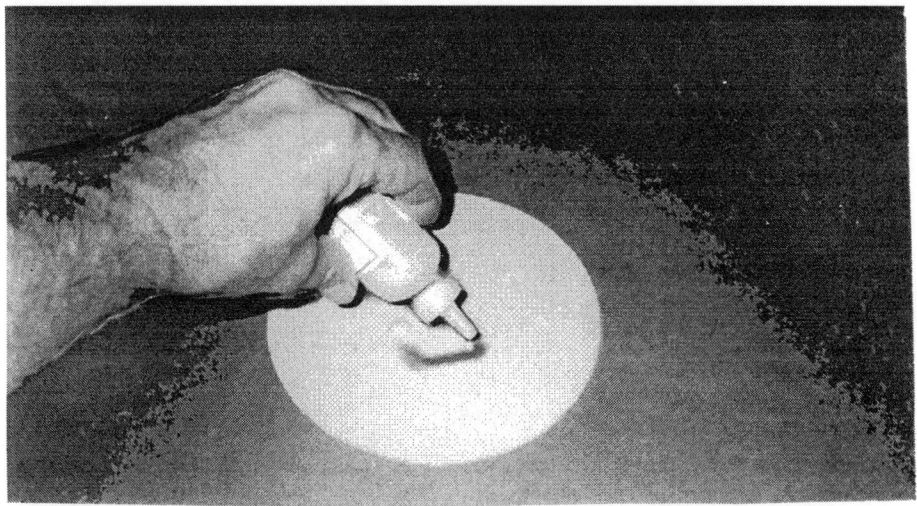

Small squeeze bottles are excellent dispensers for applying measured amounts of polish on a lap. Several varities are available.

disk to proceed to the next prepolishing task, or 2) placing a polishing film slip disk of smaller diameter permanently over the prepolishing lap and making the few up and down clicks to prepolish and polish with no further lap changes.

Polishing methods are also changing in much the same way for cabbers. Many are moving away from messy polishing powders in favor of Bruce Bars and colloidal polishing paste suspensions. The powder just involves too much messiness to suit their needs—and the paste-like polishing formulations have the additional additives which contribute to a faster and superior polish..

Much of the impetus for polishing pastes of all kinds no doubt arises from the almost universal popularity of diamond grinding and polishing products. Diamond grits which make polishing a cleaner operation are available as coatings or individual convenient pastes that come nicely packaged in hospital type syringes. Recent breakthroughs in metallic oxide colloidal pastes now allow chemical polishes to be quickly, cleanly and conveniently dispensed from a container without the addition of water. The elimination of the water as cooler-lubricant assures more consistent "damp-dry" surface conditions as well as contributing to a neater working area.

What's really appealing to gemcutters is the ability to apply

Master Gem Polishing

these chemical oxides and diamond pastes easily and neatly in measured amounts. Further, unlike precoated films where surfaces wear out unevenly and rather quickly, the polishes can be finger spread and moved over the polishing surface. With the ready availability of thin plastic and metal polishing films in combination with diamond and oxide pastes, a pair of scissors and 5 minutes time can provide a whole selection of polishing laps.

Colloidal Silica . . .

Awaiting only a minor technological improvement or two to become a nearly universal lapidary polish, colloidal silica increasingly is finding applications in lapidary.

This remarkable new polish was introduced to lapidary by the American Society of Gemcutters after a series of intensive laboratory examinations at the University of Arizona. A fast acting polish that is especially useful for materials over 7 Mohs hardness, colloid-

A worn belt makes an excellent prepolishing tool for polishing difficult cabochons. It's best to avoid new belts for fine prepolishing because they often tend to attack the stone a bit too aggressively.

Master Gem Polishing

al silica's only major gem polishing deficiencies seem to be a high viscosity (it's very thin and runny) and a somewhat elevated pH level.

Buehler's Ltd, one of the major producers of colloidal silica, sells special polishing pads (called Mastermet™) for use with its polish. The shortcoming with these flat, perforated pads arises from the fact that they were not originally designed for lapidary use but rather for polishing computer silicon wafers. The jump from wafer to gemstone surface isn't all that great as many cabbers have discovered. For faceters, it's a different story. Other than for polishing a large table facet, the perforations allow small facets to drop into or through the perforations...and there is also the ever present danger of edge rounding.

Cabbers have little problem with the Mastermet™ polishing pad, but for faceters it presents problems that are most difficult to overcome.

For cabbers, though, the characteristics of the cloth pads can be made not only acceptable but almost desirable. When placed against a soft backing, they will bend just enough to follow the rounding of the cab surface and build a superior polish.

Still, the principal complaint about CS use from both cabbers and faceters remains with the high viscosity issue. Fling from the centrifugal action of swiftly turning laps and wheels contributes to excessive loss of the silica polishing liquid. Under these circumstances, a gemcutter must carefully manage the polish supply on the wheel so the polish is not too quickly exhausted.

Recognizing this drawback, researchers continue their efforts with various chemical thickening additives and formulations. Some of the new permanently suspended silica solutions appear promising.

In the meantime, gemcutters have innovated their own responses to the silica problem, largely because the polish does such a fine job. These innovations include using colloidal silica on Mylar/acetate. For some reason the silica tends to remain a bit longer on the soft matte finish of the two plastic types.

To cut down on fling loss, other gemcutters use masking tape to build a sort of coffer dam on the outer edge of a thick polishing plate. With this paper barrier up, the centrifugal force hurls the sili-

Master Gem Polishing

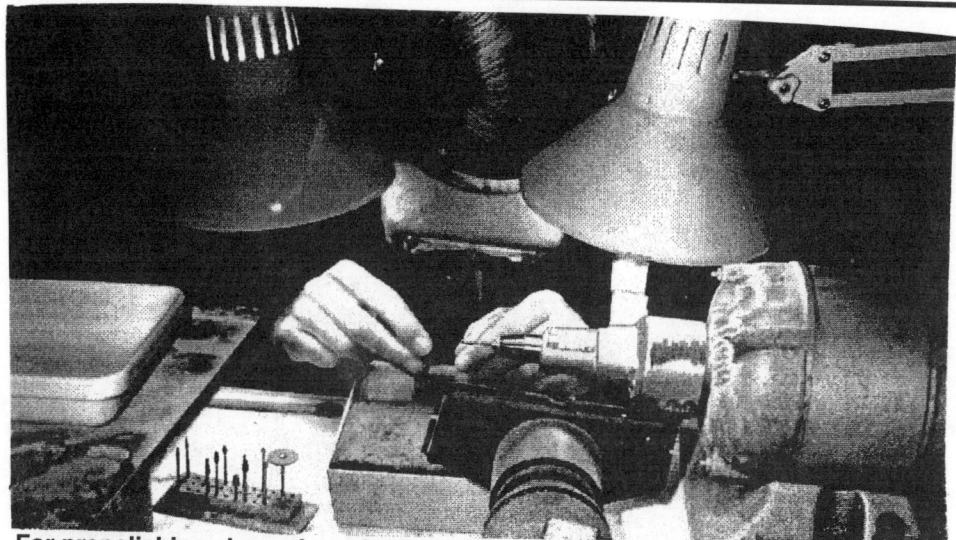

For prepolishing channels and other small, complex work, use a small silicone wheel rather than a rubberized sanding disk. Rubberized wheels leave a smudge or frosting on the mineral which is almost impossible to remove.

ca against the barrier where the gemcutter can swing the stone into the outer edge and work the polish back onto the lap.

The dam idea has been especially popular among gemcutters because colloidal silica actually improves in polishing action after being used a number of times. Some gemcutters report they have re-used colloidal silica up to a dozen times. The swarf? It's apparently the material that improves the silica's polishing action.

More Details on Flat Facets. .

When a faceter places a facet against the smoothing or prepolishing lap, does s/he really eliminate flatness concerns?

The evidence indicates an answer of "no."

A lap, regardless of hardness, can—if exposed to enough pressure—allow a small hard facet to "tilt" into or, in the case of plastic, indent itself despite the hard, flat base underneath. This kind of action is an open invitation to curved planes or rounded edges. That you don't want.

When a design calls for flat facets, that's what should be cut and it often pays to assure a facet's flatness, especially all large ones You can inexpensively make your own mirror setup to check facet

Master Gem Polishing

polishing progress. For specific instructions on making and using a mirror, see page 215. For a speedy solution, buy a section of thick, flat mirror anywhere from 1" to 3" square. The thickness makes viewing easier because the image appears lower in the mirrored reflection.

Using a section of mirror to assure flatness in a planed surface represents an old machinist's tactic, a trick that also has a long use history in lapidary. The mirror can be used, especially in repair work, to locate a facet precisely and then—using machine controls—to accurately identify index, angle and height. If you wish to check on an item's flatness, just wet the mirrored surface and place the facet in question against it flat-to-flat. What works better than water is a smear of tooth paste or even Maalox on the facet. As the matchup squeezes all the liquid out, you can see plainly the outline of the facet. Any non-flat area in the facet will fail to squeeze the toothpaste out and this condition will be visually evident. The mirrored reflection will produce unmistakable visible information about the specifications of the facet's surface.

As you seek to improve your polishing technique, don't be overly concerned by the relative Mohs level of the various plastic or metal carrier materials. Their virtues offer some true benefits and they can do a good job on stones in any Mohs hardness range. Even with thin films, once you've pre-polished a tier it's a simple matter to drop the thin plastic film over a smoothing lap, click up a few times to compensate for the additional thickness and then polish (again, consider "boosting" any impregnated or coated laps with a shot or two of oxide or 14,000 diamond paste)

As suggested earlier, if you're using a standard 8" prepolishing lap, it's convenient to drop a 6" diameter thin plastic or metal slip disk on top after adding some water to provide the necessary suction. A few clicks on the vertical cheater is about all that is necessary to adjust back and forth between pre-polish and polish. The faceter is immediately ready to commence either operation.

Polish Pastes Can Boost Polishing Ease ..

Bruce Bars come in handy for boosting the polishing action of polishing carriers. They are available in all the desired metallic oxide polishes. For self made thin film disks as well as felt and leather pads, a Bruce Bar or colloidal or diamond paste is about the

Master Gem Polishing

only effective strategy. They not only enable you to "paste" the polish on the surface in controlled, convenient amounts but the container packaging contributes greatly in keeping a work area clean and tidy. As always with pastes, remember to go easy on the water flow, though, because it washes away the soluble pastes.

One approach used by professional cutters—it works on both a faceter's polishing laps and on an expandable rubber wheel or belt—consists in marking the laps or belt with a grease pencil and then applying standard sized Aluminum Oxide Bruce Bar to the one side or ring. The remaining polishing area is treated with Linde A Bruce Bar. This combination, incidentally, is dynamite for YAG. Isn't Linde A really micronized alumina? If so, why a two-mesh? Well, Linde A is a chemically refined hexagonal shaped alumina whose particles are superior for gem polishing than those of standard cubic shaped aluminum oxide particles.

It's been mentioned before, but it bears repeating again. Alu-

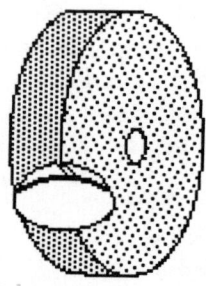 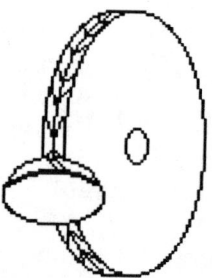

Use edge of fine SC wheel to cut channels and sharp felt tip edge to polish. Be sure to cut channels in single motion to avoid extra planing which is difficult to polish

The best way to polish Munsteiner-like channels is to cut them with a single motion (so as to leave no extra planes) and then polish with a corner or sharp edged felt pad containing a somewhat thick polishing paste.

Master Gem Polishing

mina oxide is the one metallic oxide polish that can pretty much be mixed with any other of the metallic oxides—and the resulting combination will produce superior results. When you run into a polishing challenge and the stone simply won't respond, try adding a pinch or two of aluminum oxide. This will often do the trick. Incidentally, thin polishing disks should be dedicated: a different one for each polish type.

Contemporary Polishing Theory...

If both the Beilby Layer Theory and the Diamond Scratch Theory have been largely debunked as explanations for polishing gem stones, what is left? Is there any theory that scientifically addresses the how and the why of gem polishing? The bulk of trade comment about polishing historically has been mostly anecdotal with few introductions of verified fact.

For the past three years, I've been conducting research with

Can cabochon cutters use Pellon effectively? Yes, just cut a ribbon of material and fit it around an expandable rubber wheel. Use superglue to attach the ends: it holds powerfully. Pellon is a good carrier for wet polishes.

Master Gem Polishing

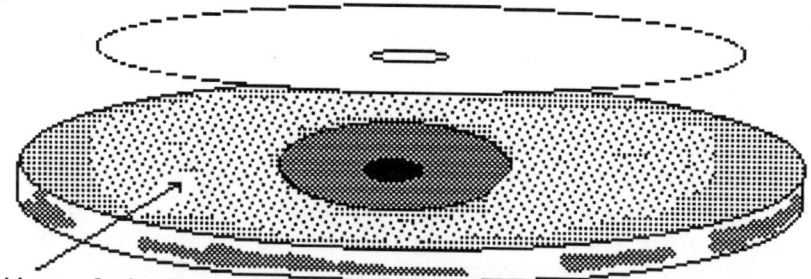

Use plain tap water or olive oil as an adhesive to hold thin plastic or metal films to the base lap.

Olive oil also makes an excellent temporary adhesive for holding thin metal or plastic films to a base lap. Water has been the traditional adhesive used.

thin polished crystal specimens and a 600x microscope. I've also been monitoring the Library of Congress, the U. S. Patent Office, the National Institute of Standards as well as the research performed at the University of Arizona and by the Japanese optics industry.

From these various scientific sources, there seems to be emerging a more contemporary theory that addresses the field of mineral polishing The theory seems based on the realization that any <u>blunt</u>, <u>uniform</u> and <u>consistent</u> abrasive element is capable of producing a smooth, polished surface on any gem crystal(s).

As an example of modern polishing theory, consider the "stress stone" that many men and women carry in their pocket. Years ago, I had my own stress stone and it had no other function than to be available for rubbing in my bare fingers, to while away a few moments when the hands and perhaps the mind had nothing else to do. In short order, that ordinary stone took on a smooth, polished surface—just from the action of my fingers. The Beilby and scratch theories

Master Gem Polishing

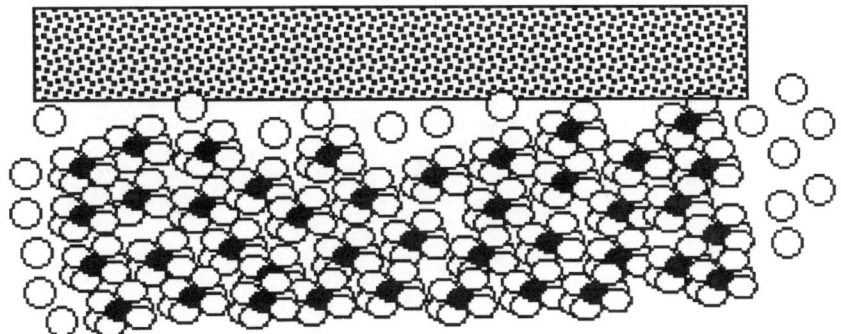

As the polishing element moves over the crystal surface, chemical interaction prompted by pressure and friction perhaps induce the molecular layers to shift their lattice positions, filling in vacancies and honing off peaks. What results is a glassy, polished surface.

never quite convinced me that separately or collectively they could explain how soft human flesh alone could polish a hard agate.

The explanation is: my blunt fleshy finger surfaces working consistently over time, expose the stone's surface to a uniform surface exerting vertical and horizontal pressures that did not equal or exceed the ultimate compressive strength of the stone material (that's why no "chips" popped out) until the rubbing forces interacted to remove and/or rearrange the atomic lattice of the stone's surface to a smooth, polished surface.

Is this explanation stretching the issue? Probably not. Considerable scientific evidence exists to show that polishing takes place because the polishing agent is hard enough, abrasive enough and persistent enough to rearrange the crystal's surface profile so that peaks are clipped off and valleys are evened off...forming a smooth, polished surface.

Ever wonder why a new 1200 diamond lap, wheel or belt cuts and scratches so aggressively until it's been "broken in"? You can't even effectively pre-polish with such a new lap because it's virtually impossible to predict the depth of the many scratches.

Master Gem Polishing

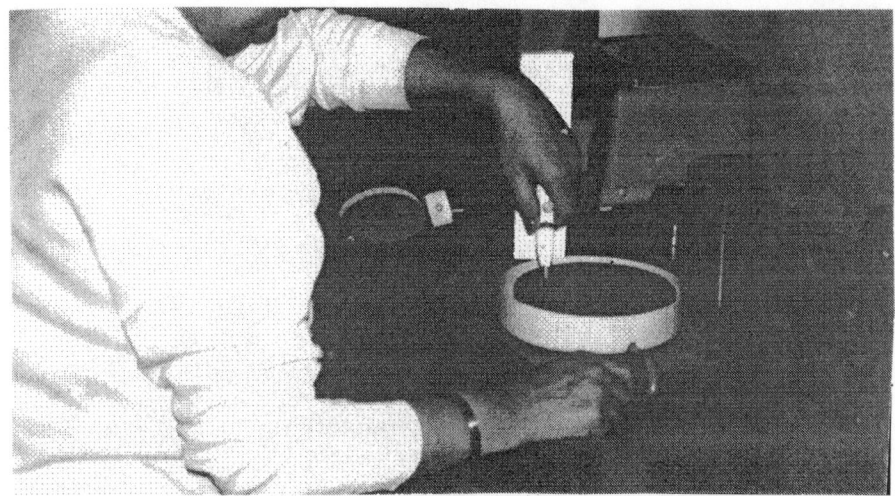

Only when hand pressure is consistently applied with appropriate pressure will a crystal surface take a polish. Polish occurs when heat, friction, polish and pressure interact to rearrange the existing atomic lattice so peaks and valleys are evened out.

Why must a pre-polish or polishing lap be "broken in" anyway? Isn't breaking in a lap a nice way of saying that you're breaking off the irregularly embedded shards and sharp points into <u>blunt</u> edges that are of <u>uniform</u> depth? When these blunted, uniform particles are <u>consistently</u> moved across a crystal face, they produce an evenly modulated surface. In polishing, the particles are so tiny that their collective action consists in removing some and repositioning or rearranging other atoms in the crystal surface until the surface has been planed, bludgeoned, or smoothed *i.e.*, it is polished.

That's what crystal polishing is all about. It's goal is to reposition crystal atoms by a smooth, uniform action of the polishing agent. Cutting or scratching—the mark of Mohs hardness—is only incident to this achievement.

Too much of gemstone polishing thought is directed toward Mohs rank. The vital element in explaining polishing action is indentability as measured by Knoops as well as Brinell, Rockwell and Vickers. These rankings measure the compressive strength of materials. The electron microscope proved that every crystal is comprised of atomic lattices arranged in a structure often resembling the shape of that crystal. How close the atoms are to each other, sometimes re-

Master Gem Polishing

ferred to as the packing order, varies with the grain. This explains why a facet will suddenly not polish in a stone that had been polishing with no difficulty a moment earlier. The direction changed so the packing order changed and rather than polish, the facet wants only to pit or develop cavities. This happens with corundum, tourmaline, and peridot all the time. Yes, with colored stones, like diamonds, direction is significant.

Understanding the atomic personality of crystals is the first step in conquering the mysteries of gem polishing. Scratching or inducing a glassy layer different from the rest of the crystal doesn't explain things. Plastic deformation or "slip"—the response of the atomic lattice to adequate pressure—might provide an answer. The blunt, uniform thrusting of the polishing particles applied with appropriate horizontal and vertical pressure, the electron microscope shows, literally uses mutual attraction of stone and polish to rearrange layers of atoms. This action causes the crystal atoms to slip and slide, filling in molecular vacancies in some cases, planing down other interruptions until a smooth, glassy surface is produced.

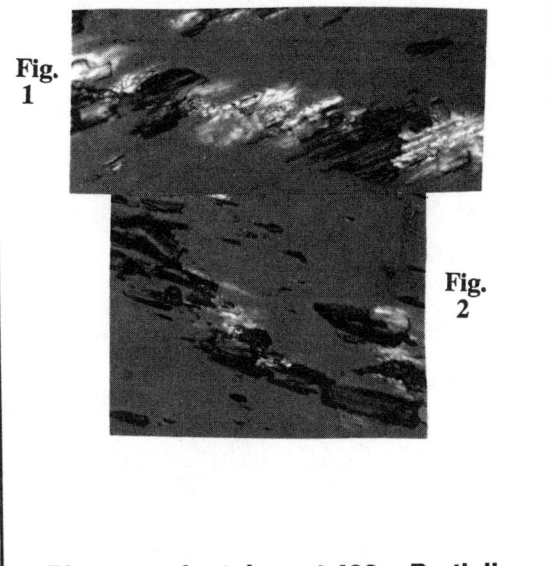

Photographs taken at 400x. Partially polished andalusite.

As indicated earlier, the packing arrangement of crystal planes parallel to any given facet explain the difference in speed and difficulty of polishing. Illustrations of partially polished andalusite above demonstrate this. Fig. 1 shows typical pitting that occurs on a plane or grain direction where excessive pressure and compression made it easier for the crystal segments to pop out rather than slide. The dark spots in Fig. 2 are reflective zones beneath the stone surface caused by stress strains just prior to spalling.

Master Gem Polishing

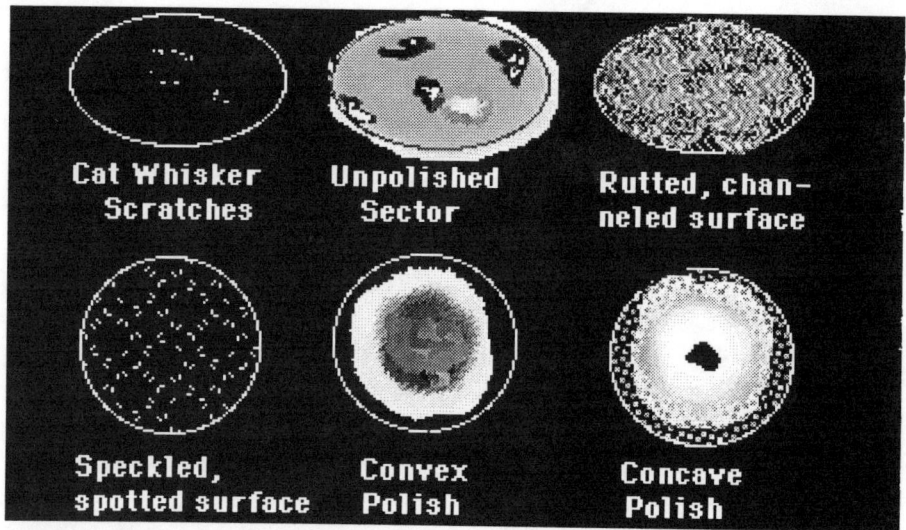

It's beneficial for any gemcutter to learn to interpret the conditions of a mineral surface as it undergoes polishing.

Why are blunted, uniform level polishing particles superior to sharp edged ones? The former equalize vertical pressure over a wider area of crystal and enhance layer movement and/or deformation. Sharp tips at random depths will more likely exceed the crystal's ultimate compressive strength and cause irregular chipping or pitting.

Polishing Jade Isn't That Tough...

Jade has an undeserved reputation. Many gemcutters insist it is a problem mineral so far as polishing is concerned.

For other cutters, jade could more accurately be described as tough to grind but easy to polish. It's all in the approach, the jade experts say, and the approach to jade is quite a bit different than, say, the approach to agate.

Keep in mind that jadeite and nephrite have fibrous structures and this gives the two species extraordinary toughness. It won't chip when ground and usually won't even break if it's dropped to the floor or ground. Indeed, Chinese artisans have used jade blocks as anvils for centuries. It's softness minimizes dents and mars and its toughness allows it to stand up to heavy pounding abuse for years without appreciable wear or tear.

Because jade can also withstand considerable heat with no danger, many gemcutters when polishing it allow heat friction to build. The reasoning is that polishing action *i.e.,* molecular flow, takes place much easier when the mineral's temperature is elevated.

After being roughed in on a coarse wheel, jade should be finished with 400 silicon carbide grit or 600 diamond grit. Once this operation is complete, go to a belt sanding operation starting with 320. Finish to a high pre-polish surface with a worn 320 grit cloth or a used 1200 diamond wheel or belt.

The secret of polishing varies. Many say use tin oxide (with a touch of vinegar or diluted muriatic acid) on a hard felt buff, being careful to avoid too much pressure. Some contend that thick tin oxide or chrome oxide on leather will produce a fine high quality polish. Others mix alumina with chrome oxide on felt.

Don't overlook the benefits of polishing jade with diamond grits. The best approach for a diamond polish is to step the jade through the various grits moving progressively from 1200, 8000, 50,000 and then—if you want to try for a superior polish—100,000.

How to Interpret
Polishing Imperfections . . .

Knowing how to interpret imperfections during the polishing process is very important.

The four imperfection categories are:

1. POCK MARKS. These are the easiest to identify and prevent, caused by failure to remove enough material during the lap-polishing operation. They are actually remains of the scratches that were left by the previous cutting operation. To eliminate or manage, just use a fine cutting lap (3000 or 1200) to produce the smaller scratches that are easier to polish out. Pock marks can easily be seen with a 5- or 10-power magnifier.

2. SCRATCHES. Can be easily seen with a conventional Opti-Visor. Often quite deep scratches will need considerable sanding to remove (usually polishing simply won't remove them). Scratches aren't always caused by contamination or debris or aggregation. They sometimes result from actual burning of rough in a very

Master Gem Polishing

The best strategy for polishing large flats or table facets is to clean the stone carefully with alcohol and then hand polish it gently on an appropriately sized flat polishing surface.

small area and the resultant cragging of the burned area scars the surface. This occurs from a concentration of pressure on a tiny spot which hikes temperature and leads to burning. You can look in the dark and see scratches as little flashes of light, thanks to irregular reflection. Lap speed is a major factor with some materials scratching even with very slow rpm and light pressure. Quartz is particularly susceptible to scratching which results from burning.

Scratch avoidance tactics represent the best strategy and there are many useful alternatives.

Acid or some sort of oxidizer goes a long way to avoid scratching which is due to an accumulation of diamond swarf or chemical powder. Orientation of the stone with regard to its crystal structure may be a factor. With doubly refractive stones, most scratching is generally experienced when the stone is oriented on the dopstick perpendicular to the crystallographic axis which is generally the soft-

Master Gem Polishing

est grain direction. Also, some facets polish faster and easier than others and this occurs mostly—some gemcutters claim—in cubic structured crystals. Crystallographically that would be impossible.

Strategies to avoid scratches include reducing lap speed, better hand pressure control, reversing direction, polishing on a stationary surface, scrubbing the wheel or lap with Lava soap or some other strong cleanser, altering the amount and placement of lubrication or chemical powders and, especially, changing the powder-water viscosity. When a polish slurry becomes too dry, it's an open invitation to scratching—yet a too wet polishing environment can cause trouble too. You want it damp-dry. One final option: use a softer lap.

3. CAT HAIRS. You'll need 30- to 40-magnification power to catch these pesky surface imperfections. They are very fine and generally cover a large portion of the facet or surface. Cat hairs often run in the same direction of polish and may be formed during the polishing phase. That's why there's often mistaken for polishing marks.

The best way to eliminate cat hair problems is to clean care-

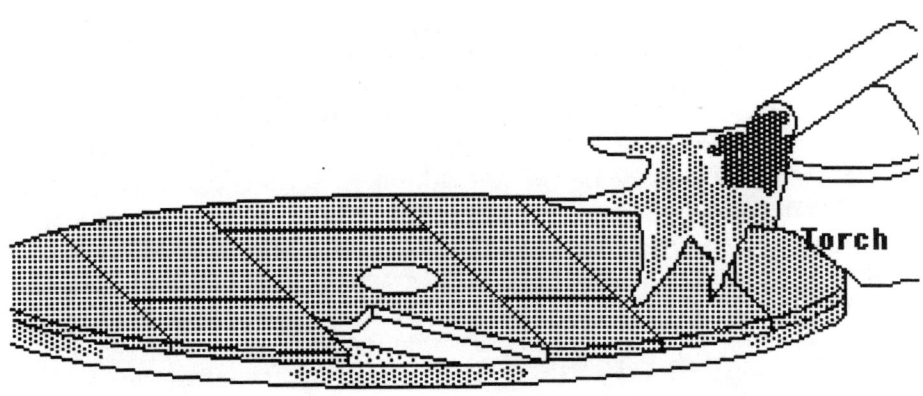

An easy technique for making wax laps is to lay up flat Kerr wax strips on a base lap and then apply a torch flames to melt and seal the seams.

Master Gem Polishing

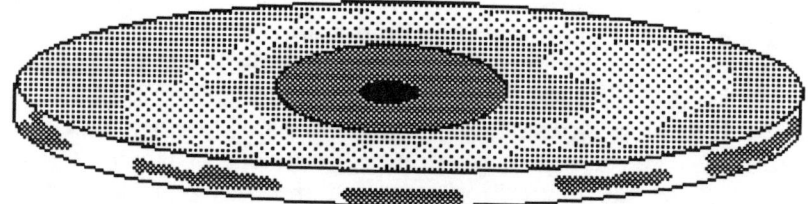

Keep in mind that tiny diamond polishing particles will sink into soft wax quickly so charge the lap with your finger tip, rubbing softly in a circular motion with minimum fluid. The idea during the charging is to maintain a tacky sensation in the fingertips so you can gauge progress.

fully the stone surface before polishing and allow a few seconds for any lubricants to "mature" or evaporate. Once found, cat's hairs are easy enough to remove: gently rub the facet or surface back and forth on a stationary lap or pad while changing the angle of the polishing surface to the stone slightly. This latter technique is referred to as "chasing cat hairs" (and polishing marks!) off the lap.

    4. PEBBLE FINISH. This kind of surface imperfection occurs very infrequently and is extremely difficult to observe, even with the required 40-diopter. Without strong magnification, you only know you have a pebble finish by the generally unsatisfactory performance of the polished surface: somehow it doesn't come alive as it should.

    Pebble finish may actually be due to the orientation of the crystal structure itself. It'll pop up in one stone while another identical one—cut and polished in the same manner—has no problem. Use 100,000 or even 200,000 diamond grit to eliminate pebble finish (often found after you've just removed some cat's hairs). The reason pebble finish is so hard to diagnose is that the scratch is less than the wavelength of visual light.

Cliff Jackson's Wax Lap . . .

For faceters wanting their own wax lap here is a method by the late Cliff Jackson for producing your own. This procedure appeared some time ago but the information is still timely:

Using Kerr's jewelers master pattern carving wax, medium blue with a small amount of paraffin added, cast the wax nearly 1" thick in disk shapes so the finished lap has substantial strength.

One you've cast the wax into the desired thickness:

1. Score the surface moderately with one wheel of a small knurling tool

2. With a waterproof laundry marking pencil, make a circle two inches from the center. The area from this rim circle to the center is for 50,000 diamond grit. In the area outside the rim circle you'll put 8,000 diamond grit.

3. Apply the 50M grit by sprinkling the diamond powder over the inside area and adding several drops of lighter fluid. Rub the diamond into the wax with a gentle rotary motion of the finger. Gentle is an operative word here. You don't want to press the tiny particles below the surface. Pressure should be just enough to anchor them into the top surface. Use the fluid sparingly so you can rub diamond in and feel tackiness as the lighter fluid evaporates.

4. When you've finished the 50M grit, repeat with the sprinkling and the lighter fluid for 8,000 grit on the outside. Be careful because you don't want to contaminate the finer grit area. It's a good idea to use paper to cover the 50M section while you work on the outside rim.

5. When you've finished rubbing the diamond grit into the wax, polish the lap—working from the inside toward the outside. Polish with a moderately high rpm using water with a heavy concentration of dishwashing detergent. All surfaces of the lap must remain wet with the rpm maintained so any 8,000 particles will spin away and off.

6. For any crystals you intend to polish on your wax lap, first fine grind them at least with 1200 lap. Only when the crystal is properly pre-polished and ALL scratches or imperfections have been

Master Gem Polishing

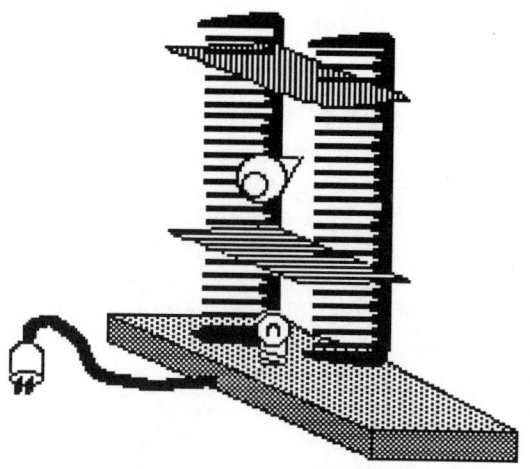

To make your own polariscope, affix two combs into a block of wood and then slide the polarizing material between the comb's teeth. A small clear bulb (you can even rig a penlight) at the base will provide the light needed. Polariscopes are invaluable for finding the optic axis of mineral specimens.

removed should you proceed to the 8000 grit polish and finish up with 50,000.

7. If you experience any scratching, change the lap direction. The wax laps are good for fluorite, barite, cerussite, sphalerite, calcite, amber and sunstone.

How to Make a Polariscope...

Making your own polariscope isn't that tough. Of course, it's always best to obtain a commercial instrument. Still, you can make one with a pair of combs stood up on end and glued onto a slotted piece of wood block.

Once the glue has set up, use the comb's teeth as "holders" and slip the two pieces of polarized film into the teeth. For light, simply thread a small clear Christmas tree bulb through the bottom of the polariscope as shown in the illustration.

Master Gem Polishing

Even with this simplified setup you can find the crystallographic and optic axes with the best of them. Total cost of the homemade polariscope: $2.16.

How do you find the optic axis of a stone with a polariscope? You turn the polarized film until a view down from the top appears darkest (with the little light bulb on now!).

Roll and turn the stone until locating in a horizontal plane where it blinks sharply four times—light, dark, light, dark—and you're pretty much on the axis. Now twist the stone until the blinking is sharpest *i.e.*, the dark and light are strongest and the light changes occurs quickly, abruptly. When you have the stone blinking as sharply as possible, the optic axis is running from your eye to the light bulb right through the stone. For the best polish of a doubly refractive gemstone, you're usually best off if you orient the stone so that the table is perpendicular to this optic axis. Why?

The optic axis in a doubly refractive crystal is the direction

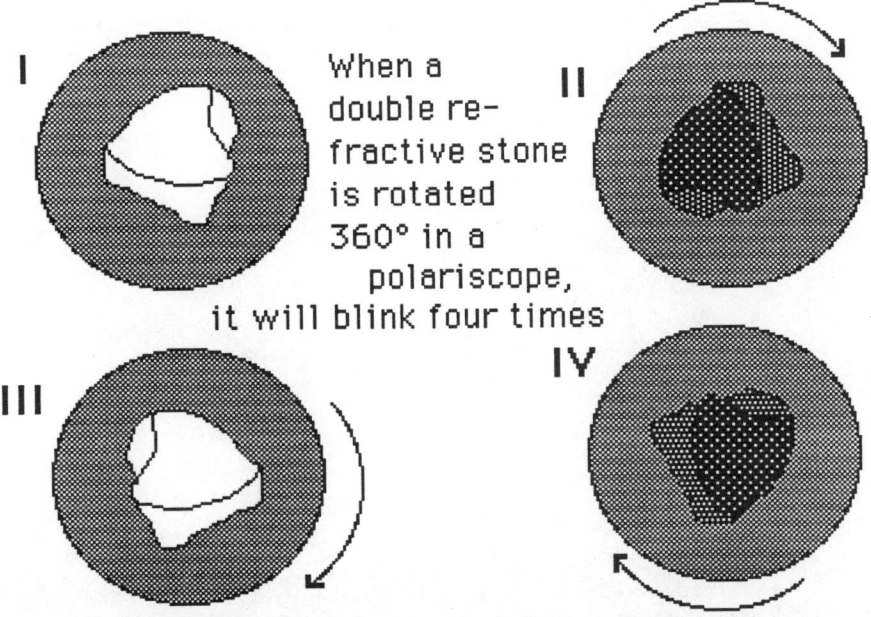

When a double refractive stone is rotated 360° in a polariscope, it will blink four times

Looking for the blinking sequence when viewing a gemstone through crossed polaroid filters is the traditional technique for locating a gem's optic axes. A refractometer is also helpful for locating optical axis direction.

Master Gem Polishing

where light conducts itself in the most singularly refractive manner. In most gem types this means the best and clearest color will often be found parallel to this axis. Also, noticeable double refraction *e.g.*, facet doubling as observed in zircon and tourmaline, is minimized. Some theories contend that the grain is also best in this direction and encourage polishing to take place easier. There's been no hard evidence to support this latter contention.

When orienting a doubly refractive stone to take best advantage of the optic axis, you will need some knowledge about the differences between uniaxial and biaxial gems. Both types are doubly refractive stones, of course, but uniaxial gems have only one optic axis while biaxial gems have two optic axes. Uniaxial gemstones crystallize in the trigonal, tetragonal and hexagonal systems. Their single optic axis is often in the same direction as the principle plane in which case the optic axis and the crystallographic axes are essentially identical. As for biaxial gems, they form in the triclinic, or-

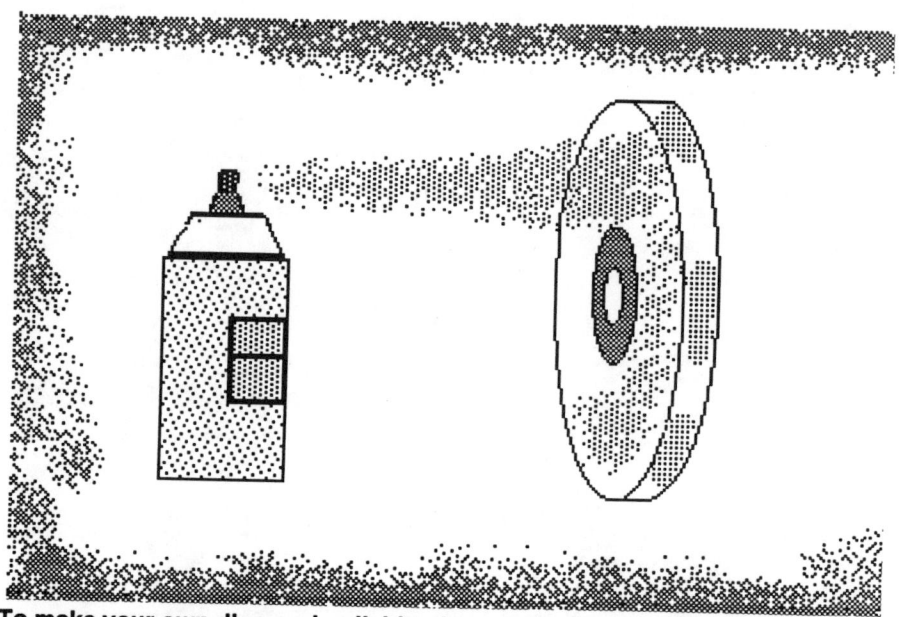

To make your own diamond polishing lap, place a lap on a horizontal—or slightly inclined—surface and apply three to six separate coats of zinc spray paint, sprinkling small amounts of the desired diamond grit on each coat between drying spells. Then burnish with a smooth, hard stone.

Master Gem Polishing

Before using a Mehanite cast iron lap, burnish off the metal jaggies with a chunk of flat corundum while the lap is running at moderate speed. If you fail to prepare the surface, you may get scratching or at least polishing marks. It should be burnished, too, if you intend to apply a thin wax coat on the metal.

thorhombic or monoclinic system. One of the optic axes is generally stronger than the other and it is this optic axis you want when orienting a DR gemstone for best optic performance. The sharpness in the blinking effect under a polariscope will reveal which axes is strongest. When it comes to uniaxial gems, the single optic axis in such a gem runs parallel with the principle or longest plane—and this is the direction gemcutters should prefer.

Each gemstone should be evaluated carefully for its strongest optic axis. Aberrations are possible, too. The above observations are neat and compact, but you can run into a paradox now and then. Some gemstone types such as topaz, for example, may be biaxial but with neither optic axis in a direction parallel to one of its crystal planes. Many experienced gemcutters and/or gemologists use a refractometer to locate the various optic axes, watching for what is called a shadow edge through the instrument's viewer.

Making Your Own Diamond Polishing Laps...

When you find yourself trying to put a finish on a nice synthetic spinel that isn't exactly cooperating it's time to enter on your wish list an order for a 50,000 diamond polishing lap.

Rather than spend time on a wish list, though, you could spend some time to make yourself one.

It's much easier than you think. Once you familiarize yourself with the procedure you'll see that it's just as easy to make sanding and grinding tools the same way. With a 2"-3" wide section of large diameter PVC pipe you can make a diamond cabbing wheel.

All you need are these items:

First, a 1/4" thick section of Glastic or Plexiglas or a flat disk shaped piece of 1/8" thick aluminum—any of which you can buy at a hardware or electrical supply store. These serve as your base lap.

Use a needle to prick any bubbles that develop on the paint surface. A magnifying glass enables you to loup the surface quickly. A small pen knife can also be used to trim up the edges of the disk.

Master Gem Polishing

Second, a can of zinc spray paint (galvanizing paint is the same thing),

Third, a 5-carat vial of diamond powder of your grit choice. We'll assume you wish to make a permanent 50,000 diamond polishing lap.

The above is all you need—plus about an hour of your time. If this all seems a bit incredulous just keep in mind that you will be duplicating much of the process that is used in making commercial resin bonded diamond laps. The technology is not at all overpowering. The only difference will involve the use of zinc paint—a good, tough paint that can withstand a lot of friction, heat and abuse.

The major unbreakable rule when using a paint spray can is this: <u>always keep the paint spray can moving</u> . . . so you get an even, smooth coating on the master disk.

Not just for spraying up polishing laps, the rule with a paint spray can is: always keep the can moving. This avoids overspray, bubbles, and a host of other difficulties...caused by pausing.

To make a master lap follow these steps and techniques:

On the flat section of material you've chosen for the master lap, trace a 6-inch or 8-inch outline using a standard lap. The center arbor hole can be drilled out later, but mark it at this time also. It's usually recommended that you cut the arbor hole out and then fit the section onto an arbor and draw the 6" or 8" perimeter while the piece is spinning. This way you make certain the arbor hole is centered properly.

Next, put your diamond dust into a small bottle which contains a fine sieve or screen. When you later must sprinkle the diamond dust down onto the wet zinc paint surface you want it to be dispersed evenly, not developed into clumps. An accepted procedure for applying diamond dust from a vial is to spank the vial lightly with an index finger so you dispel a measured amount each time. Of course, nothing beats a good, fine sieve.

Shake the zinc spray can well. On the section of base lap where you want the wet zinc paint surface, spray the paint evenly in short bursts—not in sustained spraying that leads to clumps. Working about a <u>foot away</u> from the disk, apply a single coat.

Master Gem Polishing

Remember: Always keep the can moving, never stop to spray in one spot. Apply pressure on the spray valve and—moving the can slowly and steadily—cover the disk with a thin coat of zinc. By keeping the can moving and squeezing off short bursts of paint you avoid paint running or an uneven coat thickness.

After you finish the first coat over the entire surface of the disc, put the spray can down. Sprinkle some 50,000 diamond cut over the surface: not too much now but about 3/4 to one carat. Allow the coating to dry, get tacky actually, before you apply the second coat. Just how many coats are you going to put on the disk?

Plan on applying a minimum of three coats. That will provide a reliable working thickness. Inasmuch as you should dust each coat with diamond particles, a three-coat thickness containing diamond particles provides for a long lasting lap.

Once the first coat has set up, spray on the second coat—again keeping the can constantly moving. Now the lap should take

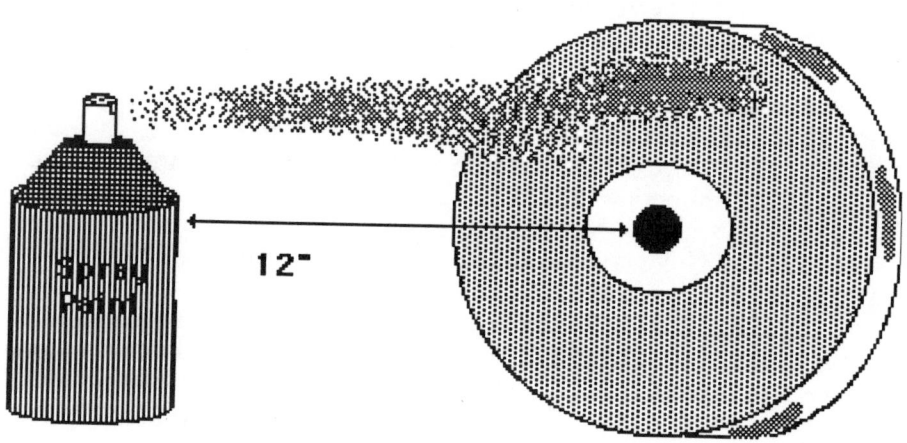

The proper way to use a spray paint can is to hold the nozzle about 12 inches from the surface to be painted and then keep the spray can constantly moving slowly in a regular, disciplined motion. If you pause or stop while spraying it'll invariably create an uneven condition or a puddle.

Master Gem Polishing

on a definite silvery zinc hue. After a light one-carat diamond sprinkle, let this coat dry, then apply the third coat. When you finish the third coat, pick up the container with 50,000 diamond dust and lightly sprinkle a couple of carats of diamond on the wet zinc surface. This is the heavy working coat and can use extra diamond.

On average, you'll want to use a total of about 4 to 6 carats on each lap. It depends, of course, as to the number of coats or how much diamond grit to use but you don't need a lap saturated in diamond dust or paint. Truth is, too much diamond dust leads to scratching and lack of performance. With a lap turning over 1500 rpms or so, it doesn't take but a few diamond tips to cut into a stone. Six is the maximum number of coats you should apply.

Apply 3-6 coats of paint and diamond to the base lap. Sprinkle at least one carat of diamond on each coat and allow it to partially dry before spraying on the next coat. Put extra diamond on the last coat.

With each of the zinc coatings, keep the spray orifice a good 12 inches from the lap surface and move the can continuously around the lap. Not once should you stop, pause or slow down. Each pass must be done completely and smoothly. Just in case there does occur during the spraying a tiny imperfection such as a ridge, bubble or uneven surface while applying the zinc paint, pin prick the imperfection or bubble—later. You want a final uniform coating and with as few blemishes as possible. Use a magnifying glass to go over the surface if you must.

Note: *It may sound excessively pedantic but practice applying paint with a spray can before you attempt to spray up a lap disk. Become familiar with the personality of a spray paint can before you go for the real thing.*

A small pen knife or sharp, flat edge of metal is excellent for scraping off the outer edge of the lap where some of the paint may have slopped over. It's often best to wait a few minutes until the paint is tacky—or even dry— before doing this touch-up.

Avoid Area Surface Touch-ups...

You won't need area surface touch-ups with three or more evenly applied coats of the hard zinc paint, so don't be tempted to spray on a bit of extra paint later to an area that you think got deprived. As emphasized earlier, just keep the can moving...don't stop...maintain the same distance from the spray nozzle to the lap surface...and don't be in a hurry. You may have to go around twice —as most disk makers do—to get a nice coating. Take your time.

After you've sprinkled the last bit of diamond on the lap set the disk aside. Allow it to dry for at least 24 hours. Then take out the disk, put it on a machine, and turn the rpms up full. Use a rounded agate block and gently dress the lap—with a plentiful flow of water lubricant. As mentioned before, if there are any irregularities in the surface, the agate block will hone them down.

Plus you'll be exposing diamond for the polishing action. Don't press too hard on the agate: all that much pressure isn't necessary because you're just rounding things off a bit. After the agate step, the lap is ready to use. Put it on the machine, turn on the water to cool and lubricate—and you're ready to polish.

Can grinding laps really be made with this same method?

Absolutely. Just use a coarser diamond grit. That's the only variable. The technique can make a fine lap or PVC rim wheel. If you make a lap in the shop this way, don't sweep the lap when in use. Get into a ring and stay there. That way you won't transfer any irregularities in the lap onto the stone and have a devil of a polishing job. As indicated, smoothing the lap with an agate helps.

Colloidal Silica is Outstanding Polish ...

Colloidal silica, thanks to a lack of marketing effort, is still largely unknown in the lapidary trade. Such unfamiliarity is a tragedy because the chemical is one of the best gemstone polishes available. It will bring up a fine, even polish on any gemstone short of the diamond.

That's saying a lot, but CS will actually perform that well. About a year ago, *American Gemcutter Magazine* introduced the chemical to gemcutters.

Master Gem Polishing

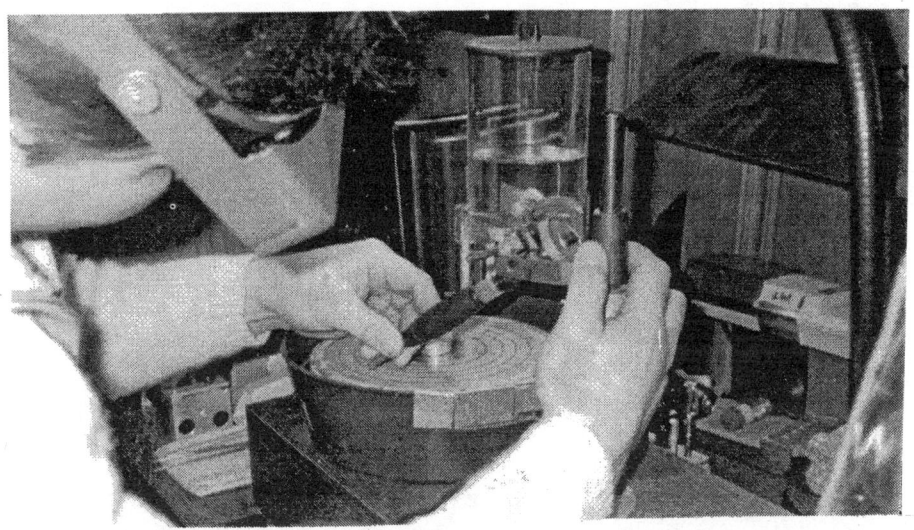

If you seem to experience too much difficulty with cat whisker scratches and polishing marks, consider the advantages of polishing in a lap or wheel that has beeen marked with "rings." Rings offer maximum control.

To fully test the efficacy of this new polish, the American Society of Gemcutters in 1988 arranged for ASG gemcutters to purchase test kits from Buehler Ltd., the Chicago based corporation which makes the product and complementary polishing pads.

A number of kits were sold but none of the members reported back on their experience with CS. ASG also purchased a kit and enjoyed extraordinary results on harder cab materials but particularly with such hard minerals as corundum and chrysoberyl.

What may have turned off the gemcutters who initially tested colloidal silica were the polishing pads, called Mastermet™, that were used. These pads most definitely were not the type of polishing pads that lapidaries use. As a result, early results may have been a bit less than anticipated. Plus, many gemcutters—those who are faceters—were probably unhappy because the process isn't as easily useful for general faceting.

It's simply outstanding for polishing a large table facet, though, especially if the table is the first facet cut or its edges protected. For faceters, who for one reason or another, want to polish

Master Gem Polishing

the table first, there can be no better choice that colloidal silica as the polish. Large facets such as a table facet are troublesome at the very least when it comes to polishing with traditional techniques. The need to bring a large area flat-to-flat on a polishing carrier can be most difficult. That's why many faceters who choose to finish a faceted stone by doing the table facet last often are forced to "walk" a table facet across a hard polishing wheel *e.g.*, polishing a little at a time and applying the cheater until the table is finished.

To polish a large cab or a table facet with CS technique is simplicity itself. You first want a polishing pad material that will hold the highly viscous liquid well. This could be a Mastermet™ or a hard Pellon cloth, leather, felt, plain cloth...anything that will hold moisture. Felt and cloth such as muslin and canvas often do the best job for polishing cabochons with CS but seldom demonstrate effective application in faceting, even for polishing table facets.

Using a rubber cement, a peel-off type rubber adhesive or a spray adhesive, attach cloth type pads to a Lucite or rubber disk.

Many repeatability difficulties can be reduced by using a one-lap setup, dropping a thin metal or plastic film lap over the prepolishing lap. Contamination isn't a serious issue because one lap is always higher than the other, and usually of a different type abrasive material.

Master Gem Polishing

Mastermet™ on a Lucite disk works well, with leather or cloth on a rubber disk—and keep the pads well wetted. When you apply the colloidal silica make certain you have plenty of CS on the lap so it remains wet.

Bring the table down onto the pad and give the facet—or an area on a cabochon—a series of 5-second, medium pressure passes. A couple of passes should do it. If the gem surface has been properly pre-polished, the brilliant polish should soon jump out at you.

Pressing the gem surface into the soft, saturated polishing pad creates a rounding. It's this aspect, of course, to which many faceters object but which cabbers find to their liking.

Just what it is that allows CS to produce such a rapid, fine polish remains somewhat of a unique chemical mystery. Certainly, the polish is equal to a 50,000 diamond grit polish. There's another minor problem associated with CS. The chemical has a very high pH so it has the capability to cause some skin conditions for certain indi-

Wiping off a stone's surface before proceeding to a finer wheel or lap is sound lapidary practice. Contamination problems arise when you don't keep the working stone surface clean before moving up.

viduals. In addition to that, the chemical will crystallize out. It's fine particles can penetrate open skin pores and perhaps initiate some itching once the liquid turns crystal. Many gemcutters don't wear gloves, saying the crystallization causes merely a sandy sensation and no more. Until you've checked out your own reaction, wear gloves! Rubber surgical or plastic gloves are fine for working with CS—or just to keep your hands clean.

If cabbers use a horizontally mounted wheel there will be a certain amount of splash off involved. Cabbers thus are warned to wear a mask and safety glasses while polishing with a wet CS polishing pad.

Again: the results are exceptional but there are safety demands. It's a matter of making a trade-off, because there are few polishes as effective as the new colloidal silica. As for wearing safety glasses, that's just good common lapidary sense. Every gemcutter should wear glasses at all times. A crystal splinter or powder particle in the eye isn't all that much entertainment.

Willems' Hollowed Out Cab Polishing Wheel...

There is yet another carrier option available to cabbers who would like to test colloidal silica. This is the wooden internal polishing wheel for cabochon polishing described years ago by J. Daniel Willems in his 1948 book, *Gem Cutting*.

Study the illustration on page 111. This wheel has the "...advantage that it will retain any polishing agent which on other wheels is thrown off the periphery almost as rapidly as it is applied." Willems emphasized that the centrifugal force of the running wheel would distribute the polishing powder equally all around the wheel and then keep it there.

I made such a wheel out of basswoood, lined it with canvas and Willems is right: it does retain. Of course, centrifugal force doesn't work perfectly. It throws the polish slurry against the rounded areas and you'll need to "scoop" every now and then with the stone to transfer polish back onto the flat back section. I'm sure innovative cabbers would be able to test other polishing agents. I tested polishing action on the bare wood and the results were disappointing. (Of course, the wood hadn't been soaked in paraffin.)

It goes without saying that any cabber wishing to make

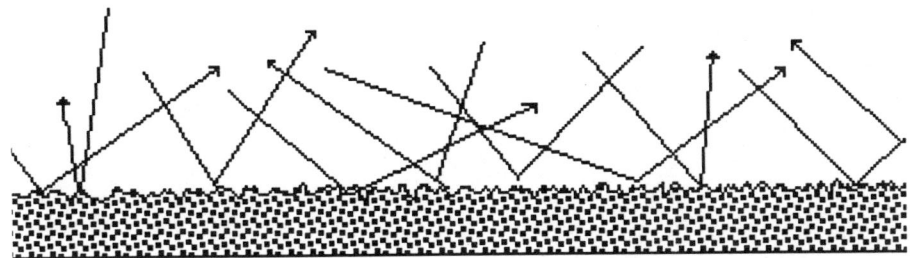

To bring out maximum luster and reflectivity in a gemstone, the surface must be highly polished so the light rays will reflect uniformly in a parallel manner. Helter-skelter light ray action—defined as diffused reflection— arises from an irregular finish or irregularly placed subsurface particles.

and use a Willems wheel might want to boil the wheel in paraffin before using it with any of the colloidal polishes or other water carrying polishes. It can, of course, also be used directly with diamond pastes, but the running surfaces soon become a bit bumpy and need trueing from time to time.

Techniques on Using Colloidal Silica Polish...

Colloidal silica may be an excellent polish for large flat cabochon areas and table facets, but it demands some special handling.

Gemcutters continue to experiment to bring out the qualities that this potentially fine polish possesses. One gemcutter who has done some serious testing with the polish is Certified Supreme Master Carl Childers of Lubbock, TX. Here are some of Carl's findings:

"I have had good results with the Buehler black polishing pad (Mastermet™ for cabochons). I have also learned about the problem of surface hardening of polishing pads I have tried.

"My best results have been with a Crystalite Poly Pad (Crys-

Master Gem Polishing

The Crystalite DMD™ lap with a 260 outer ring—and a 1200 inner ring—offers fast, easy preforming capabilities, allowing a faceter to swing back and forth between coarse and fine grinding without repeatability problems.

talite also produces colloidal silica polish) with a foam back on a master lap. I can run the lap at 200 to 500 rpm and, using my left hand, I can charge the lap with the colloidal silica bottle while polishing the dopped stone using my right hand. I now also run the lap faster and use lots of pressure on the stone."

Carl shared his colloidal silica with a colleague who got good results using a Poly Pad on a 6" vertical lap. The friend is the one who came up with a reconditioning of the hardened surface. Here's how to recondition a polishing pad that contains a hardened film of colloidal silica polish: wet the pad on the lap and turn on slow speed. Using a good pocket knife, scrape the hardened surface until it's soft again (use a mask and plenty of water).

It's probably a good idea, too, to cover your eyes when working with colloidal silica. It's a better idea even to cover your eyes with any other polish for that matter. Hardened silica crystals aren't especially nice to get in your eyes. Something as simple as merely scraping a pad could cause the hardened silica to split up abruptly and then fly around a bit. If this does happen, if you do get some CS in your eyes, just splash liberally with plenty of water to flush the

Master Gem Polishing

eyes out. There's no burning or pain, just a "something in my eye" type condition...that's bad enough!

Additional Techniques With CS...

Whenever you visually inspect a gemstone and see tiny spots on the surface, the interpretation usually means that the polishing action has failed probably because of an inadequate prepolish. You'll observe this phenomenon most often when polishing corundum. It's rather like a speckled condition, slightly translucent.

Such a spot condition usually involves an excellent candidate for polishing with colloidal silica. As you read earlier, CS has a pH of 9.8+. That's slightly higher than a strong hand soap. This alkalinity has some good news and some bad news.

The good news is that the high pH contributes greatly to a fast, smooth polish, often regardless of a mineral's hardness. Pushing any polishing situation into the high pH area will generally produce superior polishing action. That's what prompts corundum to respond so quickly to a colloidal silica. The bad news about high pH is that some people with sensitive hands may need to wear gloves. For most individuals, getting CS on the hands can cause a certain grittiness sensation, and occasionally some itching. In both cases, it's just a matter of washing your hands.

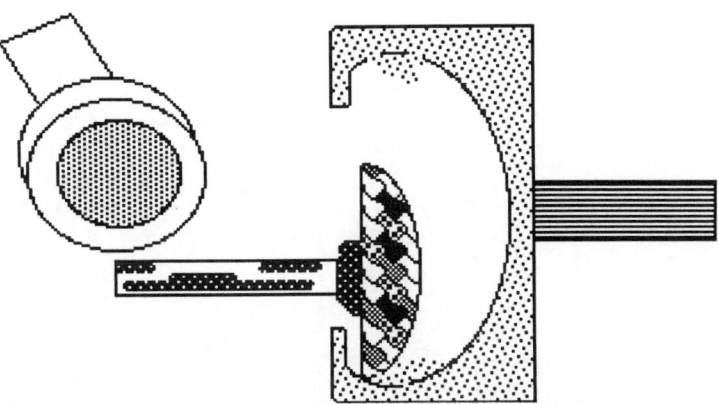

The Willems cabochon polishing wheel features a hollowed out recess so rounded surfaces may be easily worked, while the liquid polish remains trapped. These wheels are generally self-made for obvious reasons.

Master Gem Polishing

Gemstone Specifications List

(Author's Note: Some of the information in these Gemstone Specifications List is taken from the book, "The Art of the Lapidary," by Francis J. Sperisen, published in 1950. I have added to this list with some of my own data to bring it up to date.)

Minerals Used as Gemstones

Achroite	Carmazul	Fluroite	Lazurite
Adularia	Carnelian	Fowlerite	Lepidolite
	Carnelian onyx	Garnet	Limonite
Agalmatolite	Cat's-eye	Golden beryl	Malachite
Agate	Chalcedony	Goshenite	Mala-cuprite
Alabaster	Chert	Graphic granite	Marcasite
Albite	Chiastolite	Grossularite	Melanite
Albite sunstone	Chlorastrolite	Gypsum	Moldavite
Alexandrite	Chloromelanite	Hambergite	Moonstone
Almandite	Chloropal	Hauerite	Morganite
Amatrice	Chromite	Hawk's-eye	Mother-of-Pearl
Amazonite	Chrysoberyl	Heliotrope	Myrickite
Amber	Chrysocolla	Hematite	Nephelite
Amethyst	Chrysolite	Hiddenite	Nephrite
Anatase	Chrysoprase	Howlite	Novaculite
Andalusite	Citrine	Hyacinth	Obsidian
Andradite	Copal	Hyalite	Odontolite
Antigorite	Coral	Hypersthene	Oligoclase
Apatite	Cordierite	Iceland spar	Oligoclase sunstone
Aquamarine	Corundum	Idocrase	Morganite
Aragonite	Crocidolite	Ilmenite	Olivine
Augelite	Danburite	Indicolite	Onyx
Aventurine	Datolite	Ivory	Onyx marble
Axinite	Demantoid	Jacinth	Iolite
Azurite	Diamond	Jadeite	Opal
Azurmalachite	Diopside	Jargoon	Orthoclase
Basanite	Dioptase	Jasper	Pearl
Benitoite	Dumortierite	Jet	Pearl blisters
Beryl (clear)	Emerald	Kinradeite	Pectolite

Master Gem Polishing

Beryllonite	Enstatite	Kornerupine	Peridot
Bloodstone	Epidote	Kunzite	Phenacite
Bowenite	Essonite	Kyanite	Plasma
Brazilianite	Euclase	Labradorite	Pleonaste
Cairngorm	Feldspar	Lapis lazuli	Prase
Californite	Flint	Lazulite	Prehnite
Pyrite	Samarskite	Spessartite	Topazolite
Pyrope	Sapphire	Sphalerite	Tortoise shell
Quartz	Sapphirine	Sphene	Tourmaline
Quartzite	Sard	Spinel	Utahlite
Rhodosite	Sardonyx	Spodumene	Uvarovite
Rhodochrosite	Satin spar	Staurolite	Variscite
Rhodolite	Scapolite	Steatite	Verdite
Rhodonite	Schorl	Talc	Veruvianite
Rock crystal	Sepiolite	Thetis hairstone	Wernerite
Rubellite	Serpentine	Thomsonite	Williamsite
Rubicelle	Siberite	Thulite	Wollastonite
Ruby	Smaragdite	Tiger's-eye	Zircon
Rutile	Smithsonite	Titanite	Zoisite
Sagenite	Sodalite	Topaz	

Master Gem Polishing

Major Gemstone Species and Their Varieties

CHALCEDONY

Agate
Banded agate
Eye agate

Fortification agate

Iris agate
Moss agate
Riobbon agate (striped agate)
Variegated agate

CORUNDUM

Ruby
Padparadsha

Sapphire
Golden sapphire

GARNET (group)

Pyrope—
Almandine—
Grossular—

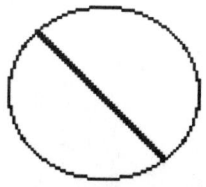
Smoothing Marks

Aggregate Scratches

Polishing Agent

Lap Surface Channeling

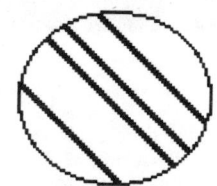
Lap Contamination

A scratch's personality reveals the lap or wheel condition that created it. Lap contamination always crosses the entire surface: thick polish paste causes intermittent scratches, and swarf aggregation inflicts deep, short gouges.

Master Gem Polishing

JASPER

Agate jasper
Brecciated jasper
Moss jasper

Orbicular jasper
Ribbon jasper
Variegated jasper

BERYL

Emerald
Morganite
Heliodor

Goshenite
Aquamarine

TOURMALINE

Achroite
Chrome tourmaline
Dravite
Indicolite

Verdelite
Watermelon tourmaline
Rubellite
Schorl

OPAL

Black opal
Boulder opal
Common opal
Fire opal
Harlequin opal
Hungarian opal
Jasp opal (opal jasper)
Mexican opal

Moss opal
Nevada opal
Opal matrix
Opal prase (prase opal)
Opalized wood
Water opal

White cliff opal

QUARTZ

Amethystine quartz

Asteriated quartz
Chrysocolla stained quartz
Chrysocolla inclusion in quartz
  (gem chrysocolla)
Gold quartz
Magnesite inclusion in quartz
Mariposite inclusion in quartz
Milky quartz
Citrine quartz

Petrified wood (also silicified, agatized, or jasperized wood)

Quartz cat's-eye
Rose quartz
Rutilated quartz
Sagenite
Smoky quartz
Tourmalinated quartz
Venus hairstone

Master Gem Polishing

TRANSPARENT GEMSTONES
(For Faceting)

Achroite	Cassiterite	Hyalite	Rhodolite
Adularia	Danburite	Idocrase	Rock crystal
Albite	Datolite	Indicolite	Rubellite
Alexandrite	Demantoid	Jacinth	Rubicelle
Almandite	Diamond	Jargoon	Ruby
Amber	Diopside	Kornerupine	Sapphire
Amethyst	Dioptase	Kunzite	Spessartite
Anatase	Emerald	Kyanite	Sphalerite
Andalusite	Epidote	Moldavite	Sphene
Apatite	Essonite	Morganite	Spinel
Aquamarine	Euclase	Obsidian	Spodumene
Augelite	Fluroite	Opal	Topaz
Axinite	Garne	Orthoclase	Topazolite
Benitoite	Goshenite	Peridot	Tourmaline
Beryl	Hambergite	Phenacite	Wernerite
Brazilianite	Hiddenite	Pyrope	Zircon
Cairngorm	Hyacinth	Rhodozite	

STONES THAT REQUIRE SPECIAL CARE IN HANDLING, DOPPING, CUTTING OR POLISHING

Adularia	Brazilianite	Hiddenite	Smithsonite
Albite	Chrysocolla	Jet	Sodalite
Amazonite	Copal	Kunzite	Sphalerite
Amber	Coral	Labradorite	Sphene
Apatite	Dioptase	Lapis lazuli	Spodumene
Augelite	Euclase	Malachite	Turquoise
Azurite	Fluorite	Opal	
Benitoite	Gypsum	Satin spar	

GEMSTONES THAT ARE HARD AND DURABLE

Achroite	Beryl	Chrysolite	Flint
Agate	Bloodstone	Chrysoprase	Garnet

Master Gem Polishing

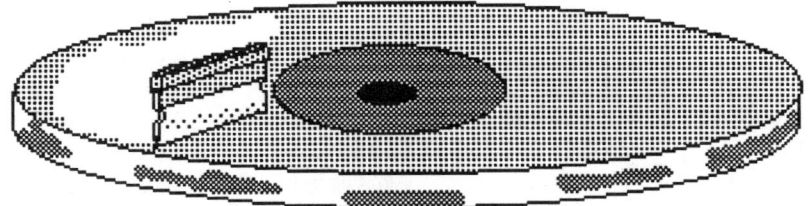

Removing a contaminant from a polishing lap or wheel surface can often be accomplished by scraping the turning wheel with a flat edge or knife blade. A 10x magnifier can sometimes help to locate the culprit.

Alexandrite	Bowenite	Citrine	Golden beryl
Almandite	Cairngorm	Corundum	Goshenite
Amethyst	Californite	Danburite	Grossularite
Andalusite	Carnelian	Diamond	Hawk's-eye
Aquamarine	Chalcedony	Dumortierite	Heliotrope
Aventurine	Chloromelanite	Emerald	Hematite
Bazanite	Chrysoberyl	Essonite	Hyacinth
Idocrase	Olivine	Rhodolite	Spessartite
Indicolite	Onyx	Rhodonite	Spinel
Jacinth	Peridot	Rock crystal	Tiger's-eye
Jadeite	Phenacite	Rubellite	Topaz
Jargoon	Plasma	Rubicelle	Topazolite
Jasper	Pleonaste	Ruby	Tourmaline
Kornerupine	Prase	Sapphire	Vesuvianite
Melanite	Pyrope	Sapphirine	Zircon
Morganite	Quartz	Sard	

Master Gem Polishing

Nephrite   Quartzite   Sardonyx
Novaculite   Rhodosite   Siberite

FINE GRAINED, TEXTURED GEMSTONES

Achroite	Chrysoprase	Jargoon	Rubicelle
Adularia	Citrine	Jet	Ruby
Albite	Coral	Kornerupine	Rutile
Albite sunstone	Cordierite	Kunzite	Sapphire
Alexandrite	Corundum	Melanite	Sapphirine
Amber	Danburite	Moldavite	Sard
Amethyst	Datolite	Morganite	Sardonyx
Almandite	Demantoid	Mother-of-Pearl	Scapolite
Anatase	Diamond	Obsidian	Siberite
Andalusite	Diopside	Oligoclase	Spessartite
Andradite	Dioptase	Oligoclase sunstone	Sphalerite

Good polishing lap and wheel maintenance calls for scrubbing the polishing surface vigorously with a scouring pad and soap.

Master Gem Polishing

Apatite	Emerald	Olivene	Sphene
Aquamarine	Epidote	Onyx marble	Spinel
Augelite	Euclase	Opal	Spodumene
Axinite	Fluroite	Orthoclase	Thetis hairstone
Benitoite	Garnierite	Peridot	Titanite
Beryl	Grossularite	Phenacite	Topaz
Beryllonite	Hambergite	Pleonaste	Topazolite
Brazilianite	Hessonite	Prase	Tourmaline
Cairngorm	Hiddenite	Pyrope	Uvarovite
Carnelian	Hyacinth	Rhodizite	Vesuvianite
Carnelian onyx	Hyalite	Rhodolite	Zircon
Chalcedony	Idocrase	Rock Crystal	
Chrysoberyl	Indicolite	Rubellite	
Chrysolite	Jacinth		

STONES THAT ARE DIFFICULT TO POLISH

CABOCHON

Cat's-eye	Hematite	Nevada opal*	Sapphire
Cassiterite	Labradorite	Pyrite	Smithsonite*
Dumortierite	Lepidolite	Ruby	Sphalerite*

FACETED

Albite	Chrysoberyl	Hematite	Sapphire
Alexandrite	Chrysolite	Hiddenite*	Sphalerite*
Apatite*	Demantoid	Kunzite*	Sphene*
Augelite*	Diamond	Kyanite*	Spinel
Benitoite*	Dioptase*	Peridot	Topaz
Brazilianite*	Euclase*	Pyrite	Zircon
Cassiterite	Fluorite*	Ruby	

*Stones that require extreme care in handling

Master Gem Polishing

Some gemcutters insist on wearing safety glasses when polishing with colloidal silica or acids. It's a good idea to wear safety glasses anytime you're cutting a gem. Flying gemstone fragments can be dangerous.

STONE WITH GRANULAR TEXTURE, COARSE OR UNEVEN GRAIN
(proneness to undercutting)

Agalmatolite	Chromite	Lapis lazuli	Sepiolite
Alabaster	Chrysocolla	Lazulite	Serpentine
Amazonite	Dumortierite	Lepidolite	Smithsonite
Antigorite	Enstatite	Malachite	Sodalite
Aventurine	Gold quartz	Mala-cuprite	Staurolite
Azurite	Graphic granite	Marcasite	Thomsonite
Azurmalachite	Gypsum	Myrickite	Thulite
Basanite	Hawk's-eye	Nephelite	Tiger's-eye
Bloodstone	Heliotrope	Nephrite	Turquoise
Bowenite	Hematite	Novaculite	Utahite
Californite	Howlite	Odontolite	Varscite
Carmazul	Hypersthene	Onyx marble	Williamsite
Chert	Iolite	Wollastonite	Zoisite

Master Gem Polishing

Chiastolite Jadeite Pectolite Ilmenite
Chlorastrolite Jasper Prehnite
Chloromelanite Kyanite Pyrite
Chloropal Labradorite Rhodonite

GEMSTONES THAT POLISH SWIFTLY WITH COLLOIDAL SILICA (CS) ON FELT
(Cabochons)

Black onyx Carnelian Chrysoprase
Crystaline quartzes Enstatitie Hematite
Jasper Lapis lazuli Lepidolite
Moonstone Obsidian Opal
Rose quartz Scapolite Sodalite

GEMSTONES THAT POLISH BEST WITH COLLOIDAL OXIDE POLISH PASTES

Colloidal CeOx (Cerium Oxide) on Felt

Collodial Cerium Oxide
Agate Black onyx Carnelian
Chrysoprase Crystaline quartzes Enstatite
Hematite Jasper Lapis lazuli
Lepdolite Moonstone Obsidian
Opal Rose quartz Scapolite
Sodalite

Colloidal TinOx (Tin Oxide) on Felt

Garnet Opal Sunstone

Colloidal ChOx (Chrome Oxide) on Leather

Azurite Chrysoprase Idocrase
Jade Lapis lazuli Malachite
Serpentine Tourmaline Turquoise
Unfractured emerald Unfractured iolite

Master Gem Polishing

Polishing is usually a messy operation simply from using too much of everything. Cut down on the speed, amount of polish and water, and pressure. You'll get best polishing when you practice "...less is best..."

Colloidal AlOx (Aluminum Oxide) on Leather

Azurite	Beryl	Cassiterite
Chiastolite	Chrysoberyl	Corundum
Howlite (difficult)	Jasper (difficult)	Enstatite
Granite	Hematite	Idocrase
Iolite	Lepidolite	Jade
Malachite	Rhodochrosite	Rhodonite
Serpentine	Sillimanite	Spinel
Tigereye	Topaz	Tourmaline
Turquoise	Variscite	Wonderstone

Understanding Luster as Component of Polishing . . .

The gem term luster is an important one to gemcutters. Without it there would be no accurate way—however difficult it would be to measure luster in mathematical terms—to describe the appearance of various gemstones.

Luster is the term which describes the surface of a gem material in reflected light. It is divided into two principal groups: metallic and non-metallic. In describing the surface of a gem, gemcutters and gemologists use these terms to define the quantity and quality of light reflected off a gem's service:

Adamantine—the highest, brightest luster, seen only in diamonds and gems with the highest optical potential such as a refractive index of 1.9 to 2.5.

Subadamantine—bright, brilliant luster seen often in well polished rubies and sapphires.

Vitreous—bright reflective luster that is most common among colored stones, especially those with refractive index of 1.3 to 1.8 found in glass.

Greasy—bright but definite greasy appearance, some not well polished jade will show this kind of luster.

Resinous—attractive luster but lacking brightness, such as found in amber and some other organic type gem.

Pearly—distinctive surface appearance seen on the cleavage planes of materials that have a pronounced good cleavage or smooth reflective surface.

Silky—appearance produced in minerals with a fibrous structure.

Dull—this is the luster term which describes the lack of brightness...often seen in some matrix-type cab materials.

Metallic—bright, brilliant luster as one would expect from light reflecting off a metallic surface such as Hematite, iron pyrite, etc.

The luster of the diamond and the pearl are truly unique. As the only popularly available—and hard—gem crystal that displays an adamantine luster, no other substance can be polished more highly or sustain its polish over a longer period of time than the diamond.

It is this luster which gives diamond its incredible excitement.

In a lustrous pearl you can block the light source with your head and, holding a strand of fine pearls about 6"-9" in front of you, see your head and shoulders in the pearl's surface.

Keep in mind that while many gemologists associate a gem's

Master Gem Polishing

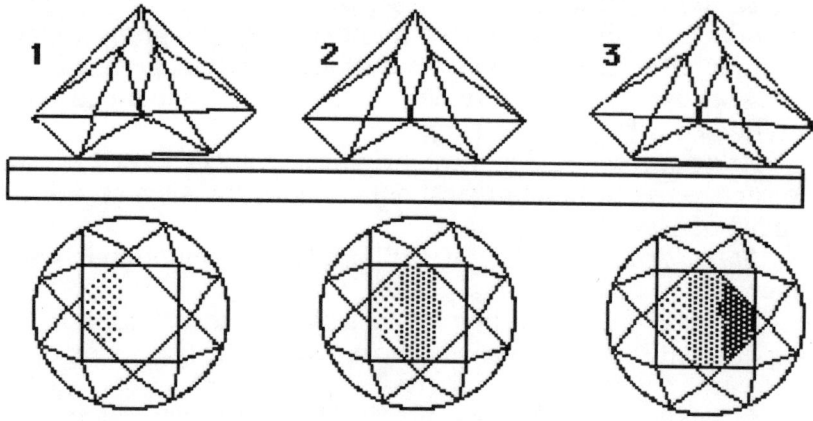

Encountering difficulty in polishing a large, flat surface or table facet, some cutters elect to "walk the facet" across a flat polishing surface. This is done by polishing progressive bands of the facet until it has been completed. This sometimes leaves slightly visible edges on the crystal surface.

luster with its hardness, the hardness is only one element in the formula. Equally important in the personality of a gemstone's luster is the stone's refractive index and its sometimes transparency. Admittedly, a diamond's hardness allows it to be given a remarkably smooth and accurate polish so that light rays are reflected and refracted with discipline and uniformity. Many gemstones, though, have a low Mohs yet exhibit adamantine luster because of their high RI *e.g.*, sphalerite, sphene, etc.

     The high RI also represents only a portion of the success formula. The surface must be highly polished for the luster to perform best. The French physicist, Fresnel, computed the quantitative components of reflectivity and he found that a gemstone simply failed to offer its best unless and until its surfaces consisted of a surface polish that would encourage light rays to deflect with uniformity. It is this aspect alone that leads many gemcutters to seek out the highest possible polish for a given gem type. It is not impossible to apply a fine 100,000 or 200,000 diamond scratch polish—usually the fine grits work best on hard stones—on a lower RI stone so as to give it the appearance of a mineral type with a much higher RI.

Surface and RI then remain two of the three important elements in producing a gemstone's luster potential—but polish is the most important of the three.

Handling Pesky Polishing Problems . . .

Ever have trouble polishing peridot, enstatite, lazulite, diopside, sinhalite, kornerupine—or any other gem types containing magnesium?

Ever wonder why these particular gems whether cabbed or faceted are the ones that constantly pose such aggravating polishing challenges not related to grain directions?

The answer is already provided: it's the magnesium. These stones are alkaline (having a pH greater than 7) because of the magnesium. Alkalinity of a specific level on the surface of a gem can produce all kinds of problems. Test after test shows that when a gem material itself is alkaline at its so-called isoelectric point the polishing action stops. That's the real reason why vinegar and diluted acid solutions mixed with the drip water prove so effective with these stones. The acid changes the pH factor, lowering alkalinity at the polishing surface to a level lower than the isoelectric point.

When you mix a little vinegar in with some synthetic tin oxide you have an outstanding peridot polish. As the pH factor approaches a lower normal the polishing action improves dramatically.

For the opposite reason, colloidal silica is different. It has a pH of nearly 10. It's this high pH that gives the chemical such a super polishing capability. For magnesium containing gems and others that respond to acid addition, the chemical action now takes place under controlled alkalinity conditions: the water and acid have low pH and this increases the hydrogen concentration. Hydrogen aggravates dislocation *i.e.*, fractures related to ductile hardening of the material. The result is more rapid removal—microscopic to be sure—of material which produces the desired polish.

The validity of this observation was established by laboratory testing. In a series of timed experiments, corundum was exposed to diamond grit. Each run was for one minute duration and consisted of 180 diamond grit against sapphire. The speed of the lap was two meters per second with 22 pounds per square inch on a 1.2 centimeter area. What clearly comes through in these experiments is the impact of pH on removal. With a pH factor of "0" some 15 milligrams were removed. When the pH was at 7-8—regarded as the isoelectric point or completely neutral—only 10 milligrams were removed. At higher pH, the removal went back to 14.

What do these timed runs prove? Only that pH extremes exert a beneficial influence on polishing by encouraging removal.

Understanding Polishing Marks ..

Round and round goes the polishing lap or wheel.

On each revolution, you expose your stone to that gremlin of the craft...the maker of an abrupt, treacherous scratch. Don't mislead yourself either: the culprit isn't always too much hand pressure. It's often a lap or a polishing condition.

Following are several more additional pointers on interpret-

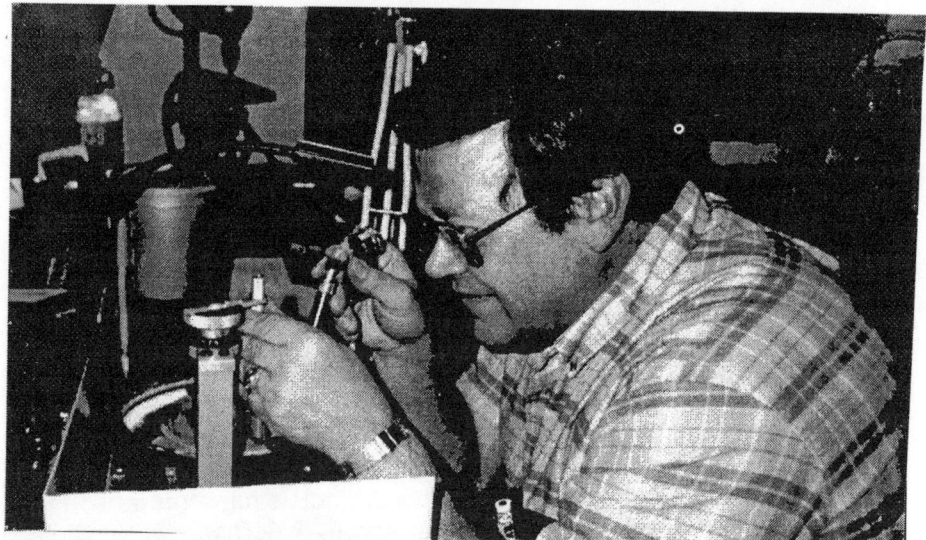

As a stone approaches final polish, don't hesitate to "loupe it." A magnified examination of any polish will often reveal conditions that are not apparent to the naked eye. The Opti-Visor is an excellent magnifying tool for gemcutters, but remember: it's magnification is only about 2x or 3x.

Master Gem Polishing

ing gemstone surfaces.

Every gemcutter knows that cleanliness and careful work habits represent the best safe guard against contamination. To assure that aggregation doesn't cause scratches, they'll usually mix a little vinegar or diluted muriatic acid in with a chemical oxide polish. Still, the real problem with a contaminated polishing surface is that no amount of vinegar will correct the situation. The lap or wheel must simply be cleaned thoroughly.

When you do encounter a scratching situation, take a careful look at the affected facet. Knowing how to read the scratches and marks on a stone will generally tell you what the problem is. Once you know that, you can start finding a solution.

For example, come up close on a stone and study the scratches carefully. Let's say they proceed completely across the polished surface from one edge to the other.

When you see scratches or gouge marks that start in the middle of the surface and then proceed in a straight line to the edge, it's a sign of the kind of polishing scratch that a bit of vinegar or acid can't help. When the scratch runs all the way across the entire surface, that is definitely the sign of a contaminated lap.

If you can't see and remove a contaminant from a polishing lap or wheel, the best alternative is to scrub the the polishing surface vigorously with a scouring pad...preferably steel wool.

Yes, contamination is serious but you don't always have to take the lap off. Sometimes you can see—or feel on the lap or wheel with a practiced finger—whatever it is that's causing the trouble. If your polish is thick or in a pasty form you might be able to find an aggregation that's balled up and is slicing into the stone.

The first step in getting rid of contamination is to try and pinpoint the approximate location of the contaminant. Hold a polished stone to the revolving lap, making sure you keep the stone in one position. If it doesn't scratch in that position, move it in closer to the nut, checking out the entire area this way. If the contaminant

Master Gem Polishing

is embedded in the lap or is remaining in one position this will generally give you a pretty good idea of which ring contains the trouble.

Work on a lap from the outer edge, moving slowly toward the center. In the case of a diamond belt or pad, work in from one side to the other. After each inch or so lift the stone and study it for a scratch. Carefully study the polishing surface. Put your finger tip down and scrape for a hard buildup. If you detect a ball of hard particles pick it off. Don't try to crush it in place.

Try viewing the surface with a 10x magnifier and see if you can detect anything embedded into the surface. Put a loupe down close, slowly moving the lap while you study the surface.

As a last resort, turn on the water flow full strength and wash off the lap with a scouring pad so it's free of all debris and polish. Give it another intensive investigation.

To make certain you don't lose your place, try using a felt tip pen to draw rings. Hold the pen to the surface and turn the motor on slow. As the lap revolves, the pen can trace a series of rings. This way with the restricted view of the magnifier you need only to keep your vision and attention between the colored ring lines and you

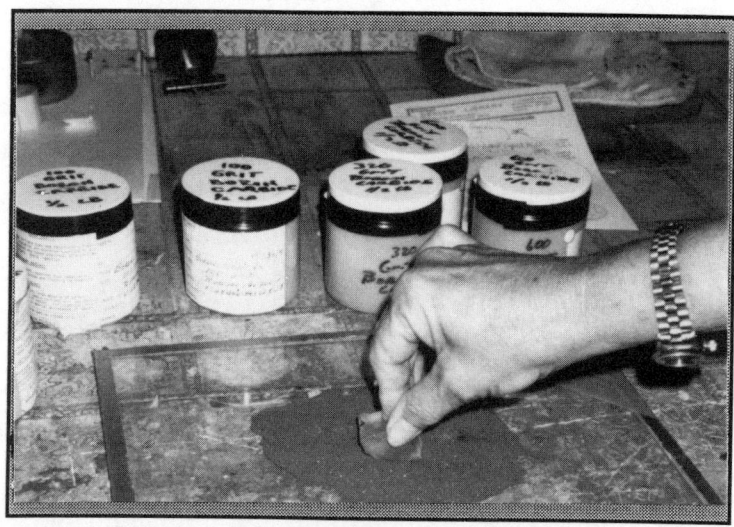

A section of plate glass or Plexiglass is all that's needed to perform hand lapping. Silicon carbide is the abrasive of choice. Don't overlook the benefits of boron carbide. BC particles break down readily, producing smooth finish.

Master Gem Polishing

won't be repeating yourself.

If still unsuccessful, turn the motor on and gently scrape the surface with a sharp blade such as a razor blade. Somewhere on that lap surface a hard tip or particle is sticking up and it should reveal itself to you on the flat, sharp razor's edge.

Should the razor fail, here's a good last resort: score the lap well and the odds are that a scoring slash will cut through or into the contaminant, dislodging and removing it. You may never know the what and where of your problem but you just might cure it anyway.

So, as a last resort remove the lap and score it with a hacksaw blade. A hacksaw blade is not a good device—normally—for scoring because the scores aren't deep and consequently they have a short life. For trying to remove a contaminant, a hacksaw blade will give comprehensive scraping coverage. When you review the lap it should be obvious that the blade's teeth have sliced into an awful lot of lap surface.

Try polishing the stone again. No scratches? Chances are the contaminant has been removed. A good tactic at this juncture calls for adding some vinegar to your polish before you resume. The acid will work against aggregation before it can form—which is a nice way to avoid another long session in removing contaminants.

Only after you've tried the previous steps have you reached the point where it's time to take the lap off the machine off and give it a good scrubbing.

> **Because it's relatively inexpensive to make your own polishing laps or pads, it is always a good idea to have available a set of dedicated lap, pads or belts...for just that occasion when needed.**

A bit of soap will assist but what you really want is to scrub that surface vigorously with a harsh scoring pad. It'll cover the entire surface and probably wear off or wear down the contaminant. So scrub vigorously. Don't spare any elbow grease so the surface will show the results of a thorough cleaning. Once you're certain that its as clean as you can get it, put it back on the machine and test polish a stone. It should polish with no difficulty now. The steps you've taken will clean up a contaminated lap or wheel in the majority of cases.

Dedicated Polishing Pads a Good Strategy...

Incidentally, despite the raging opinions on both sides of this issue, dedicated polishing laps, belts or pads remain a good strategy for any gemcutter. Some experienced cutters go so far as individual vinyl bags to hold their dedicated tools—and this is a procedure well worth duplicating.

When you get a carrier-polish combination that seems to work for you, your best tactic is to protect this personal breakthrough. It's the one, dependable way to return to a winning combination time after time. Dedicated laps, pads or wheels as a strategy aren't all that expensive either. Dedicating laps seems most reasonable for cutters who prefer diamond pastes or diamond powders.

Cutters who polish mostly with oxide powders tend to shy away from the strategy of dedicating because it isn't especially necessary. These individuals might find, though, that dedicating a lap to a specific polish gradually improves the lap-polish combination's ability to produce results. Polish enough with a particular combination and over time you'll find that a lot of powder particles work their way into a lap surface.

Methods For Managing Repeatability Problems...

It's easy to think up big troubles when it comes to polishing. For example, consider lining up a table facet—a rather large one at 17mm to 20mm, for instance—precisely on a ceramic lap.

Now most people don't like the ceramic lap because they can't get it to polish, sand, perform or do much of anything except stimulate exasperation. A number of America's finest faceters earnestly encourage other faceters to throw away this worthless excuse for a polishing lap or use it for some worthwhile purpose such as a test object for sledge hammer blows or as a hot plate for coffee cups.

Some of the new ceramic laps, whose manufacturers claim a slightly more porous surface which holds the diamond particles in place, are said to be an improvement over the old computer ceramic disks. That may or may not be true. One thing is certain, the ceramic lap has proven itself a monumental nuisance to break in and use for many faceters.

Getting a big table down flat and into a polishing mode on

Master Gem Polishing

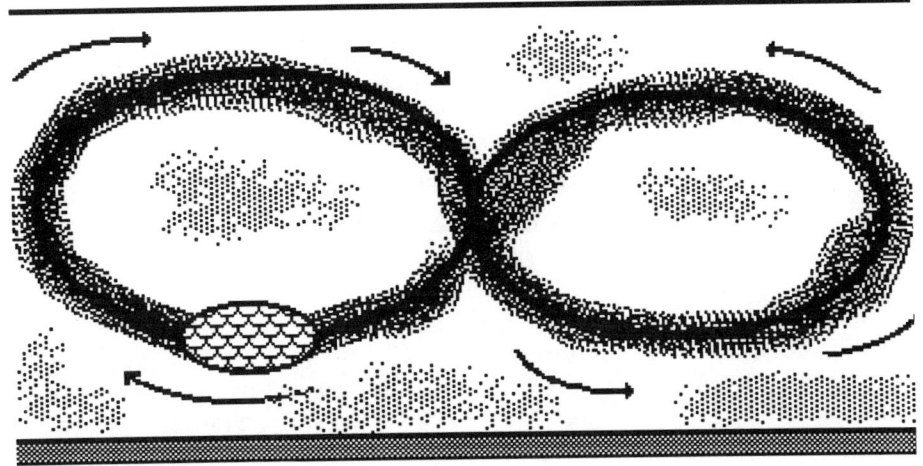

To polish large flats or table facets, a section of glass or Plexiglas will provide the polishing surface. Follow a figure "8" motion with moderate pressure to equalize pressure on all sides.

any lap—aggravated by a hard, ungiving surface and a potential lack of adequate porosity—is no easy task. Indeed, just trying to polish the base of a large cabochon against a flat surface offers plenty of trouble. That's why experienced cabbers prefer an expandable rubber wheel or a belt and rock the cab base against the polish carrier.

The faceter or flat worker has no choice. S/he must use a flat polishing surface.

Partial Polish...

Following traditional practice with any polishing lap, a faceter can try a half dozen adjustments and still a large flat table polishes only in one section or corner. Faced with such a challenge, many faceters occasionally opt for the longer, more unpleasant task of "walking" the facet across. To "walk" a large facet across a flat polishing surface means to polish a facet in a series of parallel bands, using the cheater to advance the stone to each new band until the polishing task is complete. A careful visual inspection will sometimes reveal each band afterwards.

Master Gem Polishing

Therefore, getting any large flat area polished in the traditional way isn't exactly what they call a pleasant job either. Too many variables enter into the task...runout, non-flat surfaces, unequal pressure, etc. If you persist in polishing in the same orientation, meet points or edges may disappear.

A number of factors are responsible for the inability to achieve automatic flat-to-flat orientation of large crystal surfaces.

Why do you get such variations even if you've been careful about repeatability? The most obvious answer, of course, might involve the so-called variation between the run-out of the prepolishing lap and that of the polishing lap. It's called lap variance.

Then, too, you could have cut the table in one ring on the lap and you're now bringing the table down in another ring for polish.

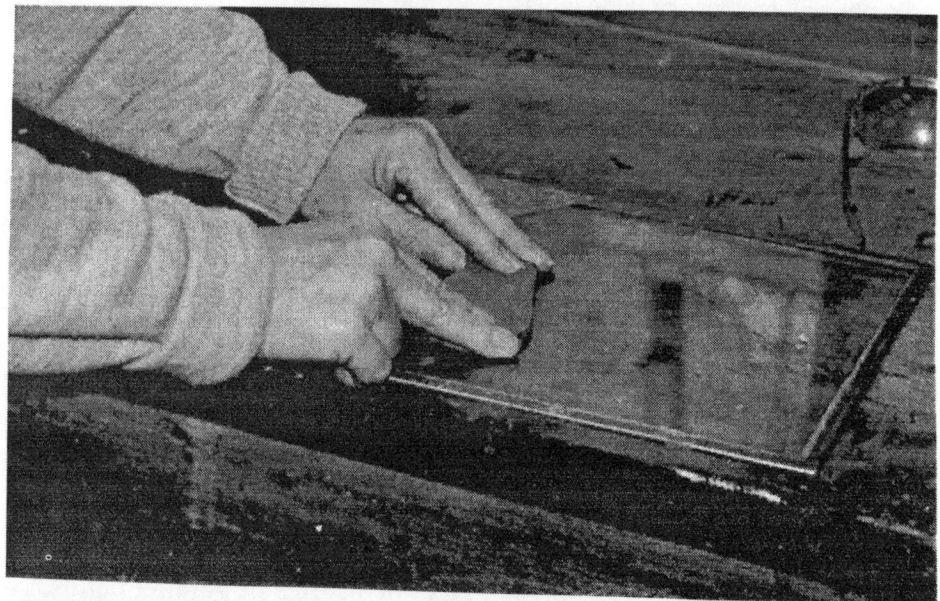

The key to hand lapping large surfaces is even application of pressure on the stone. It's a good idea to use both hands when performing this kind of lapidary work.

Master Gem Polishing

That could introduce the variance.

Speed may be the culprit. Usually a faceter prepolishes at a faster speed than for polishing. This, obviously, can introduce cheat. After all, many top cutters use lap speed and position as a poor man's way of cheating. Move a facet in close to cheat left, move to the outer ring to cheat right. Or speed up the lap for right cheat...or slower for left.

It should therefore be obvious that there are many ways to force a cheating situation on yourself—and the bigger the facet the more likely to have such a problem.

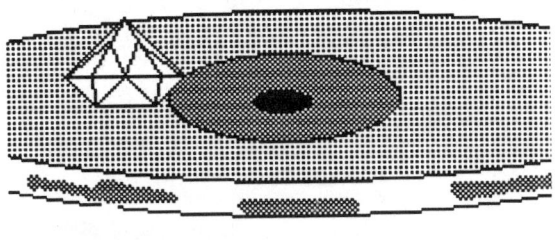

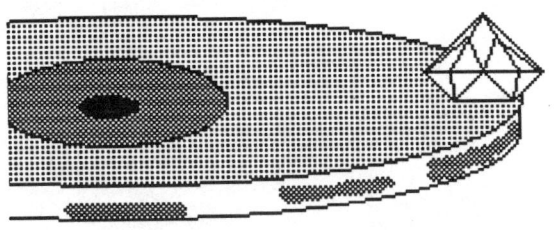

When you need to cheat, don't reach for the machine controls. Move to the inside of the lap to cheat left, and move to the outside to cheat right.

Here are some tactics to consider to avoid the most obvious repeatability problems:

1. Did you return the stone to the same lap position *i.e.*, ring area, used previously?

2. Did you change the rpm? Speed changes introduce slight cheating...and the bigger the stone the greater the cheat

3. Is the lap currently in use accurately parallel with the previously used lap? Even a thin 3 or 4 mil film lap or a belt can introduce cheat.

4. How about uneven hand pressure? If you lean a bit more on one side, it can introduce cheat. Because of so much reliance on hand holding, this is a problem that cabbers must constantly guard against

5. Has the lap thickness changed? This is basic, but it will invariably introduce significant cheat if left unmanaged.

6. Is the flat area unusually large? If a flat covers too

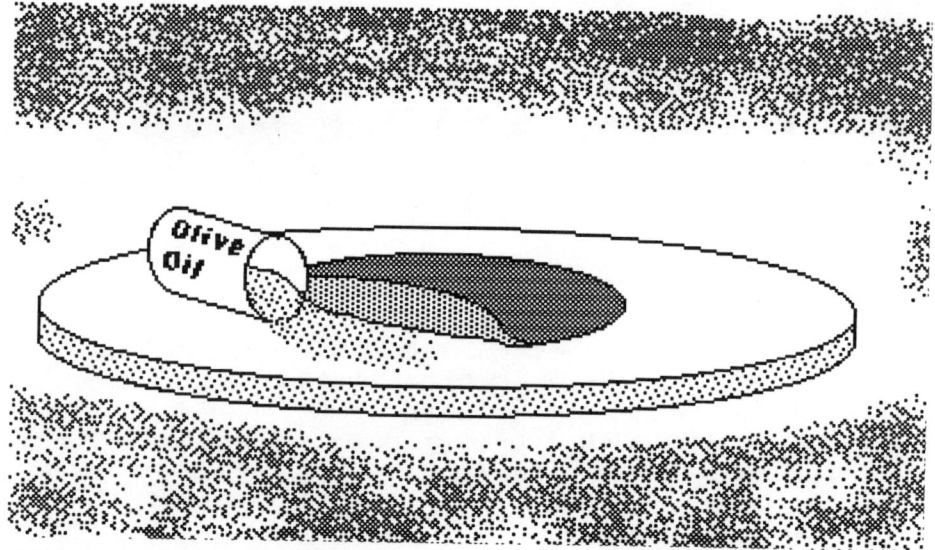

Don't throw out that ceramic lap. It makes an outstanding master lap for thin metal or Ultralap™ polishing films...with olive oil as the adhesive.

much polishing surface it is subject to different speeds and therefore cheat. Perhaps you should apply a crust or edge protection and use a different, softer polishing surface.

Wear Glasses...

The primary lapidary rule is: *wear safety glasses anytime you polish*. Do most gemcutters wear safety glasses all the time?

Probably not. But they should. Gemcutters have known for years that when working on silicon carbide or diamond wheels—especially the coarse ones where chips are flying despite a coolant—safety glasses should be worn. The same holds true with polishing materials whose fineness can fool. Wear glasses: it's good advice.

Use Superglue to Avoid Edge Rounding Problems...

If edge rounding on softer materials is such a serious shortcoming when polishing, is there is a strategy to avoid the problem?

Master Gem Polishing

Is there any way that the table on a finished faceted stone or the edges of a cab cut fantasy or Munsteiner cut can be polished without running the danger of rounding off the edges?

There is a good technique. It involves cyanoacrylate glue and some ordinary baking soda. If you wish to polish a prepolished table facet or a large flat cabochon surface using as a base a felt, leather, Pellon polishing pad or a Moyco Spectralap with colloidal silica, or any other kind of suitable polish, you need first to protect the edges before commencing with any polishing operation.

This is done by placing the stone table or flat down on a piece of Mylar pressed flat on a section of plate glass. Polyester film is inert so most glues won't stick to it effectively.

To protect the stone's or table's edges, place some soda on a tongue depressor-like stick and pile the soda against the stone all the way around the table, making a small embankment. Be sure to fill in the space at the intersection of the stone and the Mylar.

Now squirt superglue into the soda. The mixture of glue and soda will immediately form a hard crust. When you lift the stone away form the Mylar (the crust won't stick to it) you'll see that the crust is even with the surface of the table. It will be attached to the

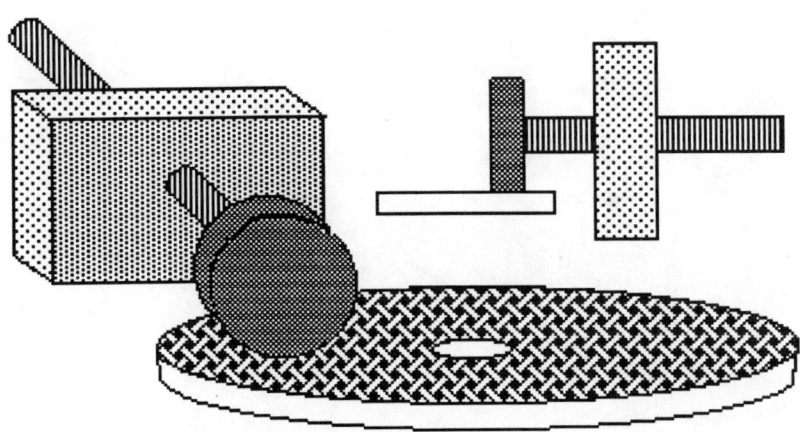

A simple block of wood can be used for fashioning small wooden and plastic abrasive wheels—and the technique also works for preforming gem shapes.

Master Gem Polishing

upper crown row of facets adjacent to the table, but not to the table itself. In the case of a cabochon, the crust will attach to the girdle or top. The polishing action can not get to the edges because the crust will protect them during the polishing process regardless of the softness of the pad carrying the polish.

CA Forms Crust...

A cyanoacrylate has a powerful affinity for baking soda. That's why when you squirt the CA onto the soda a hard crust is immediately formed. **Note:** *this crust forming tactic is a good trick to remember when you want to use CA to fill in open cavities between a dop stick and a piece of rough.*

Because the crust is formed around the table as well as atop the section of Mylar, no bond will form between the Mylar and the CA. That way, the assembly lifts off easily.

Now it's safe to use virtually any kind of polishing surface,

Thin copper disks are excellent for polishing many gems, and after easy finger chargedthey can be mounted directly on the prepolishing lap for fast, convenient polishing immediately following the prepolishing operation.

hard or soft, because the polishing action can work only on the unprotected portion of the stone. When faceting, lock a dop into a 45 degree adaptor, check for a good flat-to-flat match and turn on the motor. Given a good facet-to-carrier match, it doesn't take long to complete a perfect polish free of edge rounding. Cabbers will need to show a bit of caution about tipping the cab lest the jagged edges of the crust catch the soft polishing material and wrench the dopstick out of your hand.

You Can Make Your Own Copper Polishing Tool...

Wouldn't you know it? Just as you are about to finish up a corundum carving or a nice faceted cut in a peach colored cubic zirconia (CZ), you realize that no copper polishing plate is available.

Experienced CZ cutters insist that copper with diamond ranks as one of the better CZ polishing combinations (many corundum cutters claim the same superb results from copper-diamond). A CZ polishing catastrophe doesn't await the gemcutter who doesn't own a copper lap. Nor does anyone suggests that every faceter rush out and buy every lap for sale. CZ can be polished on any one of a number of combinations.

The fact remains that many useful lapidary tools can be self-made and a copper lap can usually be done inexpensively, too. Many copper polishing disks have been fabricated from sections of copper-clad circuit board purchased at Radio Shack or other electronic supply houses for a few dollars.

Essentially these circuit boards are epoxy-filled Fiberglas sheets about $1/16$-inch thick, with a thin sheet of copper bonded to one or, sometimes, to both sides. The price you'll pay for a section of this material depends on the thickness of the copper which is the most expensive ingredient. Even the most costly is quite inexpensive compared to buying a solid copper disk.

Making your own lap is as easy as scribing a circle. Use a compass or trace around one of your own laps to get the desired diameter. You can use a jeweler's saw to cut the circuit board. Sometimes, the saw blade will leave the edges a bit rough but this condition can be sanded away with a bit of emery cloth later.

Master Gem Polishing

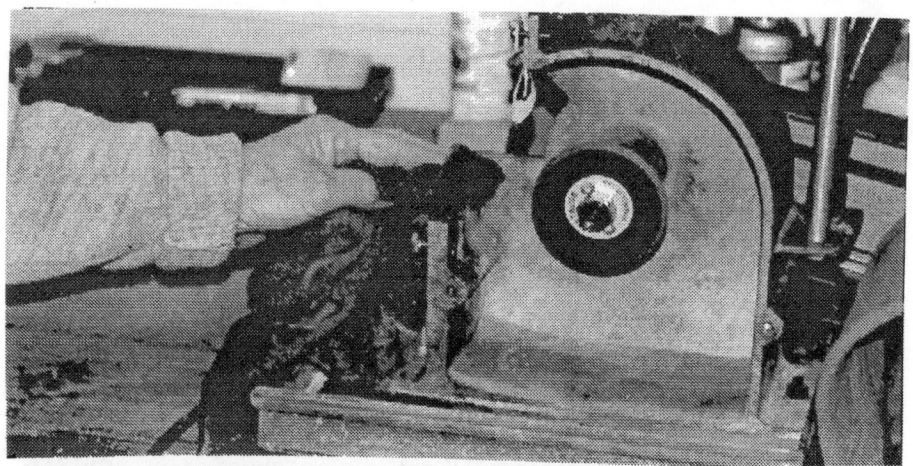

The first rule of lapidary is: keep your equipment and tools clean. Wash up often being particular to remove splash and swarf.

Drill out the center arbor hole. A jeweler's saw will do the trick but as long as you must drill out a starter hole anyway for the blade you might as well cut the size hole you need. It has to be slightly larger than the screw so the disk will slide on and off without getting hung up. Also, you want it only slightly larger than the screw thread so you don't get any wobbling when the disk is in the machine.

Mark the center hole with a nail punch. Let the punch hole serve as your guide for the drill press. Drill the arbor opening, wriggle it around the drill a few times to open up the hole a tiny bit. All you have to do now is charge the lap with diamond polishing grit and it's ready for use.

The nice thing about one of these light little disks is that even if it is out of round a little there won't be any bothersome vibration because of the lightness. If out of roundness from the sawing does bother you, just run the lap at a moderate speed and hold a fine file to the edge. It'll true up quickly and easily.

Note: Some gemcutters, including cabochon cutters, buy tissue thin copper plating for the purpose of making laminate polishing films, similar to the coated Mylar films. You can cut the copper into disks (for laps) or strips (for belts around a wheel) with a pair of scissors (razor blades are better because they don't bend the severed ends over). For disk or lap use, place the copper in a thick book for a week or two to flatten it out. For wheels, the copper ends overlap and are epoxied. Smooth the overlap a bit to avoid bumping. Charging with fine diamond polishing grit is performed with your finger tips.

Make Polishing Strips, Too . . .

You can also use copper circuit board material to make polishing strips. A gemcutter—particularly one who does a considerable amount of repair work—can use these strips to touch up scratches, imperfections...that sort of thing...while the stone is still in the mounting. Someone who specializes in repair cutting will bless the few minutes invested in making a strip needed for that one, difficult polishing task.

While you're at it, make a series of strips about $1/4"$ to $1/3"$ wide and a couple of inches long. Smear some diamond paste on them—and they make beautiful spot sanders and polishers.

Fine Grits Can be Embedded With Finger Charging...

Write the grit identification on the fiber glass or plastic base. By identifying each strip you don't run into contamination problems.

What makes these small strips so easy to make is that you can often charge them with your fingers. It's not universally practiced but diamond grit smaller than 260 can easily be rubbed into copper with your finger tips. A 260 grit takes only light rolling pressure from a steel wheel to be worked into the copper metal.

Take 1200 grit as an example. Just put a little diamond powder in the palm of your one hand, touch an olive oiled finger of the other hand to the diamond dust and transfer the powder to the copper surface. Spread it ... don't place it in one place... and then rub the particles into the copper. You don't even have to rub hard. You can use paste, of course, but it's just as easy to load up a copper disk with dry or oiled powder—and a lot cheaper, too.

For repairs, and even for general touch up on stones, keep three strips on hand...325, 600 and 1200. With these strips available you can touch up a nick, a scratch or a pit, smooth up a girdle, even refine the girdle's shape to fit better into a setting. In a pinch, you can polish a rounded cabochon with a strip...certainly complex cabs.

There's a strange thing, too, about diamond as an abrasive or polishing agent. The strange thing is this rule: less is best. You put too

Master Gem Polishing

much diamond on any kind of polishing surface and it won't do the job nearly as fast as applying a limited amount.

Get in the habit of using a minimum amount of diamond. Remember that the prize winning faceters spritz diamond polish on a ceramic lap and then wipe off the lap surface with a paper towel before proceeding with polish. For a strip, use just the amount of diamond that will stick once or twice to a finger tip —and the strip will do the job much better.

Also, stone carvers and engravers can use tiny strips like this. There are plenty of tough spots that a carver gets into, spots where s/he'd like to have something small and/or flexible to allow for preparing the surface for polishing. A small strip like this will come in very handy for such prepolishing as well as polishing work.

Wire Diamond Polishing Tools . . .

Wire polishers also have a place in the sculptor's tool inventory. To make such a tool you need only a small wooden dowel for a handle and a 2" long section of $1/8$" or $3/16$" diameter copper wire and some diamond grit. Hammer down flat one end of the copper wire and file it to attain the desired square, knife or rounded edge shape. Insert and glue the opposite end in the wooden dowel and the tool is finished except for charging with diamond. When you have an area or corner in a gemstone carving where a revolving wheel or burr simply won't reach, reach for your wire polisher. These can be made in almost any configuration and the copper stalk—just like the stalks on old fashioned diamond cutting dops—means you can bend it repeatedly to conform to the job needs.

Place a little diamond on the flattened part and you can prepolish even the most difficult places. Commercial copper laps or hard nickel bonded strips aren't a bit better than the ready made ones just described. **Note:** *avoid brass which makes a poor lapidary carrier.*

Unlike a solid copper or tin lap, the circuit board lap can't be scored, can't be resurfaced, won't stand for any rough treatment or gouging, and will probably wear out rather fast if you cut a lot of corundum and CZ on it. For the price difference, though, a solid copper lap can't touch these little hand made ones. Further, it's a great convenience to dip the finger into diamond powder and then finger apply a

Master Gem Polishing

booster charge directly to the lap.

That goes true for the diamond sanding strips and wires. Sure the commercial ones last longer, but you don't use strips or wire polishers that much. Furthermore, the self-made ones are inexpensive, quick and easy to make. They're nice to have on hand for that one, important moment when you need them.

After all, you know there's never been a better tool than having the one you need at the moment you need it.

Hand Lapping Skills Solve Polishing Difficulties . . .

Every gemcutter, sooner or later, comes up against the need to lap or polish a flat piece of mineral.

It happens to cabbers more than any other cutting discipline. That's because a flat section comes right out of the slab saw and it's pattern and colors, texture and finish are such that it demands some creative work.

Middle of Flat Polish Problem. . .

The only trouble with large, flat sections is this: most lapidary equipment—except for flat lappers—just isn't built to apply a polish in the middle of a flat of any substantial size. This difficulty applies also to the polishing of large table facets. On the larger flat sections that one normally encounters with slabbed or cabochon materials, certainly a belt or disk sander won't work up the center. Effort will do justice to the edges but in the absence of a regular flat lapper the center forever retains a somewhat unfinished, frosted appearance. A hand tool is seldom the answer.

What is clearly needed is a large, flat, hard surface upon which the stone can be flat lapped. Yes, a flat lapping machine will do nicely but unless you do a lot of flat work, you probably shouldn't invest in such equipment. That leaves hand lapping as the only viable alternative. It's a skill that most gemcutters should develop. This is increasingly true for faceters, many of whom are catching on with the trend of cutting and polishing the large table facet first.

Although boron carbide is extremely brittle and particles break down rapidly, it's super abrasive qualities prove invaluable for loose grinding tasks...because it has the ability to grind and pre-polish

Call that big facet on top by any name you choose, it's still a large, flat—and it poses considerable challenge to anyone trying to apply a consistently fine polish all over its surface.

Equipment Needed For Hand Lapping..

You don't need much in the way of equipment for hand lapping. A section of plate glass or Plexiglas plastic will do for the grinding surface.

At this point, you have some new technology that might help. It's customary to use silicon carbide grit for taking the stone or mineral through the grinding and prepolishing operations. Diamond is also excellent for lapping but you'd best get a flat piece of cast iron with a polished flat top surface for a grit so hard.

A third option—and one that isn't used all that much by lapidaries—is to use boron carbide (BC). Rated as a super abrasive, BC is much harder and much more brittle than silicon carbide. Both the

Master Gem Polishing

hardness and brittleness represent great benefits to hand lapping.

The BC will grind much faster and the brittleness means that the grit particles will gradually break down. The technique for using boron carbide as loose grit to finish minerals is no different than working with silicon carbide. You simply put a small amount of BC on the glass, plastic or steel surface, add some water with a dropper to produce a thick slurry and begin lapping.

Coarseness of the grit you choose to use varies with the hardness and the surface condition of the stone. For table facets, the initial cutting is generally accomplished on a lap in a faceting machine (you probably want speed and careful hand control so you don't mess up the desired orientation of the crystal). Once the large table flat has been cut it can probably be hand lapped much more easily.

For large mineral sections, the first grind should be to smooth out the saw cuts and bring the surface to a uniform flat consistency. The grit grains will break down under heavy use after a few minutes and may need to be replenished. You can feel the lap condition getting finer and performing less abrasive work as you proceed. Use a

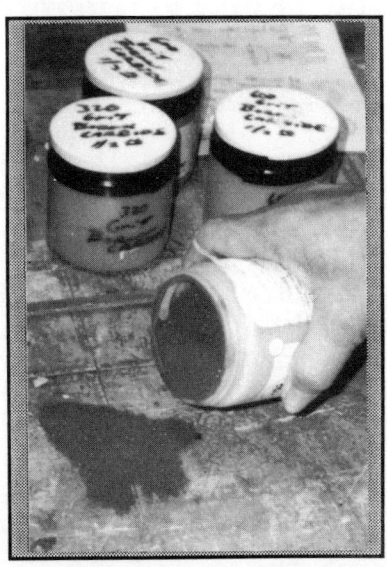

Boron carbide (BC) is superhard but it is very brittle, breaks down quickly and easily. Use it for loose grinding where it performs best.

figure "8" or at least circular lapping motion so the flat stone surface remains in the slurry. Change directions often and don't be reluctant to use some moderate pressure so the grit can "bite" in.

After about five minutes of grinding (you can start at 80, 100 or 200...at 260 for table facets or flat areas that have already been flatted in a machine) wash off the stone and inspect it. Hold the surface nearly parallel to the sun or a bright unfrosted light. The shadows will reveal any saw or coarse grit marks that haven't been completely removed.

The Halogen lamp by General Electric provides superb illumination for gemcutters. The bright, extremely white light is quick to dramatize any imperfections in a smooth finish. Warnings on the radiation danger from these lamps appear considerably overstated.

It's always a good idea to use a water soluble ink when marking gem crystals and minerals with a pen marker. If the ink penetrates the stone specimen's porosity, you want to be able to remove it with water.

You can mentally mark any areas that need work or paint them with a water soluble ink. Why a soluble ink? The last thing you want is for a permanent ink (spell that "dye") to penetrate any porosity or surface openings and take up permanent residence in the stone.

All surface irregularities must be removed at these early grinding stages. Any remaining scratches will become prominent when you get to the pre-polish and polishing operations—and these steps don't remove a lot of material. They aren't intended to remove.

Fine sanding for hand lapping operations is generally 600 grit but you can obtain even finer particles in boron carbide because of the readiness of the particles to break down under pressure and friction. Final polishing operations can be performed with colloidal silica on Pellon, Ultralap™, or even on a wheel in cabbing fashion (if the edges have been protected by "crusting." For information on crusting, see pages 38 and 160. Large flats are best polished on glass, steel, stiff plastic,wax or sometimes on cloth. The reason these kinds

Master Gem Polishing

of polishing materials are used in lapping is that a leather polishing disk, pad and wheel often can't work the center adequately.

If you do decide to try, use a metallic oxide polish—preferably a Bruce Bar which offers an easy way to get polish onto a damp wheel. If that doesn't work, switch to a slurry of water and alumina. Or, use the polish selection that is most suitable for the mineral type you're working with.

Recently, some gemcutters have opted for the use of Cubic Boron Nitride, a superabrasive under the name of Borazon. This is indeed a fine abrasive because its hardness is half that of diamond. This makes it the second hardest known substance, far harder than corundum or Boron Carbide.

Nevertheless, you gain little by using CBN in place of these other abrasives. CBN offers about the same cutting characteristics as BC with much greater expense. CBN is expensive. Boron carbide is much less costly—and does the same job *i.e.*, starts out as a brittle large particle grit and then progressively breaks down under use.

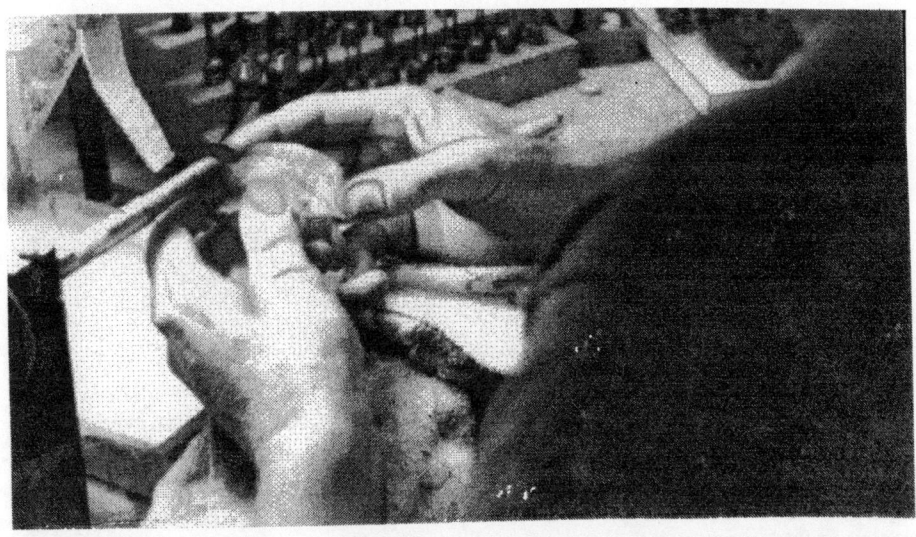

Pick and position your lighting carefully. Proper illumination will enable you to make accurate evaluations of polishing tasks—only so long as the lamp has been positioned properly. Good lighting is a must for polishing.

Another Method to Make Your Own Diamond Paste...

Here's another approach for making your own diamond past. You can save plenty of money with this one. The commercial syringes containing diamond mixed with a water soluble paste are expensive. No doubt about it.

Professional gemcutter Don Cook of Norfolk, NE, had no intention of paying out good money for a product he could more easily make himself. Here's how Don makes his own paste:

He uses plain old grocery store olive oil and loose diamond powder. The olive oil is purchased at the store, and the loose powder is bought cheaply in 100 carat vials.

Says Don, "I mix the two in a plastic teaspoon. I put 5 carats of diamond powder in the spoon and add 4-5 drops of olive oil. I mix it with my finger to a very thick slurry and then apply that in dabs with my finger, rubbing the solution over the entire surface of the lap. No big deal. I just rub it in and spread it with my finger.

"It takes only a few seconds to charge a lap and then you might have to recharge it after a stone or two. That's a small price to pay, though, for the rewards you get with diamond polishing...the inexpensive kind."

Is it worth it? Well, a pint of olive oil will last for years the way you'll be using it. Loose diamond boart, of course, is quite inexpensive. You'll hear this elsewhere but don't bother with liquid detergent in place of the olive oil. You don't get good polishing results with the detergent.

Good Use For Ceramic Laps...

Don't throw away that old ceramic lap that was originally produced as a computer memory disk. It's valuable as a master lap.

Without (often with) proper porosity, your ceramic disk sometimes isn't worth a tinker for polishing gemstones. As a master lap for thin metal and plastic films, though, it's found an inviting home in lapidary.

(**Author's Note:** *This marvelous idea in utilizing a ceramic lap as a base lap for thin plastic films works equally as well—better, say some faceters—with thin metal polishing disks.*)

Master Gem Polishing

Even the porous ceramic laps should be limited in use to polishing only a few stones at a time. After 4-5 stones they'll start to scratch your stones. Ceramic laps, say experienced gemcutters, are great for working on a single competition stone—but they're lousy and unreliable as production laps. Get a good cast iron lap if you want production even if they aren't good for softer stones. If you want the neatest, fastest, and least troublesome polishing setup you've ever experienced, try using the combination of ceramic master lap and thin plastic film laps.

Willard Augsburger of Shreveport, LA, a longtime gemcutter and teacher of electronics, came up with the idea—and pure joy—of using the ceramic lap properly. The idea is: use the ceramic lap as a master lap for an Ultralap™ or your own self-made thin metal or thin plastic film laps charged with diamond or metallic oxide polish. This combination will produce a polish action that is incredibly quick and excellent—and even less of a hint of edge rounding. Talk about a beautiful combination.

... the key to the thin plastic film idea is: *you put olive oil —not water—on the ceramic lap as the adhesive...***The olive oil will grip the plastic on the surface of the ceramic lap like glue—and you get the sharpest facet edges you've ever gotten.**

Now, here's Willard's genius on this idea. Yes, you can use an Ultralap™ or any thin metal or plastic disk (frosted side up) and charge them with diamond paste—or with one of the new colloidal oxide polishes—and place them on the ceramic lap. First, though, and this is the key to the thin film idea, *you put olive oil —not water—on the ceramic lap as the adhesive.* Wipe the olive oil on the ceramic surface with your fingers and then squeegee it back off the surface with a razor blade. Now lay the thin film disk on the coated surface. The olive oil will grip the film on the surface of the ceramic lap like glue—and you get the sharpest facet edges you've ever gotten in your life.

To keep the thin films polishing you merely charge them as needed.

So, don't throw away those old ceramic laps that you couldn't get to work right. They're dynamite—although admittedly expensive—as a master lap to hold thin film disks for one of the better polishing combination you can imagine.

It's a good idea, too, to refrain from throwing out a diamond or oxide Ultralap™ when it fails to polish anymore. Without the need to use copious amounts of water to maintain the suction that promotes adhesion to the base lap, these worn out disks can be given a new life with a charge of diamond paste or a colloidal oxide paste. Commercially coated diamond plastic films by themselves, of course, aren't all that cost effective, efficient or long lasting for sanding or prepolishing, but the polishing disks can be made acceptable as rejuvenated polishing disks.

As for thin metal polishing laps, the olive oil also provides a powerful suction here, too. Just place the metal polishing disk atop the olive oil treated ceramic lap as you would a thin plastic film, and it will hold well.

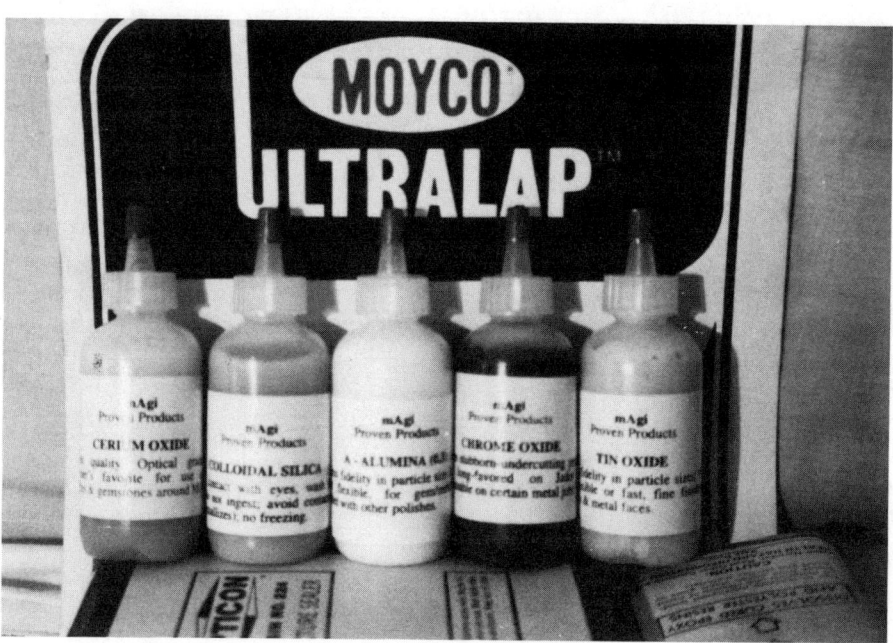

Tips on Corundum Polishing . . .

How do you polish corundum?

That's a question asked by many gemcutters.

If you want a good, brilliant polish with a minimum of difficulty, just go to cast iron laps for polish using 14,000 diamond paste. Cast iron with 50,000 diamond grit will also polish corundum in a hurry, as long as you've given the stone a good 600 or 1200 pre-polish. Many gemcutters prefer the 600 grit for pre-polish. They contend that 1200 merely slakes off surface material and doesn't materially improve the pre-polish finish. Be a bit cautious, though: a cast iron lap with even fine 50,000 will do some cutting, too.

You can also use a Crystalite Last Lap with 14,000 for corundum. This combination works well because the metal pelletized resin surface offers the level of hardness that's needed to get the corundum to take a polish.

As usual with any gemstone, pre-polish is the key. Pre-polishing on corundum at 600 will usually suffice. Some faceters urge 1200 and even 3000 pre-polish but it sometimes won't pre-polish because you often get on the basal cleavage. With corundum when you try to pre-polish against the C axis with a fine grit the direction is sometimes so hard it won't abrade: it will polish.

Plus, a 3000 disk will wear out too quickly running against something as hard as corundum. When polishing a small corundum consider using 50,000 diamond on a Last Lap, after a 1200 pre-polish. For bigger stones, go right to the cast iron lap...that's the real corundum polishing workhorse. How about spinel or chrysoberyl? Use the same approach as you do with corundum...cast iron with either 14,000 (for rapid polish) or 50,000 (for a bit slower and finer polish or for smaller stones).

More on Polishing Corundum . . .

Corundum is the second hardest substance on earth and it often poses major problems for the unwary gemcutter.

The major rule to observe when polishing corundum is this: because of its hardness and toughness the material must be adequately pre-polished. Failure to produce a surface suitable for polishing lies behind most of the failures to get the fine subadamantine polish that corundum features.

Master Gem Polishing

Pre-polish corundum with at least 8,000 grit, say award winning faceters. This can be done on a phenolic lap with a small amount of olive oil as lubricant, they claim. Perhaps! I've never had luck beyond 1200 with a prepolish because the corundum starts to slake off. Maybe it's my hand pressure...or the lap...or...or...or

Many faceters finish polish on a Fast or Last Lap with 50,000 grit for the final polish. They claim to fine sand the finish

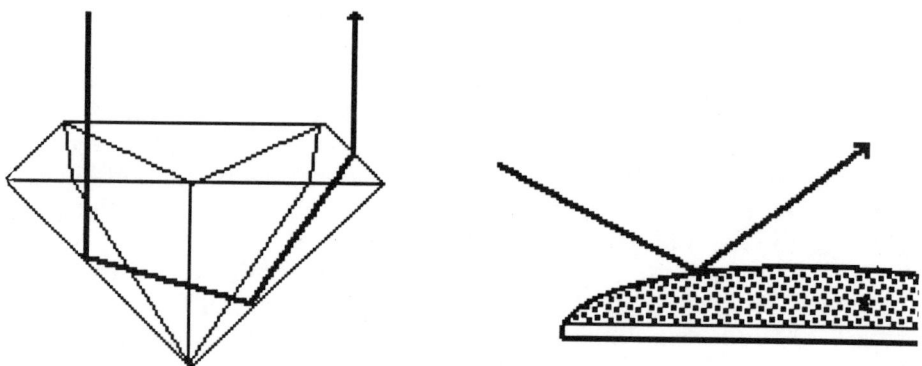

Transparent stones depend mostly on a smooth polished finish for achieve spectral diffusion and thus maximum visual effect. Cabochons depend on spectral diffusion, too, but often tiny subsurface particles also produce irregular ray deflections called diffuse reflection to product its full optical impact.

with 1200 in order to clean up some meets and accelerate the final action. Whoa, say others who contend that they go to a fine diamond polish direct from a 600 prepolish. Some cutters succeed with 1200 prepolish, polish with 14,000 and then remove any polish "frost" by finish polishing with alumina on a tin-lead lap. The best advice is: test your own corundum prepolishing techniques—and grit sizes.

Diamond polish is about the most effective agent for working on corundum (and spinel!). Also, don't overlook the benefits of diamond polish on a copper lap (that's one of the slick ways to get a super polish on CZ, too). For more on polishing corundum, particularly with a ceramic lap, see page 251.

Glass Polishing Similar To Gemstone Polishing...

Polishing theory is a subject that maintains a high interest level among gemcutters.

At one time the lapidary industry thought it had all the answers. Polishing, the experts told us, could be explained on the basis of two theories:

a) the *Beilby layer theory* — this theory contended that crystal polishing was the result of a thin layer, different from the rest of the stone, which smoothed out as a result of the interaction between polishing agent, heat, and friction. It essentially was aimed at explaining powder or oxide polishes.

b) the *scratch theory* — this theory contended that polishes were the result of finer and finer scratching on the surface of a stone material until the distance between the scratches was so infinitesimal that the human eye could no longer distinguish one scratch from the other—hence the surface appeared polished. It essentially was aimed at explaining diamond particle polishing.

Later research tended to merge the two theories. It was felt that neither type of polishing action was mutually exclusive. Some scratching was involved in the Beilby layer and some production of a special polished layer was involved in diamond scratching.

Finally, researchers debunked the Beilby layer. The diamond scratch theory, too, came into disrepute. Despite so-called laboratory studies that had earlier "proven" these theories, it was obvious that neither really held the answer.

They just don't explain polishing: that was the last word.

The How and Why of Polishing Gems...

Today, gemcutters exhibit reasonable knowledge about how and why a polish develops when a gemstone is subjected to certain chemicals and techniques. Science hasn't yet provided an absolutely definitive answer. It has simply observed that a fine polish develops with certain combinations and under certain conditions.

In doing research on polishing at the National Bureau of Standards on another subject, *American Gemcutter Magazine* re-

Master Gem Polishing

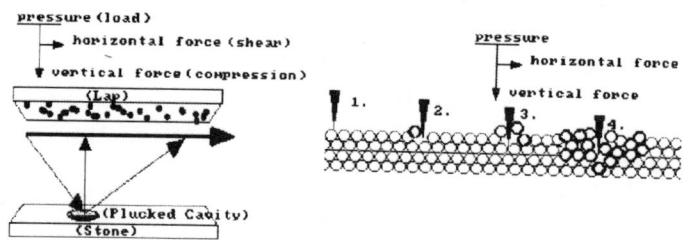

Contemporary grinding theory holds that stress created by a particle of abrasive grit results in the removal of a chip. The efficiency of the process depends on the hardness and sharpness of the grit and stone hardness.

---

searchers came across an excellent treatise in the Scientific Papers from Cambridge's University Press on polishing the glass used in mirrors, prisms, interferometers, lenses and so forth.

While much of this technical paper is dated and is directed to glass and/or quartz polishing, the techniques and explanations may be of great interest to gemcutters who seek more and better answers to lapidary polishing. It does demonstrate that changes come slowly and in increments in the lapidary polishing arena, with many of the techniques used long ago and in other industry applicable today with only slight modification.

Here is an edited summary of that treatise:

Shaping Comes First...

The glass or other material on which an optical surface is to be applied is first roughly formed to the desired shape. For example, in the case of a lens, the first step consists of cutting out a disk of glass. Then a prism is sawed or rounded to rough dimensions from a larger block. The proposed surface itself is next generated more precisely by periods of grinding with suitable laps. Finally, the surface is ground with coarse grits of either carborundum, silicone carbide or Boron Carbide to conform approximately to the specifications.

Finer and finer abrasives precede the final grinding which is performed with the finest particle. Once the fine grinding is finished, the surface gets polished to as much perfection as possible.

Theories Alike...

Theory of Glass Grinding and Polishing: Optical grinding and gem polishing are alike in that both require the use of a material which is harder than the glass. The abrasive consists of loose grits or fine powder. For grinding, the grit is worked over the surface with a hard tool, ordinarily made either of glass or cast iron. Polishing tools or surfaces are made from a softer base material.

A polishing tool for preparing precise optical surfaces is usually composed of some combination of metals, waxes, and plastics. In instances where no great precision is demanded, such polishing tools as paper, cloth and wood suffice. The grinding process itself depends upon the characteristic conchoidal fracture produced when an excessively high pressure is applied to a point in the surface of the glass. The pressure exerted on the surface by a single particle of abrasive or grit, as it is rolled about between the tool and the work, builds up stress beyond the strength of the glass, resulting in the removal of a chip. Carborundum and carbide particles were ordinarily used. Today they mostly use super abrasives *i.e.*, BC, CBN, diamond. The efficiency of the process depends primarily on the sharpness of the grits. Carborundum and boron carbide grits break down faster than silicon carbide or diamond. Still, the fractured particles have sharp edges and consequently they grind quickly.

Carborundum Grinds Faster...

Ellisons[1] says that Carborundum grinds about six times as fast as emery (garnet). Fortunately, all types of grits are available today in different sized particles and the fineness of the surface can be prepared by changing to finer grits.

The hardness of various abrasives is indicated in Moh's extended hardness scale (see Table on next page)

---

[1]Ingalls, Albert G., editor, Amateur Telescope Making, p. 74. New York: Scientific American Publishing Co., 1935.

Hardness Scales

Moh's Scale

Substance	Value
Orthoclase	6
Quartz	7
Topaz	8
Corundum	9
Diamond	10

Extended Moh's Scale

Substance	Value
Orthoclase	6
Vitreous pure silica	7
Quartz	8
Topaz	9
Garnet	10
Fused zirconia	11
Fused alumina	12
Silicon carbide	13
Boron carbide	14
Diamond	15+

From a practical point of view, we may consider that the polishing operation is a planing process[2]. The grains of abrasive appear to fix themselves automatically in the soft material of the tool, so that their crystal surfaces are parallel to the direction of motion of the tool and parallel to the plane of its surface. Thus a complex scraper is formed.

Planing action generally will start on the "peaks" or hills of a gem crystal.

As this scraper moves over the glass, the height of each

---

[2] For a more comprehensive treatment of the theory of polishing from a different point of view see the following:
  Lord Rawleigh, Proc. OP Convention, No. 1, page 73 (1905)
  Finch, G. I., "The Beilby Layer," Science Progress, 31, 609 (1937)

Master Gem Polishing

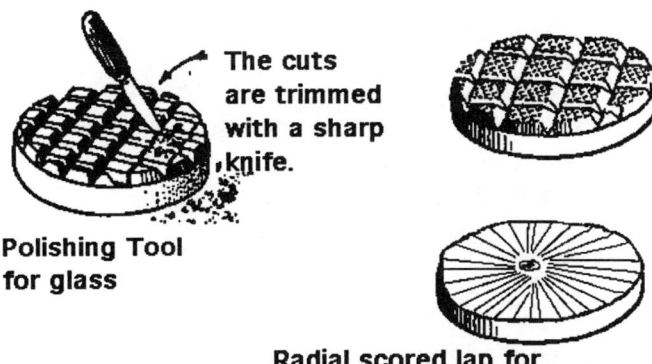

Polishing Tool for glass

The cuts are trimmed with a sharp knife.

Radial scored lap for polishing gemstones.

Scored polishing laps represent a lapidary technique taken from the glass lens polisher who cuts the rouge pads into squares to assure even, smooth exposure of the glass surface to the polishing substance.

abrasive particle is automatically adjusted in the soft backing so that it produces a fine smooth cut. The removed glass is washed away by the liquid lubricant, usually water. The planing action starts on the peaks of the "hills" that result from the fine grinding and produces a full polish there almost with the first strokes.

Continued operation of the polishing tool removes additional glass, so that the hills become plateaus as they are finally planed down to the levels of the deepest valleys.

The character of the surface on any particular plateau is not improved by continued polishing—it is to be regarded as fully polished from the first initial strokes. This is illustrated on the next page.

This particular part of the glass polishing theory is a good point to remember the next time you achieve a full polish—and then believe you can improve by just a little extra polishing effort. There is indeed a time to polish...and a time to quit.

Master Gem Polishing

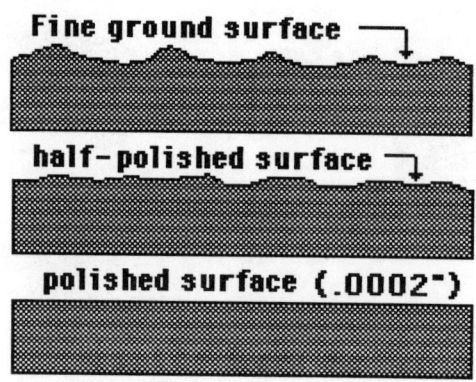

After the whole surface becomes uniformly polished, further working with the polishing tool removes additional glass. In constructing an experimental aspheric camera lens, as much as 0.0030" of glass has been removed by polishing.

Methods of Polishing. Glass can be successfully polished with almost any fine abrasive, provided a suitable soft and yielding backing is used. For some types of work such as edging mirrors where irregularities in the surface do not matter, glass is polished with a wood tool charged with carborundum or cerium oxide. Glass may also be polished with rouge, either the red oxide or the magnetic black oxide, and also with charcoal or tin oxide.

Rouge is Most Satisfactory...

For ordinary optical work rouge is still the most satisfactory polishing material. Surfaces of glass, quartz, calcite, and fluorite are often best polished with rouge or cerium oxide on wax, pitch

> **Rouge is often used for polishing glass and similar soft crystals.**

or plastic. The action of various polishing agents depends on the type of backing—cloth, paper, or pitch—plus the hardness of the

Master Gem Polishing

Before you try to polish with a Mehanite lap, burnish the polishing surface with a chunk of flat corundum while the lap is turning. This removes metal jaggies which can cause scratching.

material being polished as well as the method of lubrication.

Some agents which are indifferent polishers when used with a wax or pitch tool and lubricated with water are quite effective when used dry on a paper lap. For paper backed polishing, tin oxide is commonly used. Chromium oxide is recommended for polishing certain minerals and metals such as stainless steel which is "attacked" by rouge.

The material for the polishing tool may be a soft metal—copper, lead, or aluminum. Tools made of these metals are sometimes used for polishing thin specimens of minerals which are to be examined with the microscope. Alumina is usually employed for mineral work of this type owing to the additional hardness of the minerals.

The polishing tools for precision optical work are made of pitch or pitch and wax compounds, in contrast with cloth- or paper-faced tools used on some commercial products. Glass is polished with surprising rapidity on a cloth polisher, but it exhibits a peculiar grainy "lemon-peel" surface.

The Experience of a Mehanite Lap...

Few faceting newcomers—or non-diamond polishers—have experienced polishing with a cast iron lap. Truth is, for hard stones it's rapid, accurate, and produces minimal scratching. In colored stone cutting, the lifetime Mehanite lap is not well known. Its nearly unmatched when it comes to polishing hard stones such as corundum, chrysoberyl and spinel...providing it is broken in properly. Rub the surface vigorously with corundum to wear off metal jaggies before using it.

Mehanite is a proprietary cast iron that is made in various formulations. What makes it so valuable for faceters is the fact that it's closely grained, slightly porous, stable and resists wear. Diamond grit particles find a home in the pores, thus giving the lap its unique polishing capability.

A Mehanite lap, owing to the hardness of cast iron, offers the best polishing on harder stones. It will usually scratch softer stones.

Jarvi Tool Company of 780 Debra Lane, Anaheim, CA 92805, the maker of the Facetron faceting machine, offers newly formulated Mehanite laps. President Norm Jarvi says his company purchases cast iron blanks which were originally intended for optical lens grinding/polishing. Setting up tight specs, Norm finishes the laps for lapidary so that both sides can be charged with diamond. He recommends 3,000 or 8000 on one side and 50,000 on the other so a faceter can apply both a fine pre-polish and a final competition level polish. I prefer 14,000 on one of the sides.

If you're a gemcutter who has experienced great difficulty with ceramic laps, you may find an acceptable alternative in a Mehanite lap. It's a whiz for polishing (some people use the lap for sanding and pre-polishing by dressing the surface with a more coarse grit) all hard stones. Cubic zirconia can be a pesky polishing problem at times, but with a cast iron lap it polishes up quickly and with few problems. The same holds true for a number of the other relatively hard synthetic gemstone types.

Making Up Effective Polishing Combinations . . .

To obtain a superior gemstone polish, gemcutters must often innovate with the various components and accessories.

For example, colloidal polishes perform with outstanding results on cabochons if the right arrangement has been made between polish, flexibility of the polishing pad and the master lap. To use a colloidal polish whether it's an oxide or silica, a leather or felt pad should be adhesively attached to a minimum of 1/4" thick rubber which itself is attached to a Lucite disk (or a disk of similar strength and flatness.) Some cabbers successfully attach an Ultralap™ to a rubber cushioned polishing disk. This difficult tactic can also be used for polishing cabochons on a faceting machine.

For polishing flats or an edge protected table facet, attach the Pellon to a ceramic disk. This setup is great for cabochon bases.

When using colloidal silica, remember that a Pellon lap should be kept wet. Use a dripper that will keep the solution appearing slowly on the Pellon surface.

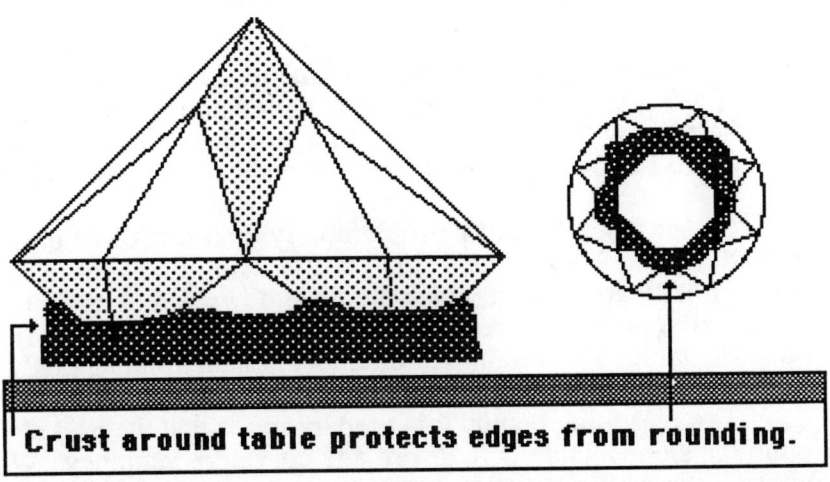

Crust around table protects edges from rounding.

When other facets are involved, to polish faceted tables with colloidal silica and a soft polishing pad, make a crust barrier around the outer edges of the table. Casting resin, epoxy or baking soda -superglue can be used.

Master Gem Polishing

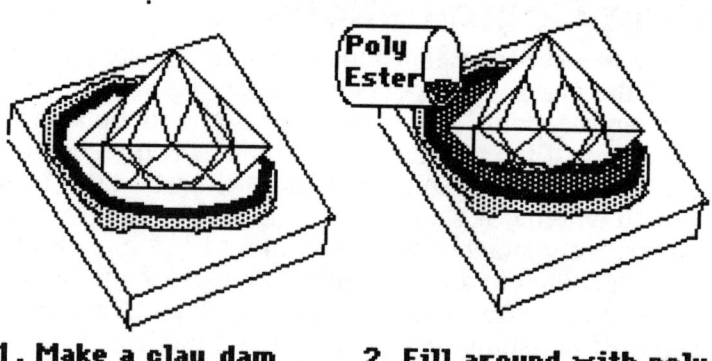

1. Make a clay dam   2. Fill around with poly

Another way to form a crust around a table facet or large flat so edges will not round when using a soft polishing carrier is to make a small coffer dam out of clay and pour in casting resin (casting polyester).

Using Casting Resin to Control Edges . . .

If a faceted stone is already completed and you wish to polish the table with colloidal silica on a Buehler's Mastermet or a felt or a hard Pellon Lap, you'll find that resin serves your purposes well.

Smear a thin film of petroleum jelly on a section of glass or flattened Mylar. Then make a small coffer dam of clay around the petroleum jelly area. Next, place the table down flat on the jellied area. Finally, pour some resin around the gemstone so that it fills in around the table. Be certain that the facet is seated flat against the jellied surface to avoid any resin seeping between the two surfaces.

The reasoning behind this preparation is that the cast resin around the stone's table will absorb any curvature tendency. When you bring the table down flat on a soft carrier, the table will polish flat and the resin crust will protect the facet edges from rounding. This same effect, incidentally, can be achieved using baking soda

Master Gem Polishing

and cyanoacrylate glue. See page 38 for more information on this technique. Pack baking soda around the table and then apply superglue. The resulting crust will also protect the table edges against rounding on any soft polishing surface.

As for cabs, you can use felt or hard Pellon on a rubber pad or Lucite or simply leather or a cloth pad on rubber. All of the materials will hold the moisture well, a vital necessity with colloidal silica. Oxide polishes, of course, work best when they are damp-dry.

Solving the Sunstone Polishing Dilemma...

For some reason, sunstone gives the average gemcutter polishing fits.

I'm not certain why...so long as the prepolishing has been performed properly. If you are having difficulties with this marvelous stone, take a few pages from the carver's book.

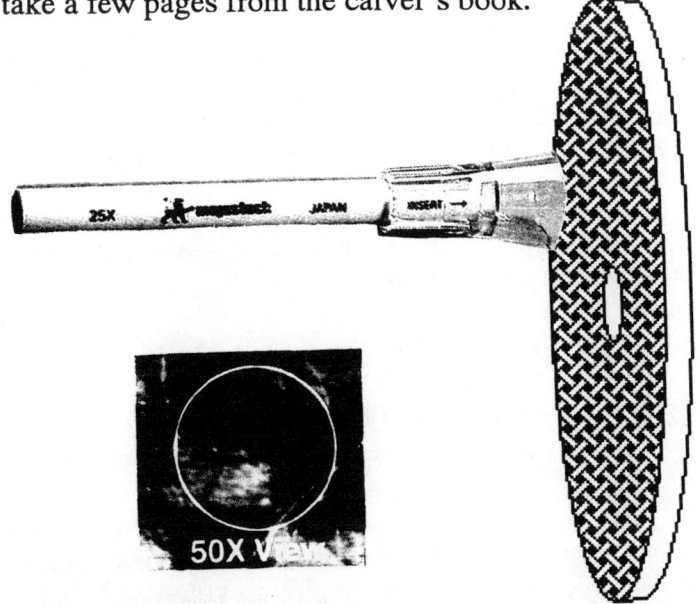

It takes a bit of experimentation to get your "looking technique" under control. Try different forms of lighting and types of magnifiers. The Opti-Visor is one of the more popular magnifying tools, but others just as good include the box loupe, triplet magnifiers and others.

Master Gem Polishing

Carvers prepolish sunstone with a well worn 600 sanding paper. If the touch is light enough, they can then proceed directly to a final polish using cerium oxide. The polish generally comes up quickly and beautifully.

If your shaping of the mineral eliminates flat surfaces, use a 1000 grit Bruce Bar on a felt wheel. This will work nicely on curved, complex surfaces. When using cerium oxide on felt, remain cautious about heat buildup. Heat not only aggravates the natural cleavage but leads to undesirable streaking. Apply light pressure with swipe polishing and keep the water flowing copiously.

For faceting, I have used tin oxide on a tin lap with considerable success. Sunstone can give faceters a fit. That's because the mineral tends to become abusive about accepting a flat surface polish. Even cutting a large facet can be a challenge. Subject sunstone to a coarse lap and it will pit and craze. If you try a diamond paste on a canvas pad, the combination will produce serious sloughing off.

If you switch to a phenolic lap, says carver Henry Hunt, you can expect the stone to abrade unevenly and display intermittent, uncontrollable spot polishing. This litany of woe can be avoided if you'll remember: rough in with a worn 260—carbide sander or diamond lap—using a light touch and plenty of water and step up through the grits, finishing with a 1200 or 3000 prepolish. Go to cerium or tin oxide on a tin or tin-lead lap—and you should have sunstone polishing under control.

Managing Light
Vital to Good Polish . . .

"Cut a little and look...polish a little and look..."

That's the rule of gemcutting.

Obviously, viewing your progress with a partially finished stone is just as vital as the cutting itself. Make a mistake so far as what your eyes tell you—or should tell you—and the likelihood of an accurate gemstone vanishes. One of the key skills in any form of gemcutting consists of the development of your eyes...to see or detect and to help interpret the condition of the work. To become proficient at seeing a gemstone develop you must maximize your eye

Master Gem Polishing

Reflected light will produce the desirable visual effect on a polished surface which enables a gemcutter to analyze the work properly. This condition comes as a result of proper orientation of viewer, light and stone

skills. In other words, you want to develop a "looking style."

How, though, does a gemcutter develop a good looking style? Much is written about how to cut. But how does one go about looking at a partially finished stone and making certain the viewing unveil the necessary information.

Lighting is Important . . .

Before any setup is confirmed a gemcutter would be well advised to consider the type of lighting. Conventional wisdom holds than a clear incandescent bulb is the best kind of light. It allegedly will unveil those tiny scratches much better than a frosted bulb or a fluorescent lamp.

Not too many gemcutters disagree with this principle. Most of them opt for a 75 watt bulb. A 100 watt bulb produces much more light. The disadvantage of the 100 watt bulb, though, lies in the "nothing in excess" principle. You really don't need that much illumination—or heat. The glare can also be excessive. You might actually miss something with so much bounce back.

Master Gem Polishing

Add to that the considerable heat from the higher wattage bulb and you can easily understand why lower illumination offers superior advantages. For maximum lighting—especially for older gemcutters—the search is on for something even better. This seems to be the quartz lights with their more narrow spectrum.

A strong case can also be made for General Electric's Halogen lighting. These lamps produce brilliant white light that is quick to reveal even tiny scratches that may go unnoticed under other strong lighting. Some minor controversy exists over the safety of the Halogen's light ray emissions. Such concern is largely unsubstantiated and the product is still on the commercial market which may indicate that the concern is excessive. One aspect about the Halogen and other high lumen level lighting is undisputable: they do tend to give off plenty of heat.

Regardless of the heat produced, many experienced gemcutters use these stronger lights (they produce less glare, too) and en-

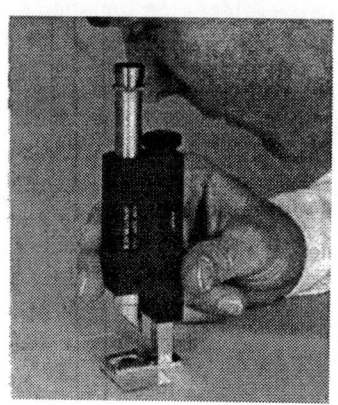
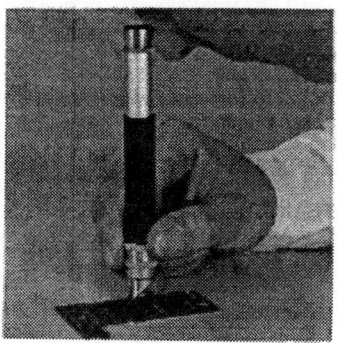

It doesn't cost all that much so consider the benefits of using a battery powered magnifier with light. Such an instrument allows you more movement freedom than a fixed light position.

joy the additional "looking" strength. A good option for gaining stronger light without so much heat is to try quartz lighting: quartz lights tend to burn cooler.

No strict answer exists for the most appropriate type of lighting. Vision requirements for every gemcutter are so different. Only experimentation will disclose what kind of lighting is best for you.

The important factor is this: experiment. Don't drop a frosted light bulb into your lamp and proceed on the basis that it need never be changed because it seems right. Yes, you can grow accustomed to unsuitable lighting. But a little simple testing might prove that you've been using the wrong kind of light and better "looking" is just around the next flick of the on-off switch.

Reflection Important, Too ...

Once a gemcutter has determined which kind of light is best, a technique must be developed. Technique is simply the coordination between the light source, the gemcutter's eyes, and the stone.

What you seek when examining a gemstone—whether faceting or cabbing—is a reflective skin created by light. Look at the illustration on page 286 where an effort has been made to define and demonstrate the kind of reflective shading and illumination types that are most suitable for gemstone inspection.

When you have the light source oriented properly to the stone, you should be able to view across the target surface under inspection. The light will reveal differences in surface texture. It will also illuminate scratches....right down to a cat whisker.

All the description in the world won't suffice until the phenomena has been experienced. A gemcutter must actually view a stone surface under a bright light in such a way that the reflection dramatizes the features that are being searched.

If you're polishing a surface, the light reflection will show at once that portion that reflects light rays uniformly and in parallel. This appearance is markedly different from the helter-skelter reflections given off by an unpolished surface. The key to "...cut and look...polish and look..." is to develop a visible awareness of these subtle differences. It's not at all difficult to keep the stone moving in front of the light and oriented to your eyes in such a way that the light reflects off properly to offer desired information.

Master Gem Polishing

For best viewing of polished gemstones, consider clear incandescent lamps arranged so the surface can be viewed in reflected light.

One Supreme Master Gemcutter, while cutting a complex shaped cabochon for competition, took his nearly finished stone out at night and inspected it with a magnifier under the full power of an automobile's high beam headlights. The powerful beams were enough to disclose several cat whiskers that the cutter's own overhead lamp had failed to illuminate.

Magnifier Use . . .

Nearly all gemcutters use magnifiers. The most popular strength is 10x except for those who use an Opti-Visor. The latter devices offers a handy headband with magnifiers between 1.5x and 3x which slip down like eye glasses. A tilt of the head is generally all that's needed to train the neck muscles and eyes to make those

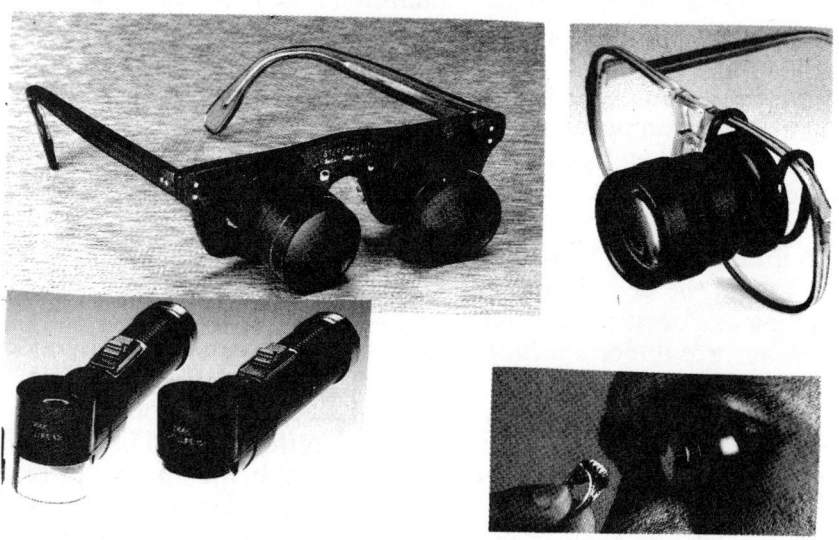

Although reflected light and a low powered Opti-Visor will suffice for most gemcutting requirements, some individuals arrange for special lighting and special magnifiers.

Master Gem Polishing

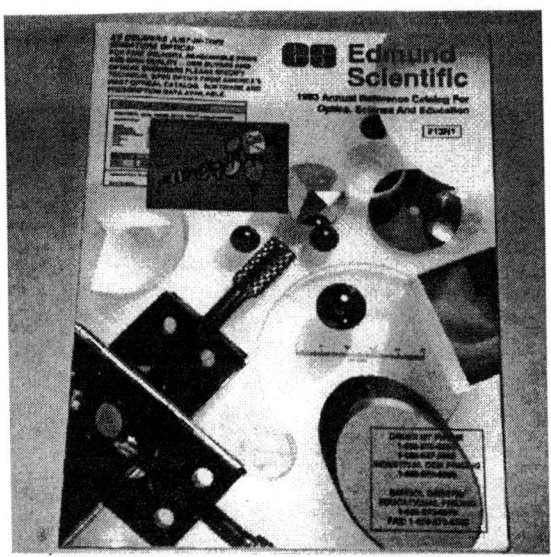

The Edmund Scientific catalog is an excellent source for optical and other scientific devices, many of which are useful in the gemcutting trades.

coordinated movements necessary to see the stone in the proper reflected light.

Many gemcutters, of course, use a loupe, either the diamond cutter's box type or the fold away loupe. Faceters generally rely more on magnifiers than do cabochon cutters or carvers. The latter use the unaided eye mostly, going to a magnifier only when encountering some type of sensitive situation. When a cabber does get in the habit of using magnifiers it is usually an Opti-Visor so as to have both hands free for working.

Options for Improving Sight...

The techniques are different, too, between a faceter and a cabber. For a faceter, the quill tends to limit the light and stone positions to the swing radius of the machine. Only a lift off type quill such as a jamb peg or an old fashioned Lee head allows the faceter to pull the quill completely off the machine.

Cabbers have this same away-from-the-machine flexibility. They are able to move the stone with total freedom. Because the stone is usually hand held, a cabber can move at will—even walk

Master Gem Polishing

away from the cabbing machine to another light source—until a suitable orientation is found that will give best viewing results.

Older gemcutters face another "looking" hurdle. This is the issue of eye glasses. A normal single corrective lens for the eyes doesn't introduce too much complication. Bifocals and trifocals do, though. I know because I wear trifocals. Depending on the line of sight, different focus configurations are at work. Not only must a gemcutter wearing bifocals and trifocals manipulate the light source, stone orientation, and eye direction but s/he must do so to accommodate that portion of the bi- or trifocal lens in use to obtain the best vision. This can be an acute problem if the cutter persists in wearing these glasses while cutting as I do.

Indeed, some gemcutters dispense with their glasses while cutting. They generally use an Opti-Visor only while cutting and inspecting. To minimize the problem of eye glasses, others have constructed their own high powered telescopic viewer. In a few cases, this consists of a barrel-like instrument which is firmly attached to the cutting machine. It permits an extremely detailed view of cutting results. Not surprisingly, such viewers are used by competitive cutters. Although some of these high powered scope attachments have been custom made you can obtain such an instrument commercially and rig it up yourself. The cost is not all that great. If interested, write in with a request for a catalog (there is a slight charge for the catalog) from

Edmund Scientific Co.
101 E. Gloucester Pike
Barrington, NJ 08007 1-609-573-6260

I recommend that you obtain a copy of this marvelous catalog. It contains many other scientific items that might challenge your inquisitiveness and inventiveness, particularly the optical tools.

Some time ago, the American Society of Gemcutters notified its 3000 members that a specialist in making surgeon's magnifiers would be willing to custom make such glasses for lapidaries—at only $650 per pair. The same magnifying glasses—or rather an entire selection of different models of various magnifying strengths—can be had from Edmund Scientific for a mere fraction of that cost.

Get a copy. If nothing else, it makes for wonderful browsing on a rainy afternoon. Besides magnifiers, you'll find a host of optical, lighting and other items equally useful for lapidary purposes.

Polishing Sapphire Cabochons...

Sapphire cabochons are tough to polish. For star sapphires, the best approach, of course, is to use a diamond charged wood, brass, or copper cups that are made for these kind of star stones.

Absent this tool or when attempting to polish a standard oval cabochon, place some 6500 or 8000 diamond grit in a curved phenolic lap and turn to a moderate speed. The polish comes up quickly. For the flat back or bottom, lap it or spread the diamond on a piece of glass and hand polish. It takes a few minutes, but the polish will come up by following a figure 8 motion to assure exposure of the entire surface. Forget about attaining a sapphire cab polish on a lead lap. It won't do a satisfactory job, and you'll get a lot of orange peel.

Some cabbers insist they can gain an effective polish with Linde A or even natural ruby powder. Maybe so. It's true that these substances will work on corundum but the results are a long time coming. Diamond remains the best polishing agent for a mineral as hard as corundum.

Polishing Rhodonite and Jade...

If you want a top polish on rhodonite or jade, use shoe sole leather or saddle leather. Cut an 8" or 10" diameter leather pad and attach it to a wood disk with the flesh side out.

Prefinish the rhodonite or jade with a worn 600 sander and then go directly to polish. Alumina or chrome oxide is the polish of choice when using a leather pad and don't be hesitant about applying liberal supply of polish on the pad. The frictional heat can be a problem for rhodonite but jade isn't effected.

There's another good use for a shoe leather polishing pad. Make up a mix of olive oil and 400 diamond grit and work the mixture into the leather with a hammer. The 400 pad will do nicely for prepolishing, and then finish up to a nice polish with 1200 diamond grit on a separate leather pad, canvas or Poly Pad.

Those who use this combination as a sapphire polish report extremely fast—and satisfactory results. The polish may need a finer grit to get a truly high polish.

Another effective option for jade polishing on leather consists of mixing up a batch of No. 1200 metal lapping compound (that's merely 1200 carborundum in grease). Smear the outside 1½ inches of a leather polishing lap with the metal lapping compound.

After prefinishing the jade on a 600 wet sanding cloth, work the stone into the compound charged leather lap with a speed of about 1200 rpm. This double prefinish produces a dull polish which can quickly be brought up to a high gloss using either tin oxide or cerium oxide polish.

The Impact of Frictional Heat...

A fine, finished polish should have a brilliant reflecting surface, free from visible scratches, pits—and intermittent dull spots.

Why the emphasis on dull spots? Cabochon cutters, more than faceters, often encounter dull spots. It usually comes from applying excessive pressure of the stone against the polishing carrier. This causes sector overheating which result in cloudy spots, dull spots. Agate is particularly susceptible to such "point friction" burning.

Avoiding overheating is why many gemcutters insist on wet sanding and polishing. The water keeps the stone cool even if the pressure control goes awry occasionally. A few years ago, many gemcutters used dry sanding papers for prepolish and it was this practice that confounded the final super polish attempts when working with jade, agate, malachite, lapis lazuli and similar types stones. With wet sanding there is little left in the polishing step other than finishing up. That's why the trend now is toward wet work.

If you have trouble with these intermittent cloudy spots, review your procedures. Work wet in the sanding and prepolishing stages and then try using cerium oxide or even extremely fine alumina on a canvas...with plenty of water to keep the stone cool.

Slow the wheel down to under 800 rpm. A slower wheel speed reduces heat danger and centrifugal force so the tendency to throw off the water-polish compound is less.

Theory—which so far isn't substantiated fully—holds that heat changes slightly the molecular structure of the stone's surface and it's this condition that imparts the cloudy or dull spotting appearance.

The Quality of Reflectivity...

The quality of reflectivity dictates the optical excellence of virtually any gemstone. For this reason, it becomes impossible to achieve a valid understanding of polishing without consideration for the role that luster plays. To polish gemstones is to modify a crystallographic surface so the maximum amount of light may reflect off the surface or allow it to enter a transparent stone <u>in a disciplined manner</u>, reflect internally, and then emerge <u>in a disciplined manner</u>. This modification, allowing light rays to move in even, uniform cadence, enhances the internal and external optical capability of the stone and thus produces the maximum *spectral reflection*.

Whether a stone specimen is transparent, translucent, or even opaque, it's capacity for reflectivity or reflectance almost always carries enormous impact on cutting decisions.

In faceting especially, reflectivity involves not only brilliance (due essentially to interior reflectance) but also luster (mostly exterior reflectance). With cabochons, attractiveness is likewise a

Three very hard polishing laps include the Mehanite (cast iron), the ceramic (compressed aluminum oxide), and Miracle (marbelized resin). The Miracle and Mehanite have enough natural porosity to house diamond particles. So does the ceramic but it must be especially formulated for lapidary.

function of a mineral's ability to externally reflect light rays off its polished surface.

Every gemcutter understands that internal reflectivity is expressed in terms of *brilliance* or return of white light. The term for external reflectivity is *luster*. White light return can be measured easily enough by simple mathematics, but much of its visual qualitative and quantitative aspects *i.e.,* visual effect, are also largely dependant on stone orientation, light source, cutting angles...plus a number of other constantly changing factors.

Technically, luster in a gemstone is defined as the optical effect created by the reflectivity of light rays from the stone's *surface,* complimented, of course, by the emergence of some internal light ray reflection. It becomes the appearance of a surface viewed in reflected light, depending principally upon the relative smoothness of the surface and upon the refractive index. The latter governs the amount of light reflected. Even though directly related to the refractive index of a gem material and often to hardness, it may sometimes be accurately appraised in the rough by the naked eye. Usually, though, luster is best revealed when the stone has been polished

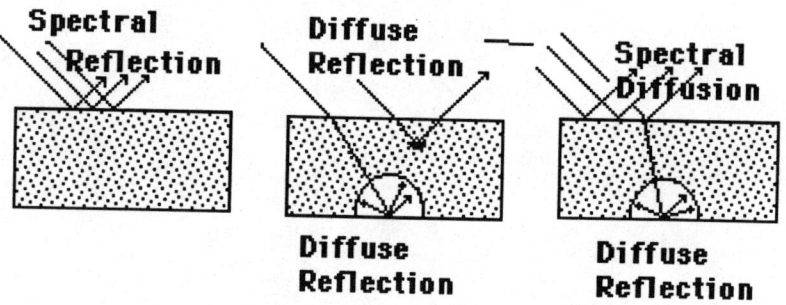

Internal reflections provide brilliance to a gemstone. External reflections provide the optical effect known as luster. For cabbers, texture—not a precise optical quality— is best dramatized by orientation and careful cutting.

Master Gem Polishing

and light rays reflect with consistent, uniform discipline (*specular reflection*). Luster may be largely subjective in its observation but fortunately all reflectivity levels are measurable. These different qualities of luster are loosely interpreted visually with sufficient accuracy that definitions at each level may be communicated without resorting to theory or instrumentation. The accepted labels for luster include in descending order:

metallic—the type of very high luster usually associated with metals (*e.g.* gold, silver, platinum) and often seen in some metallic compounds (*e.g.* pyrites, galena, hematite).

adamantine—a unique brilliant surface appearance polish observed only in such high RI gems as diamond, sphalerite, sphene.

subadamantine—the slightly more subdued appearance as seen in corundum, zircon, and demantoid garnet.

vitreous—a glass-like luster typical of the majority of gemstone (topaz, beryl, quartz, tourmaline)

resinous—a subtle polish as seen in amber

waxy—the almost matt surface typical of turquoise and jadeite

greasy—the appearance of soapstone and nephrite

pearly—the luster seen in mother-of-pearl

silky—a fibrous luster typical of satin spar

In recent years, an instrument called a reflectance meter has enabled gemologists to extract a precise comparative measurement of a stone's luster. The majority of these instruments depend on a broad band of light in the infra-red region approximating to radiation of some 950 nm which is provided by a light-emitting diode powered by a small battery. The light reflected from the surface of the specimen is received by a photo-transistor positioned at an angle of up to 30° to the beam of infra-red light. The light is subjected to a calibrated scale in terms of refractive index. **Note:** *reflectivity meters as a gem identification tool have apparently lost ground to the more reliable thermal property testers.*

While measurements of reflectivity are useful, the broad definitions and individual interpretation of experienced gemcutters and gemologists is usually sufficient. One merely needs to have viewed a diamond once to know the value of an adamantine luster. The quality

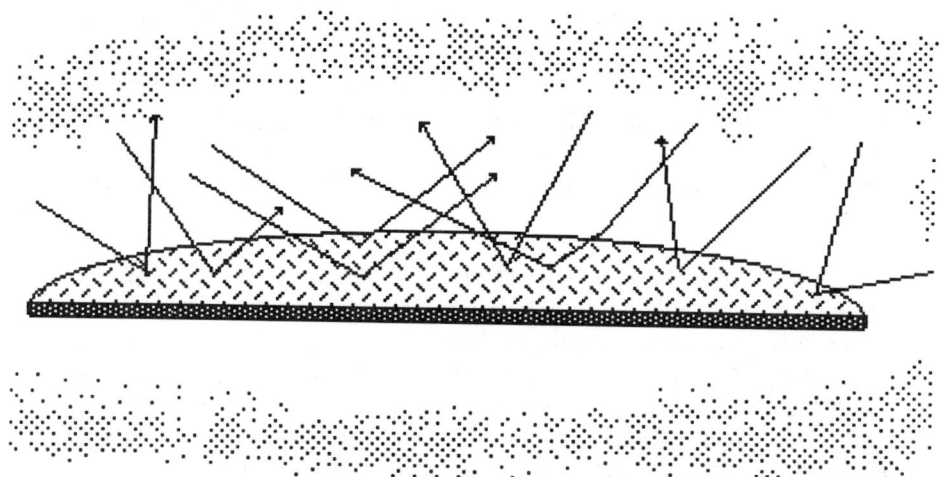

Sheen is an optical phenomenon that is produced by reflections beneath the surface of a mineral specimen. For the most part, the depth level as subsurface. When these reflections are random, it is called diffused reflection.

of subadamantine luster is also easily determined if one places a well polished corundum next to a diamond.

Sheen Different...

Don't confuse luster with sheen. Luster describes an optical effect created by light rays reflecting uniformly from a stone's *surface*. Sheen is the optical appearance created by light rays reflected irregularly from *beneath* the surface of a gemstone (*diffused reflection*).

Although both luster and sheen result from a single reflective encounter between light rays and stone they are not the same. Light rays deflected from a gem's polished surface will produce the visual effect known as luster. Light rays deflected from some other material or caused interference within the host stone cause sheen. Nor is sheen the same as the reflections causing brilliance. With brilliance reflections, a light ray follows a geometrical path through the entire interior of a stone, obeying various optical and physical laws which might involve several reflections before emerging.

As with luster, different kinds of sheen may also be described by universally accepted definitions. These include:

chatoyancy—this is the well-known "cat's-eye" effect, a band of light created by reflections from parallel groups of fibres, crystals or channels within the stone. For example, fossilized remains of asbestos fibers create channels in quartz and the mineral type is known as Tiger's Eye. A cat's-eye is usually cut en cabochon.

asterism—this is the "star" effect, a special form of *chatoyancy* created by fine parallel fibres or crystals lying along the crystal's lateral axes and intersecting each other at 60°. **Note:** the best known star stones are corundum, but a six-pointed star can also be seen occasionally in rose quartz. With quartz, the star is visible in *transmitted* rather than *reflected* light (an effect termed *diasterism*; reflected light asterism is called *epiasterism*). Four-pointed stars can be found in diopside, enstatite and some garnets.

iridescence—this is the play of rainbow-colored light caused by extremely thin layers or regular structures beneath a gem's surface. Like a thin film of oil on water, these layers interfere with the reflected light rays, reinforcing some colors and canceling others out. Precious opal displays iridescence at its best. Since 1960, it's known that opal's *play of color* is caused by millions of submicroscopic spheres of cristobalite (silica gel) which make up the stone's bulk. Spheres of 300 nm diameter reinforce light in the red-orange spectrum, and spheres of only 200 nm reinforce the blue-violet end.

Tyndall Effect—this is a pale blue light scattering caused by minute particles in a transparent medium *e.g.*, smoke particles in air. When it occurs in gems, it is often referred to as "*opalescence.*"

labradorescence—this is a form of iridescence seen in the labradorite variety of feldspar and in spectrolite. Color is due to thin flakes of feldspar in the gem's surface layer which are the result of lamellar twinning appearing in the basal plane.

adularescence— known as *shiller,* this is a bluish sheen seen in the moonstone variety of feldspar. It's another form of iridescence, also caused by lamellar twinning.

What is the Polishing Relationship?

A gemcutter may ask what reflectivity has to do with polishing. It has a great deal to do with it. Only when a surface is smoothly polished will the luster show best. That's because the specular reflecting light rays must strike the surface and then reflect in a disciplined, parallel pattern.

Furthermore, the amount of light reflected from the surface of a gemstone bears a strict relationship to the mineral's refractive index. The famous French physicist, Fresnel, demonstrated that the degree of luster or reflectivity of a gem (assuming a high, "perfect" polish) is due mainly to its refractive index, but is modified by other factors such as its molecular structure and transparency. Fresnel developed a simple equation which related a transparent *isotropic* mineral's reflectivity in air to its refractive index. The formula assumes the ideal case where both the incident and reflected rays are normal (*i.e.*, perpendicular) to the reflecting surface.

$$\text{Reflectivity} = \frac{(n - A)^2}{(n + A)^2}$$

where n is the refractive index of the material, and A is the refractive index of the surrounding medium (= 1 for air). Despite Fresnel's insistence that his formula applied to isotropic materials, it still also applies to *anistropic* materials for angles of incidence and reflectance up to 10° to the normal.

A note of interest to gemcutters is this: if the value for A in the equation is increased above 1, the reflectivity of the gemstone decreases. That explains why gemstones are often immersed in a high-RI liquid for inspection. The immersion reduces the amount of light reflected back from the surface of the stone thereby enabling the light to enter and illuminate the interior. For the same reason, a stone when immersed in such a liquid with the same RI level will virtually disappear.

As a convenience, the next section contains a list of all the most popular faceting and cabochon minerals with the percentage amount of their reflectivity worked out according to Fresnel's formula.

Reflectance Percentages For Leading Gemstones

Diamond	17.23%	Benitoite	7.58%
Corundum	7.53%	Brazilianite	5.32%
Beryl	4.78%	Chrysoberyl	7.29%
Tourmaline	5.46%	Danburite	5.73%
Quartz	4.52%	Diopside	6.29%
Andalucite	5.73%	Dioptase	6.15%
Apatite	5.73%	Epidote	7.29%

Master Gem Polishing

Euclase	6.01%	Aventurine	4.52%
Sphene	9.33%	Turquoise	6.01%
Fluorite	3.13%	Lapis Lazuli	4.00%
Hematite	27.67%	Sodalite	3.74%
Idocrase	6.86%	Azurite	8.72%
Iolite	4.65%	Malachite	9.76%
Kyanite	6.13%	Danburite	5.82%
Obsidian	3.74%	Axinite	6.50%
Opal	3.37%	Cassiterite	12.44%
Phenacite	6.01%	Sinhalite	6.82%
Rhodochrosite	5.32%	Kornerupine	6.46%
Rhodonite	7.15%	Prehnite	5.87%
Scapolite	4.65%	Petalite	4.23%
Scheelite	9.92%	Beryllonite	4.81%
Sphalerite	16.52%	Amblygonite	5.83%
Spinel	7.00%	Enstatite	6.34%
Spodumene	6.01%	Lazulite	5.94%
Topaz	5.59%	Variscite	5.19%
Tourmaline	5.46%	Hemimorphite	5.82%
Zircon	10.96%	Smithsonite	8.88%
Almandine	7.87%	Cerussite	12.26%
Spessartite	8.01%	Chrysocolla	4.00%
Pyrope	7.15%	Serpentine	4.93%
Grossular	7.15%	Ulexite	4.26%
Demantoid	9.33%	Cuprite	23.09%
Uvarovite	9.19%	Rutile	19.90%
Jasper	4.52%	Pearl	6.15%
Jadeite	6.15%	Onyx Marble	6.13%
Nephrite	5.69%	Moldavite	4.00%
Periodot	6.58%	Alabaster	4.39%
Zoisite	6.72%	Coral	6.13%
Pyrite	8.31%	Jet	6.44%
Amazonite	4.39%	Ivory	4.52%
Moonstone	4.25%	Amber	4.52%
Labradorite	4.89%		

Starting on the next page you will find a comprehensive listing of mineral types and the polishes that work best together. Note that many minerals are listed under different polishes, providing optional choices to gemcutters. Generally speaking, soft polishes work with soft stones and vice versa.

Master Gem Polishing

RECOMMENDED POLISHES
FOR USE WITH
VARIOUS GEMSTONES

TIN OXIDE

Actinolite	Agate	Alabaster
Amazonite	Amber	Amblygonite
Analcime	Andalucite	Anthophyllite
Anthracite	Aragonite	Aventurine
Azurite	Barite	Beryl
Brazilianite	Calcite	Cassiterite
Coral	Cuprite	Danburite
Datolite	Diorite	Enstatite
Epidote	Euclase	Feldspar
Fluorite	Garnet	Glass
Goldstone	Hambergite	Howlite
Hypersthene	Jadeite	Jasper
Jet	Kornerupine	Kyanite
Labradorite	Lapis Lazuli	Limestone
Malachite	Moonstone	Mother-of-Pearl
Nephrite	Obsidian	Onyx
Opal	Peridot	Petrified Wood
Phenacite	Quartz	Rhodochrosite
Serpentine	Smithsonite	Spinel
Spodumene	Sunstone	Tiger-Eye
Titanite (Sphene)	Topaz	Tourmaline
Tremolite	Turquoise	Variscite
Willemite	Wonderstone	Zircon

CHROME OXIDE

Apatite	Azurite	Apophyllite
Aragonite	Axinite	Barite
Calcite	Celestite	Cerossite
Diopside	Diorite	Fluorite
Garnet	Howlite	Iolite
Jadeite	Jasper	Labradorite
Lapis Lazuli	Limestone	Lapidolite
Malachite	Nephrite	Obsidian

Master Gem Polishing

Onyx
Rhodonite
Sphalerite
Varicite

Petrified Wood
Scheelite
Tourmaline
Wonderstone

Rhodochrosite
Serpentine
Turquoise
Zircon

Aluminum Oxide

Actinolite
Analcime
Anhydrite
Apophyllite
Barite
Bloodstone
Celestite
Rhyolite
Diopside
Epidote
Fibrolite
Hematite
Idocrase
Jasper
Lapis Lazuli
Limestone
Mimetite
Peridot**
Phenakite
Rhodochrosite
Serpentine
Sphene
Strontium Titanate
Tourmaline
Williamsite

Algodonite
Andalusite
Anthracite
Augelite
Benitoite
Boracite
Cobaltite
Danburite
Diorite
Euclase
Garnet
Hickoryite
Iolite
Jet
Lazulite
Malachite
Muscovite
Petalite
Prehnite
Rhodonite
Smithsonite
Spinel
Tiger-eye
Turquoise
Wonderstone

Amblygonite
Anglesite
Apatite
Axinite
Beryl
Cassiterite
Copper
Datolite
Enstatite
Feldspar
Hambergite
Howlite
Jadeite
Kyanite
Lepidolite
Marcasite
Nephrite
Petrified Wood
Pyrite***
Rutile
Sphalerite
Spodumene
Topaz
Variscite
YAG

CERIUM OXIDE

Agate
Anthracite
Benitoite
Chlorastrolite
Enstatite
Garnet

Amblygonite
Aragonite
Beryl
Dioptase
Epidote
Glass

Analcime
Axinite
Beryllonite
Diorite
Feldspar
Goldstone

Master Gem Polishing

Hematite	Howlite	Jadeite
Jasper	Jet	Lepidolite
Limestone	Natrolite	Obsidian
Onyx	Opal	Peridot
Petrified Wood	Pollucite	Quartz
Rhodonite	Scapolite	Sinhalite
Sodalite	Sosolite	Thompsonite
Tiger-Eye	Tremolite	Turquoise
Unakite	Varicite	Vesuvianite
Willemite	Zoisite(Tanzanite)	

DIAMOND

Beryl	Chrysoberyl	Corundum
Garnet	Peridot	Ruby
Sapphire	Spinel	Topaz
Tourmaline		

TRIPOLI

Amber Coral (Red)   Coral (Black)*

*Use jewelers rouge
** Add Acid
*** Thick Paste

Author's Note: In general terms, it appears that the composition of various polishing compounds produce little influence in the rate or quality of polishing. For example, some gemcutters prefer thick pastes when mixing oxide powders and water while others opt for a more viscous solution with less powder given the same amount of water. Tests show that both kinds work well and are equally effective, too, for translating polishing conditions into the highly desirable "damp-dry" state.

The principle rule in mixing powder is: make certain there is no lumping...that particle distribution is even throughout.

Master Gem Polishing

Recommended Combinations of Buffs, Laps and Polishes Known to Apply a Good Finish on Various Difficult Gemstone Types

Cabochons

Buff: Leather (over special wheel or backed by sponge or felt cushion)
Polish: Alumina or tin oxide(opal), chrome oxide, or mixture containing 1 part alumina mixed with 8 parts chrome oxide
Stones: Jade, amazonite, cuprite, rutilated quartz, serpentine, sillimanite, Texas Palm Wood, opal. (Vinegar or diluted acid is very effective with felt buffs), amber (leather should be used damp), aragonite, azurite, rhyolite, beryl, rhyolite, garnet, idocrase, pyrite, rhodochrosite, rhodonite, sphalerite, topaz, tourmaline, turquoise, zoisite

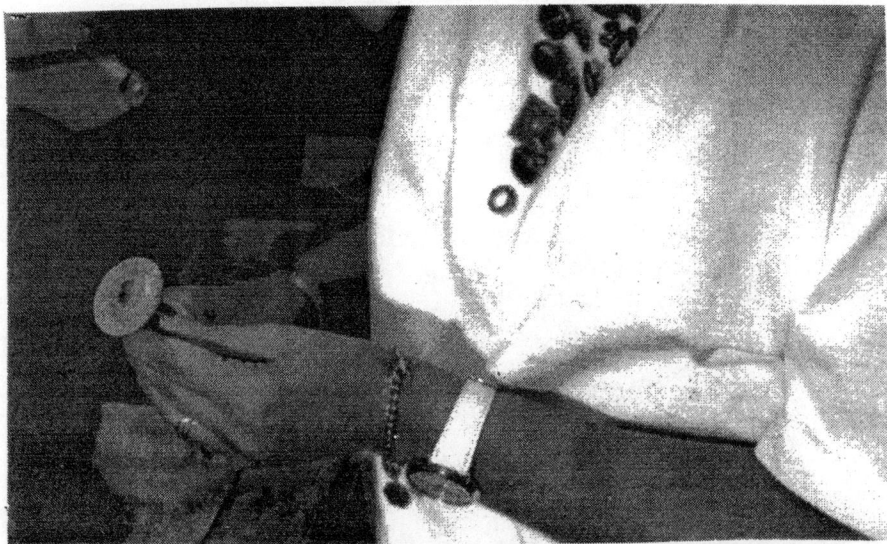

In the final polishing phase, the gemcutter must call on experience and skill because good polishing is the result of an effective combination of polish, lubricant-coolant carrier, lap and stone.

Master Gem Polishing

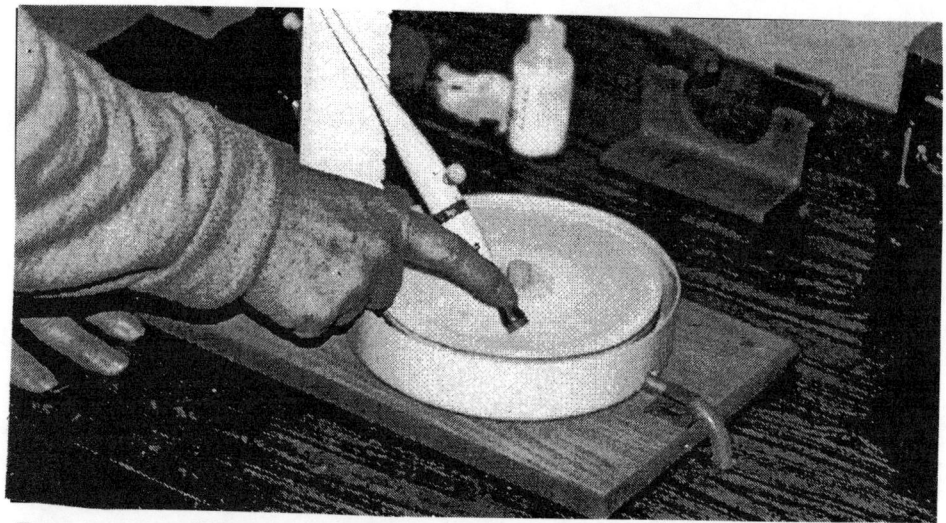

Extra pressure is often beneficial for polishing but be wary of applying excessive pressure. Get in the habit of applying a single finger to a faceted stone or use a "swipe" motion with cabochons.

Buff: Canvas
Polish: Tin oxide
Stone: Opal, jade

Buff: Muslin
Polish: tin oxide, alumina, chrome oxide mixed with a little graphite, rouge (opal)
Stone: Jade, opal, malachite

Buff: Felt
Polish: tin oxide (for jade, try using tripoli), cerium oxide (for opal, enstatite)
Stone: Jade, opal, agate, amber, apophyllite, aragonite, obsidian,

Buff: Velvet
Polish: tin oxide
Stone: Jade, opal, coral,

Master Gem Polishing

Lap: Wood
Polish: Tin Oxide
Stone: Jade, opal, calcite (alumina), fluorite,

Buff: hard Pellon
Polish: cerium oxide
Stone: opal, quartz, coral

Buff: Leather, felt, hard Pellon
Polish: Colloidal silica
Stone: Almost all stones (subject to test)

Faceting

Lap: Maple, boxwood, optical pitch, pewter
Polish: Tin Oxide
Stones: All stones, 6 Mohs and under: feldspar, glass, lapis lazuli, malachite, opal, flourite, obsidian, lazulite

Lap: Tin
Polish: Tin Oxide
Stones: Axinite, benitoite, californite, diopside, cordierite, danburite, hiddenite, idocrase, jadeite, kunzite, nephrite, phenacite, jadeite, rhodonite, sphene, beryl, quartz, chalcedony

Lap: Tin
Polish: levigated alumina
Stones: cassiterite, chrysolite, epidote, hematite, peridot, spinel, titania, topaz, tourmaline, zircon, YAG, brazilianite, cassiterite, danburite, diopside, hematite, phenakite, sphene, spinel, spodumene,

Lap: Tin or Zinc
Polish: diamond powder
Stones: corundum (also cabs), axinite, chrysoberyl, spinel, benitoite,

Master Gem Polishing

Lap: Copper
Polish: diamond powder (occasionally alumina oxide)
Stones: corundum, chrysoberyl, spinel, CZ, YAG, GGG

Lap: Cast Iron
Polish: diamond powder
Stones: diamond, corundum, spinel, chrysoberyl, CZ

Lap: Wax
Polish: alumina oxide, cerium oxide
Stone: amblygonite, anglesite, Anhydrite, augelite, barite, bauxite, calcite, celestite, cerussite (tin oxide), cinnebar,

Lap: Lucite
Polish: cerium oxide
Stone: dioptase, quartz, feldspar, iolite, petalite, scapolite, scheelite

Not just for its repeatability virtues, Ultralaps™ are finding greater use among faceters and cabbers. Their efficiency and working life can be further boosted by adding powder or even diamond paste to the coated surface.

Master Gem Polishing

Lap: Resinized metal or marble
Polish: diamond, alumina
Stones: all stones 7 Mohs or harder, especially effective with corundum, chrysoberyl, spinel.

Unique Characteristics of Polish Carriers...

Having a realistic understanding of each polishing carrier's characteristics is important for good results in polishing gems. Here are the most important carriers and the techniques that most experienced gemcutters use to put them to maximum use:

Felt—attacks stone's surface aggressively...works best on textured minerals so avoid use with those that tend to undercut *i.e.*, malachite, rhodonite, etc...builds up heat quickly when friction is involved...available as a wheel or as a pad (latter is suitable with backing disk).

Leather—a ver satile buffing material ...economical and efficient on most minerals...sheet leather is preferred although some leather wheels are sold from time to time...can be used as a peel-off pad or lashed to bowl or grooved backing disk...apply cement to the smooth side of leather (most gemcutters feel the rough side holds the polish better) ... although not as much as felt, leather does build up heat in response

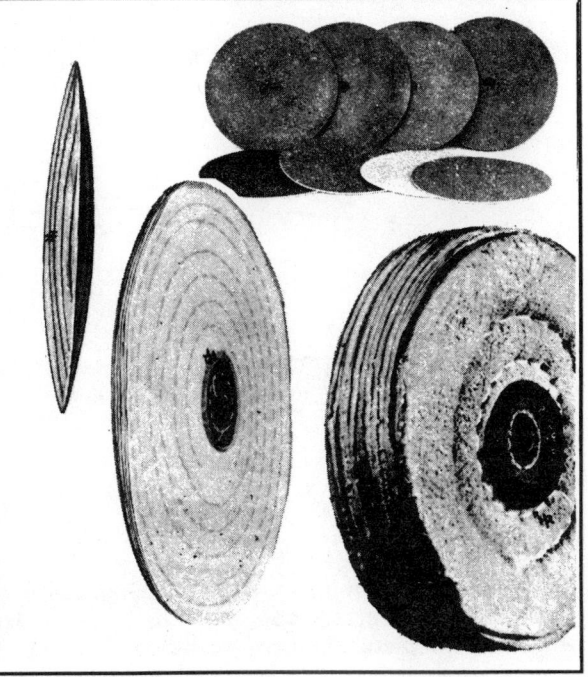

Master Gem Polishing

to friction.

Canvas—canvas is excellent for use with heat sensitive stones. It develops modest friction heat although pressure will indeed elevate stone temperature... despite cautious use, canvas still tends to wear out rather quickly...it is an excellent material for use with diamond paste or diamond spray polishes.

Pellon—Pellon isn't really a cloth: it's a plastic material and has been used for years in industrial polishing applications...can be used on backing disk loose or with adhesive...with care can also be used to polish facets (light pressure helps minimize facet edge rounding)...when resiliency is desired such as in cabochon polishing, use a cork backing...Pellon is outstanding material for use with stones that are heat-sensitive, that undercut...also good for polishing flat surfaces (that is it's major industrial applications)...extremely effective with quartz gems (no scratching). As mentioned earlier, when buying Pellon, make certain you get the hard (almost plastic

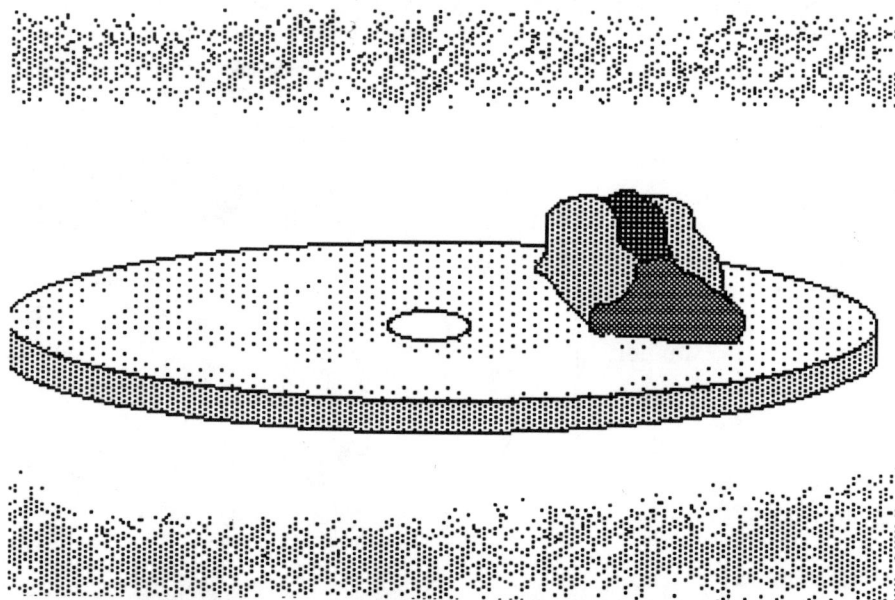

Plexiglass or Lexan laps tend to glaze over after extended use—as do ceramic laps. This glazed condition can be corrected by running the laps against a flat piece of silicon carbide.

Master Gem Polishing

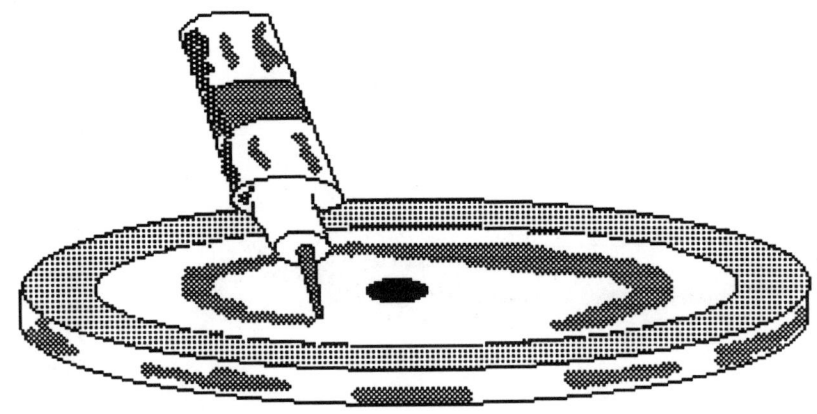

For faster polishing on an Ultralap™—and an excellent response to a stubborn facet—try adding a few short spritzes of vinegar. The addition of acid also works well on belts made of Ultralap™ plastic.

hard) type: the softer material isn't especially efficient for lapidary use.

Muslin—muslin is made in several thicknessess...retains polish very well...usually sold as a $1/4$" to 1" thick wheel in which several layers have been stitched together....best use is with soft stones that are heat sensitive...before using a muslin buff, take a knife and slit one of two rows of stitching so the edges of the buff will be loose...

Cotton Velvet—this material, which holds a polish reason ably well, is often used with difficult-to-polish soft stones...also does well when polishing a stone on its cleavage plane...velvet is preferred for polishing calcareous fossil materials such as the Petoskey stone...the long nap of the material holds polishing compound best...avoid stain proof velvet because it won't hold compound...best material is the plush type used for drapes or upholstery...

Thin Films—these materials, 3 or 4 mill Mylar, acetate, copper, bronze, copper, tin or stainless steel make fine polishing laps for use directly on the prepolishing lap...can also be placed over a rubber padded disk for equally efficient cabochon polishing....all these materials can be purchased in flat sheets and then scissored to the shape desired.

Master Gem Polishing

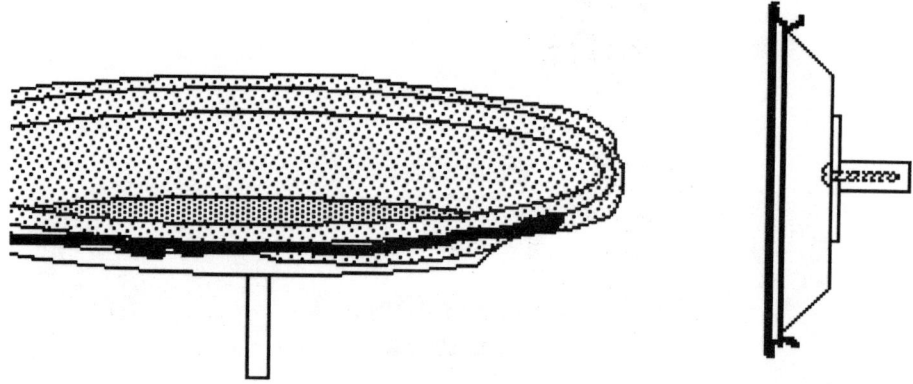

Leather for polishing can be used flat or stretched over a bowl-like device that allows the material to conform better to the stone's shape.

Other Materials—keep in mind that any material that will maintain its integrity and still hold polishing compound can probably polish gemstones. This includes wood, sheet cork, some types of vinyl, wood carpeting and other heavy fabrics including synthetic fibers.

Enhancing Tigereye...

It's not strictly a polishing application, but color enhancing tigereye can be fun—and produces some beautiful, unique looking chatoyant gemstones.

Heat treating tigereye is the safest and least expensive option.

Bleaching (with muriatic acid) and then following up with various forms of treatment such as heat treating or dyeing is a bit more involved. The acid techniques are safe enough if you follow good safety rules.

As you probably know, tigereye is an extremely versatile stone, long a favorite of cabochon cutters. Its comes naturally in a color range from golden-brown, to blue, red, blue and gold mixed.

The more rare type combines blue, gold and red.

The golden-brown can be heated to change in color to a variety of red hues. It may also be bleached to lighter shades of brown or gold (usually the practice when you're seeking a beautiful cat's eye or Hawk's eye appearance). Each piece of tigereye will react differently to heat or acid bleaching. For that reason, it's best to test the material before committing yourself to an extensive operation.

Before beginning any operation, clean the tigereye with warm water and detergent. Tigereye is non-porous so you won't have much danger of it retaining saw coolants or lubricants, but it does need to be clean for best results. To run a test, cut a sample piece or two of the slab and code them with an insoluble pen. One will be used for a heat test and the other for an acid bleaching test.

Remember that it's equally possible to color enhance rough or finished tiger eye.

It is preferable to heat tigereye after it has been cut and polished. When you heat rough, the color penetration may not be sufficiently deep (it's usually only about 1/8" deep)and this skin will probably be removed in the cutting.

Regardless if the specimens are rough or are already cut and polished, check carefully to be certain they are free of the black metallic matrix that sometimes appears in tigereye. Acid will dissolve this matrix, leaving pits or holes in the finish.

Heat Treating Tigereye...

A simple process is involved in heat treating golden-brown tigereye to a cherry red. The whole operation can even be carried out in the kitchen stove.

Place the tigereye stones in a plain container such as a metal pie pan. Put these into the cold oven with the temperature set at its highest level. Tiger eye will will begin to change color at 450° F. and by 700° F. the color change will be complete and permanent.

Check occasionally while the heating process takes place. To

Master Gem Polishing

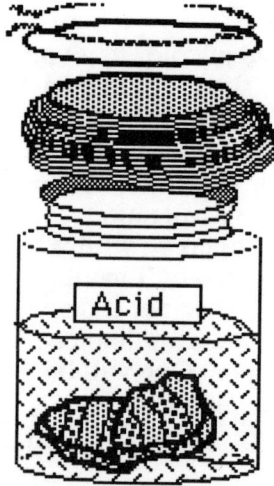
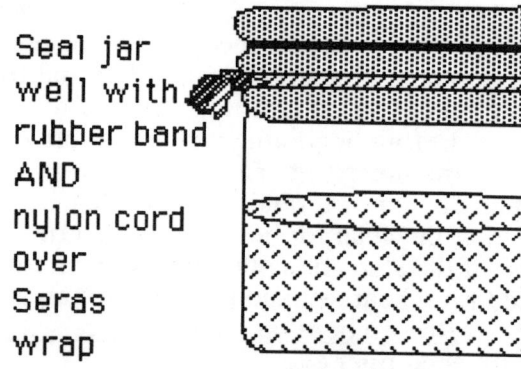

Seal jar well with rubber band AND nylon cord over Seras wrap

Place a dry tigereye in a glass jar, then cover the stones with full strength acid. Wrap the glass jar lid with six layers of Saran wrap and hold in place with rubber bands. Wrap nylon cord tightly around the bottle neck.

avoid a radical temperature change which could cause the tigereye to crack, just open the oven door a crack and peak in with the assistance of a flashlight. A thermometer could be used but it's really not necessary.

Your visual checks will be sufficient. Depending upon how much heat is applied and the amount of iron content in the specimen, the color of the tigereye will vary from a light red to a darker hue. As indicated earlier, it is preferable to heat tigereye after it has been cut and polished. When you heat rough, the color penetration may not be sufficiently deep (it's usually only about $1/8$" deep) and this skin will probably be removed in the cutting.

Note: *If you wish to treat the rough, though, plan on sanding and polishing through the heat treated layer. The contrast between red and golden-brown can often make for a most interesting cut.*

In sequence, here are the steps for heat treating tigereye:

1. Put cut and polished tigereye in container *i.e.*, pie pan
2. Place stone-pan in cold oven, set oven to highest temperature
3. Bring gradually up to heat of 700° F.

Master Gem Polishing

4. Crack the oven door slightly and visually inspect the tiger eye color with the assistance of a flashlight.

5. Turn off oven when stone has reached desired color and then leave oven door closed while stone cools

Bleaching Tigereye...

Tigereye is normally bleached in muriatic acid.
Here are a few important rules about handling acid.

- ✔ any acid should be handled only with complete protection of eyes, skin and clothing. Wear rubber or plastic gloves as well as a a face mask and a rubber or plastic apron or vest.
- ✔ with any acid, work only in a well ventilated area... away from children and pets.
- ✔ have a supply of baking soda and water (mix 1 quart of warm water with 8 tablespoons of baking soda) handy to wash off should any acid splash on the skin or work

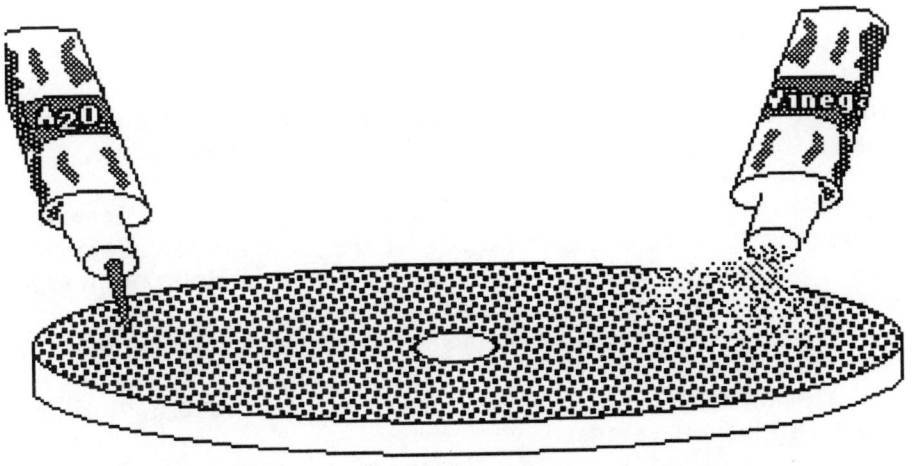

To accelerate polishing action on an Ultralap, try smearing wet alumina paste on a lap (this works fine with a Spectralap) and then allowing it to dry. For polishing, use the lap almost dry. Apply only a spritz or two of vinegar as a coolant. You'll find that this dry condition will polish in seconds.

Master Gem Polishing

        ing area...and keep it within easy reach
- ✔ if acid gets in the eyes, immediately flush with running water for 5 minutes and consult a physician
- ✔ to assist doctors in case of emergency, job down the acid type on a piece of paper where it can be retrieved

To remove all traces of oil, the pieces of tigereye that you intend to acid treat should be washed thoroughly in warm water and detergent. Dry the stones and place them in a screw lidded wide mouth glass jar (don't use a metal container!). Cover the stones with full strength muriatic acid and then cover the jar with a minimum of six layers of tight fitting Saran Wrap cover. Don't use a lid on the jar because this would create unwanted pressure during heating. Just cover the mouth of the bottle as illustrated on the next page. Hold the Saran in place with strong rubber bands. Stop any leakage of acid fumes by wrapping the bottle neck tightly with nylon cord.

The stones and acid should now be heated to between 140° and 160° and held at this temperature for 60 hours. Do not heat the acid above 160°. Higher temperature will create a corrosive gas which can cause tremendous pressure against the cover. Usually, this results in the escape of unwelcome fumes.

Whatever you do, don't use the kitchen oven as a heater. Work outside or in a separate work house. Under any circumstances, some fumes may escape and you certainly don't want these in your house. Even a small amount of acid fumes will ruin your stove.

After 60 hours of heat, remove the bottle carefully from the oven and allow it to cool before even attempting to open. After a single treatment, the acid is useless. Dig a hole in the ground and pour the spent acid into the hole. Do not empty it into the drain because it will still be strong enough to corrode metal pipes.

Once cooled, rinse the stones in running water. Now place the stones in a container of clean water and return to the oven for another session at 160° for 12 hours. This final step is to remove all residual acid from the stones.

The third and final step calls for removing the stones from the water and heating the stones in the oven at 160° for 12 hours to evaporate all the water. This last step should leave the tigereye nicely bleached to its new blond state. It is now ready to be heat treated

Master Gem Polishing

or aniline dyed.

In sequence, here are the steps for bleaching tigereye:

1. Scrub stones with detergent and warm water to remove oil
2. Rinse and dry stones
3. Place in glass jar and add hydrochloric (muriatic) acid so it covers stones with at least 1/4" layer. (wear protective gear)
4. Wrap the lidless top with 6 layers of Saran and secure with rubber band and then strong nylon cord for extra insurance.
5. Heat for 60 hours at 140°-150° (keep below 160°).
6. Remove container and let cool before pouring off and discarding acid (wear protective gear)
7. Wash tigereye in clean water, then cover with water in container and heat 160° for 12 hours to remove acid.
8. Remove from water and dry in in pie pan at 160° for 12 hours to evaporate all water.

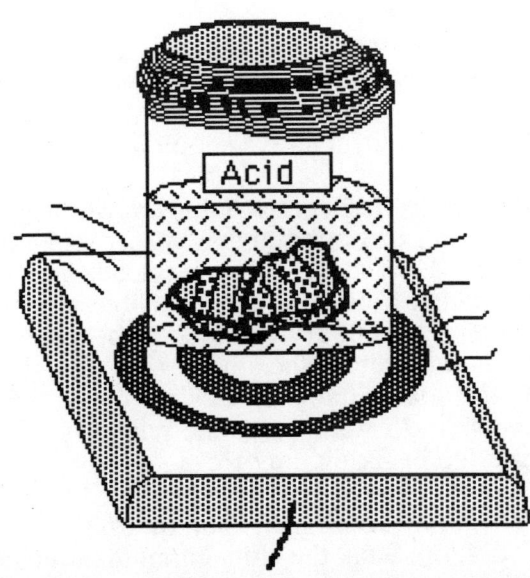

When acid treating stones, cover the jar carefully and then heat. At no time should the temperature level exceed 160° F. For safety's sake, elevate the temperature slowly. NEVER use a regular cover on the jar because such a cover would allow internal pressures to build up.

Heat Treating Bleached Tigereye...

To turn the bleached tigereye into a lovely, light strawberry color, pop the tigereye into a pie pan and place in a cold oven. Turn the temperature control to 459°. Depending on how much iron is contained in the tigereye and how much stone is involved, the heating time should be run anywhere from one-half hour to several hours.

Take occasional peeks by opening the oven door just a crack to inspect with the flashlight. When the stones have achieved the desired color, turn off the oven and allow the stones to cool slowly.

In sequence, here are the steps for heat treating tigereye:
1. Place bleached tigereye and pie pan in cold oven
2. Turn the oven heat to 450° and heat stones until the color is satisfactory.
3. Turn off oven and allow stones to cool slowly

Dyeing Bleached Tigereye...

Place the bleached tigereye in a glass jar containing enough analine dye to cover the stone.

The length of time that the stones bath in the dye solution will vary from minutes to weeks. Some stones will accept an intense coloration in minutes while others take colors only in streaks after weeks in the dye. Ideally, a piece of tigereye should be thoroughly colored within 24 hours.

This is where testing comes in handy. Stones from a single slab which don't respond to dye in at least 24 hours shouldn't be used for dyeing. They are candidates for other processes.

Because dyeing time is so unpredictable, remove a stone after only a few minutes. Wipe it dry and then inspect it for dye penetration. If it's not dark enough, return the stone to the dye, inspecting occasionally. When the stone attains the desired color, remove it from the dye, wash it off with water and wipe dry with a cloth.

The final step in fixing the color is to drive off the alcohol. Place the stone in an oven at 160° for about 12 hours. When complete, study the stone's color. Too light? Then return it to the dye and repeat the process. Too dark? Soak the stone in methanol alcohol, inspecting regularly.

In sequence, here are the steps for heat treating tigereye:
1. Place bleached tigereye in jar containing dye solution.

Master Gem Polishing

   2. Place lid on jar and inspect stones intermittently until the color is right.
   3. Clean tigereye with water and wipe with dry cloth.
   4. Place in oven at 160° for 12 hours to evaporate alcohol.
   5. If stone too light: return to dye. If stone too dark: soak in methanol alcohol.

Professional Secret on Polishing Jade...

It isn't a particularly well known secret, but jade can easily be polished without resorting to polishing compounds and buffs.

In the Orient, cutters often use flint sandpaper. Attach a section of 4/0 sandpaper to a sanding disk on which you have already mounted a sponge rubber cushion. Before submitting the stones to the paper, break it in. This can be done by sanding a hard stone—7 1/2 or 8 Mohs—until the abrasive becomes powdery.

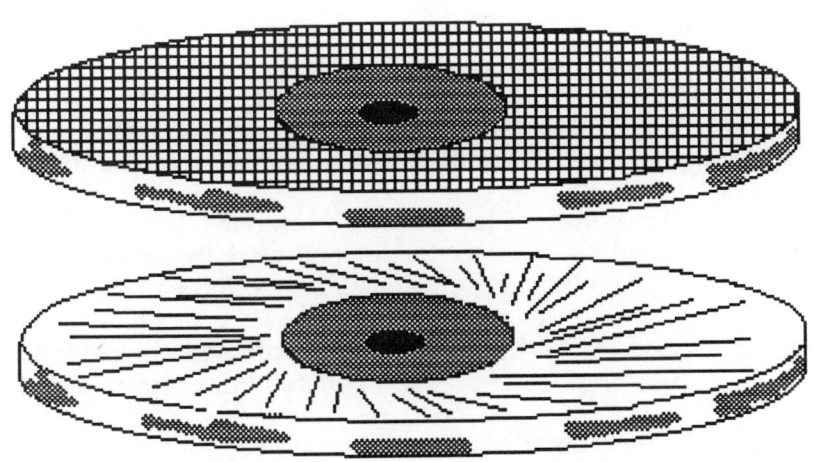

For gemcutters who regularly score their polishing laps, a cross scoring technique seems to work best of all. Use a razor blade to cut vertical and horizontal channels across the face of the lap, producing small squares.

Master Gem Polishing

Then run the disk at about 250 rpm—wet or dry. You'll be astonished at how fast and how well the polish comes up on this difficult-to-polish gemstone.

A Tip on Pre-Polishing...

Many cabbers use 600 sandpaper to pre-polish. You can improve that operation by adding a pit of water-pumice mix to the sandpaper. This, of course, won't work on real hard stones but for the average cabochon type, the pumice brings the finish to a near polish.

A good sandpaper trick, whether pre-polishing or polishing, is to paint the stone surface (this won't work on porous stones!) with a water soluble ink. The abrasive aspects of the polishing action will remove the ink, leaving evidence of where you are with the polishing operation. This same tactic can be followed through the sanding steps. It's especially helpful for getting rid of the scratches left by the final sanding steps. With this preparatory step, you avoid arriving at the polishing stage in time to suddenly discover a few tiny scratches that escaped earlier notice.

A Potpourri on Polishing...

Here are entries from my 30-year-old notebook on polishing tips for various lapidary items. You're welcome to them.

- ❑ That piece of jadeite won't respond? Try adding a little graphite to chrome oxide and work the stone with a muslin buff. Sure jade is tough, but it isn't hard.

- ❑ For stones that undercut, you often get better results working fast with a felt pad and thick alumina paste.

- ❑ Glue a small section of Moyco Spectralap on a flat stick for polishing touchups on those tiny areas that resist taking a polish no matter what you try.

- ❑ Michelangelo used oxalic acid to gain that incredible smoothness on his marble statues. Before polishing

Master Gem Polishing

onyx, mix up a batch of 1/2 teaspoon of oxalic acid to 3 tablespoons of water and add that to your polish.

- ☐ If you'd like to try your hand at polishing cabochons with coated Ultralap material or Pellon belts, just scissor out a rectangular strip, glue the ends together with superglue and fit it on an expandable rubber wheel. Works like a wonder!

- ☐ The best cabochon polishing disk setup has a 1/4"-1/2" sponge rubber pad adhesively attached to a hard backing. The polishing pad—including thin polishing films— goes right on over the sponge with rubber cement. Some professional cabbers have a series of such polishing disks—all dedicated.

- ☐ For factory type jade polishing, get a bunch of Crystal Pads and place a sequence of diamond spray or diamond paste polishes...200—600—1200—14,000—

If you have a small, complex area to polish, resist forcing felt edges, soft muslin, etc. into the area. Get a small wood or plastic wheel, smear it with polish and do the job quickly and properly. It takes only a minute or two to set up for small wheel polishing—and get good results.

Master Gem Polishing

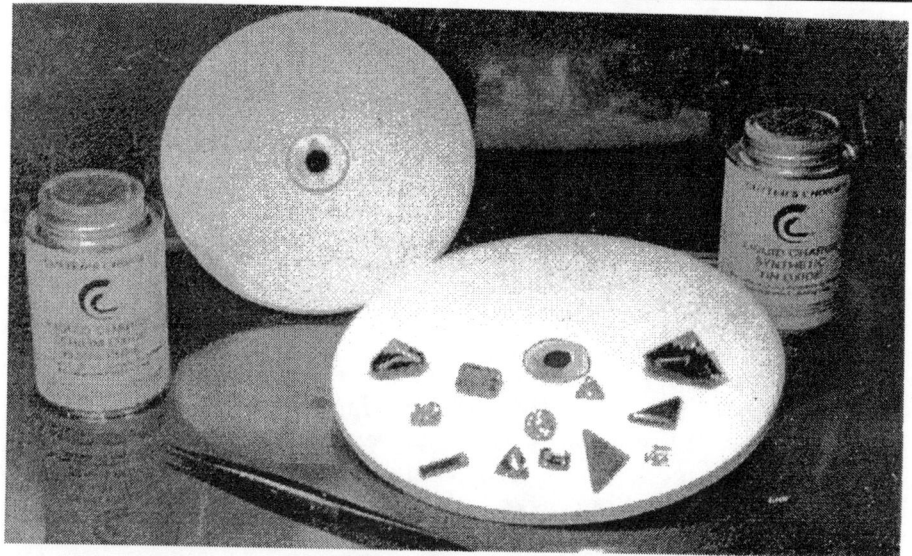

It's rather thick at 1/2" but the new mineral-resin "Miracle Polishing Lap" by Dyna Ltd of Boise, ID, promises to become a useful polishing lap for corundum and other equally hard stones, possible replacing ceramic.

50,000. Use plenty of pressure to build up some heat, and the results can be outstanding. Incidentally, alumina on canvas polish jadeite nicely.

- ❑ Say what you want, but if undercutting looms as a serious problem on a particular stone, consider the wisdom of polishing it with diamond. That way, you'll have less undercut and heat buildup...especially if you use the diamond on a canvas carrier.

- ❑ With a Mehanite cast iron lap, you should burnish the polishing surface with a piece of corundum to remove the metal jaggies before polishing on it. Also, be a bit wary of applying a wax covering to the lap surface before using. Wax can cause scratches in medium hardness stones. Mehanite, I find, is best used with real hard stones, corundum, chrysoberyl, spinel, etc. Quartz will scratch almost every time on cast iron.

Master Gem Polishing

- Hard up for a quick polish for your gold and silver? Dip these precious metals in a Coke, 7-Up, Pepsi or similar cola based drinks. Rescue the metal and wipe briskly with a dry, clean cloth. It'll work fine—if you remember to use separate cloths for gold and silver.

- Having trouble getting spinel to take a polish? Try alumina with chrome oxide on felt for cabbing and carving, and the same polish on copper for faceting.

- Everyone will tell you that alumina oxide on a well scored tin-lead lap is the key to a fine topaz polish. It is. But so is alumina oxide on cork of all things. Try it. The results are a little short of amazing...and the rounding can be controlled, too. Cabbers will zip through topaz cab polishing problems—and cleavage planes succumb rapidly and easily to the cork carrier.

- To get maximum results for polishing Australian fire opal, tin oxide or alumina in a thin slurry can be painted onto a leather buff (rough side out) on a sponge or foam rubber backing. Just keep the leather wet so friction doesn't build up too much heat.

- Everyone says use good light to inspect for polish. The best use for an ordinary light bulb is to check its reflection in the fine surface of a polished gem. That'll tell you quickly enough if there are any scratches around.

- In faceting, scratches come from delay. If a facet isn't "taking" all over its surface immediately, don't delay in cheating or making corrections. Any slight alteration in a flat-to-flat match allows swarf to ball up in front of the facet and then slide underneath, causing a scratch.

- NEVER clean off a stone or dopstick with Acetone or Attack (they're solvents if you plan to use the stick im-

Master Gem Polishing

mediately). Clean off items to be dopped with isopropyl alcohol and the adhesive will work better.

- There are some safety laws involving acids. They include:

    Always **A**dd **A**cid to water (never the reverse!)

    Baking soda and water will neutralize acids or containers that previously contained acid.

    Never mix two acids.

    Be careful how and where you use Purex in your workshop. When mixed with an acid, it produces deadly chlorine gas.

- In cab polishing, a common spray bottle is mighty useful for spritzing a measured amount of powder polish-water-vinegar mix to the wheel or lap.

- Keep firmly in mind the corundum polishes. Levigated alumina is ordinary corundum polishing material and no longer used much in lapidary. Alumina is aluminum oxide in both natural and synthetic form. The synthetic, best known as Linde A, was formerly manufactured under exacting chemically controlled conditions. Other trade names for aluminum oxide are ruby powder, sapphire powder, Diamontine, Ruby Dix, Damascus ruby powder. Alumina's efficiency depends on particle size grading and the type of particle *i.e.*, hexagonal (used in lapidary) or cubic (Linde B and not very efficient for stone polishing).

- If you have a supply of alumina, don't hesitate to mix it with other powdered oxide polishes. A popular mix is one ounce of aluminum oxide to a pound of tin oxide.

- When tumble polishing, add 2-3 tablespoons of oxalic

Master Gem Polishing

acid crystals to the mix to get a good polish.

- ☐ Getting wet when you saw that stone? Then turn the saw around and pull the stone into the blade rather than push it. Pulling tends to give better hand control anyway.

- ☐ When shaping a thin mineral slab, you don't have to saw it all the time. Use a carbide wheel glass cutter. Score the slab as you would with ordinary glass then snap it with a pair of pliers.

- ☐ If you pre-mix powdered oxide polishes and water, use a wide mouthed jar and a sponge for keeping the polishing operation neat and clean. A sponge on a stick will usually pick up a measured amount of mix and keep it from dripping while you transfer to the disk or wheel.

- ☐ Why add a small amount of liquid detergent to your polish mix? Well, the detergent makes the water wetter and this assures better spread or coverage on the lap or wheel. It gives the mix a homogeneous consistency and inhibits a leather or cloth-like buff from glazing.

- ☐ A fine, perfect polish on a gemstone can be attributed to these earlier steps:
    1. well done pre-polish so all scratches are absent
    2. proper mix of polish agent and supplements *i.e.*, water, detergent, acid, etc.
    3. combination of polish and carrier suitable for stone type
    4. proper rpm for the job
    5. maintaining appropriate "less is best" and/or "damp-dry" condition during polishing operation.
    6. consistently disciplined hand pressure on the stone against the polish/carrier.

- ☐ Thinly mixed polishing compounds are best applied to

felt and cloth-type buffs with a small paint brush about an inch wide.

Polishing Thin Slabs....

Polishing thin slabs poses specific challenges, especially when you're dealing with iris agate slabs. Pieces are just too thin and breakage is a constant difficulty.

One good alternative, sticking the thin slabs on larger pieces of rock with double faced tape, has already been discussed. This way, the larger object can easily be held by hand while you work the thin piece. Half nodules lapped across the face make ideal hand holders.

For thin iris agates, though, equal attention must be paid to the slab's preparation. Make certain that all high points and high edges have been removed. When you begin polishing, you want as good of a flat-to-flat match as you can get—if you are flat lapping. If you intend to polish on a wheel and thus make only point contact with the slab, the high point removal isn't quite so critical.

Clean the slab and the holder stone thoroughly. Work at room temperature. Depending, of course, on the size of the slab to be worked on, place two strips of $1/2$" double faced tape about 1" to $1 1/2$" apart on the thin slab.

Press the slab against the flat holder and maintain pressure for a moment or two until the adhesion matures. You are now ready to take the slab to polish. Exercise restraint on the use and flow of water: you don't want the liquid to loosen the tape bond. If there are saw marks remaining, use a flat lapper. After that you can go to a drum sander or drum leather for fast, predictably high results.

Hand lapping is the best approach for a sizable section of agate. Make up a medium slurry of cerium oxide with a spritz of vinegar on a flat glass or Plexiglass lapping plate. As is customary when doing hand lapping, move the slab in a figure "8" over the lapping surface. This assures uniform exposure of the slab's face to the lapping plate.

Make certain the lapping surface stays wet. You can feel the tug of the polish on the stone as the polish begins to dry out. With large surfaces, of course, you face an aggregation challenge so keep an eye on the lap plate.

Slide the slab off for removal. Don't try to pry it off.

Master Gem Polishing

Crystalite Introduces Resin Laps...

They're called Crystalrez™ laps.

Recognizing the popularity of less expensive resin bonded diamond technology, the Crystalite Corporation of Westerville, OH, renowned world wide for its high quality metal bonded diamond laps, in the last few years introduced a new line of such laps. The multi-layer laps represent a sort of sintered resin lap in that a thick resin coating is impregnated with diamond particles throughout.

Crystalite worked closely with the American Society of Gemcutters when developing the line. Designed as a laminate that can be attached to any of the company's aluminum base laps, the Crystalrez™ laps come as a thin unmounted resin-diamond coating on a PSA backing and a 1/2" arbor hole. Any Crystalite lap base will serve as a master lap or the company will provide an aluminum backing plate for about $20. The Crystalrez™ laps run about $30 for 6" diameter and up to $55 for 8" diameter.

What makes these laps of interest to faceters seeking easy polishing conditions is their uniform height. They go a long way toward removing repeatability difficulties because you have available a series of same-thickness laps from rough grinding to super fine polish. For convenience sake, all the laps are colored coded.

Single Lap Approach to Sanding/Polishing...

It's routine for a Bangkok faceter to turn out 150-200 faceted rubies and/or sapphires a day. How is it possible for the faceters in the Far East to achieve such tremendous production?

One major key to this process lies in their use of a single lap to sand and to polish. That's right! These faceters simply don't change laps. They cut and polish the facet on the same lap. The lap is usually a porous cast iron lap (the diameter can run as much as 12"-14" to provide simultaneous access to the wheel for a number of cutters). What's on the lap is 14,000 diamond grit, mixed with olive oil and perhaps a few other strictly proprietary liquids.

The Two Keys to Success...

How is it possible for a faceter to get production out of a single lap covered with 14,000 diamond particle size? Don't put down a polish done with 14,000 diamond grit: it represents a fine commercial polish and you'll be hard pressed to distinguish it from a polish done with finer grits. The polish usually done by a CSM or CMG it may not be: a fine, professionally acceptable polish is most certainly can be.

Far East cutting shops achieve 150-200 stones per day per faceter and this production is based primarily on the skill of the preforming operation.

The secret becomes credible once you understand how they go about achieving such high production. In the first place, top production is realized on small, hard stones. To achieve their high finished stone count, they specialize in cutting fractional or melee type stones cut from rough such as Montana sapphire and small Southeast Asian corundum.

Master Gem Polishing

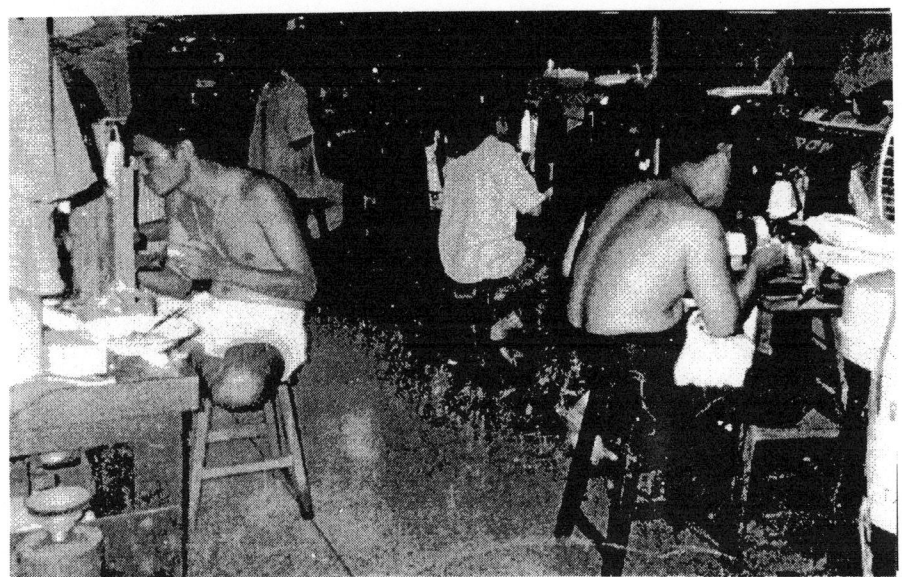

The key to single lap faceting lies with the preformer. Here, the stone must be shaped to nearly finished condition...almost always 2-tiered step cuts.

Gemcutters familiar with Montana sapphire know that rough crystals are often small and flattish. The flat surfaces serve well as pre-formed tables, particularly since the flat sections are aligned properly with corundum's optical axis. Not only do the stones come with the table already established, but optical orientation is accommodated, too. Once the stone is oriented and the best shape determined (most of the stones in these factories are small 2-tiered step cuts in order to gain the best yield advantage), the stone is turned over to a pre-former. Working with a hand turned wheel and holding the stone, the job is done quickly.

In a Far East faceting factory, the pre-former is the individual with all the skill...certainly far more than the faceters are required to demonstrate. It takes brains, good cutting technique and skills to make a successful pre-former. In the diamond trades, these pre-formers would probably be known as "blockers." Whatever they are called, they have the gemological experience and skills to take best advantage of any given piece of rough. Further, they are fully capable of shaping the pre-form so closely that what's left for the

Master Gem Polishing

faceter amounts to little more than identifying the facets, tuning up the meet points and applying a finish. With the small facets involved and the need for production, this faceting component can be accomplished with speed, accuracy and excellence.

Using standard silicon carbide (some of the better equipped shops are making the move to diamond wheels), the pre-former carefully reduces the rough crystal to a precise, nearly finished pre-form shape. Once the pre-former turns the finished stone over to the faceter (who might be called a "brillianteerer" in diamond cutting), there can be little doubt as to what shape the pre-former intends as a finished stone. It remains only for the faceter to remove a slight amount of material so as to flatten out each facet while simultaneously applying the final polish. Within minutes, the faceter—often holding the stone in his fingertips—has completed the stone.

To reach the kind of production these shops attain, dopping and manipulating machine controls would simply get in the way...consume

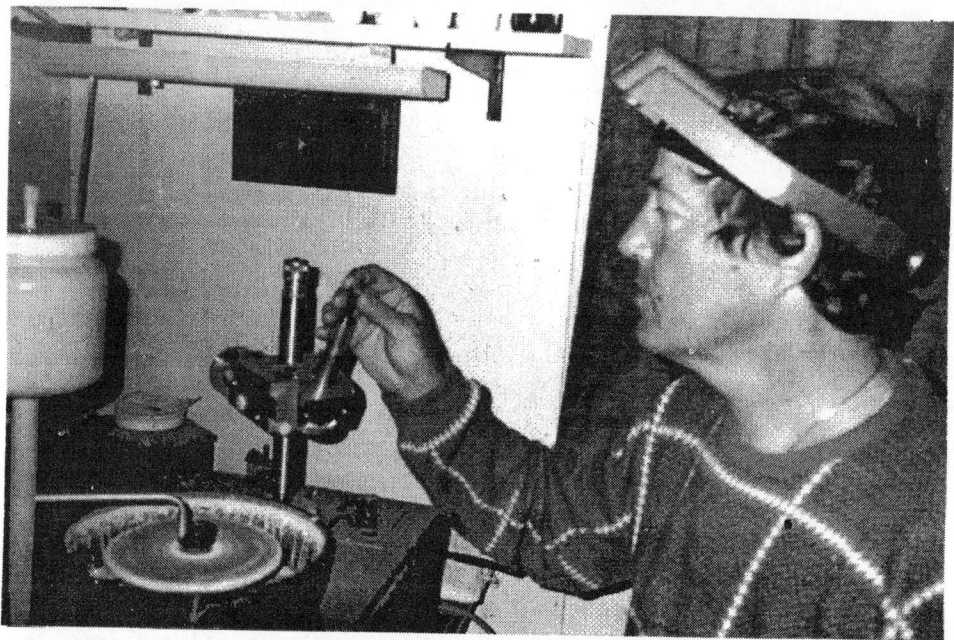

Some gemcutters may object to a 14,000 diamond polish, but this level of fineness does represent a commercial polish finish on hard stones.

too much valuable time. These faceters and pre-formers are so skilled they seldom nick a finger nail on the wheels and are perfectly capable of preforming or faceting a stone in minutes. At the small size of the melee being cut, it becomes extremely difficult to notice a slight error in a few meet points or in facet sizes or in the plan shape accuracy.

Such a fundamental approach to basic faceting is not difficult to duplicate. To obtain the best possible preform, hand hold the rough crystal and shape it using traditional cabochon technique. You're better off starting with step cuts—like the Bangkok cutters. Roundness offers a bit of a problem as perfect symmetry will be realized only by using a template or exhibiting "Italian Eyeballs" *i.e.*, the ability to visually establish or guess measurements with uncanny accuracy.

For finishing with 14,000 diamond grit, you need a smooth sanded finish going into the final polish. This saves on aggravation and time...not to mention the longer working life your laps will enjoy.

What About High Production Rates..

Can these high production systems be reached? Could an American gemcutter—one not accustomed to hand holding while faceting—learn something from this technology? In short, is there a way for Americans to cut those small Montana sapphire with less difficulty than they are now experiencing? Remember, this system works on hard, small stones...such as corundum which responds well to efforts to polishing with 14,000 diamond grit.

Yes, it can be done. As you read a few paragraphs back, you can easily duplicate the Far East system easily, using a cast iron or even a ceramic lap.

After I'd been told about the technique by ASG Member Sofus Michelsen of Bayonne, NJ, I pulled out my Mehanite and ceramic laps and began testing. Michelsen, who with famed South African diamond cutter/author Basil Watermeyer, plans to open a diamond cutting school in upper New York state, travels regularly to Bangkok with his wife. He observed the factories at work, took pictures, and told me of the fantastic production that these cutters were achieving.

As most American gemcutters know, using a single lap is not exactly earth shattering news. Jamb peggers have been doing it for centuries. The reason why American and Canadian faceters haven't flocked to this easy system is that they don't especially enjoy cutting melee and other small stones. Modern wester faceting machines are built to handle quarter carat cuts pleasantly.

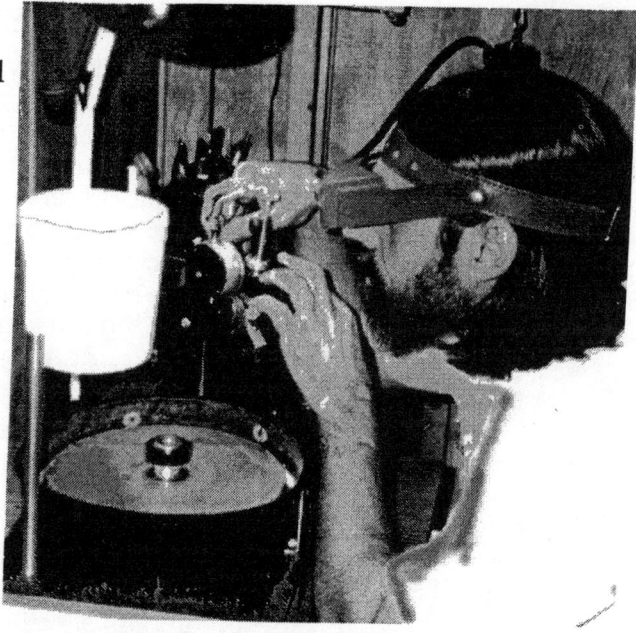

I realized, though, that this system could perhaps be dusted off, given a few new wrinkles, and introduced as a viable "new" system for repairing stones, cutting small Montana sapphires, and putting enjoyment into the task of cutting all small, valuable stones which heretofore faceters have avoided. Consequently, I took out of my rough drawer a few Montana and Sri Lanka sapphires—samples that would produce only half or quarter carat cuts—and pre-formed them carefully by hand on a 6" 600 diamond wheel, using my tiny but convenient Little Rock Rascal.

Cuts Four Preforms...

Of the four step cut preforms, I dopped up and inserted all of them one after the other into one of the prototypes of my patented Calibrated Jamb Peg™ faceting machine. Quickly and almost effortlessly, I cut and polished three stones on a ceramic lap and a Mehanite cast iron lap. The other three were finished on an aluminum lap which I'd had anodized to a black surface. Behind the anodized aluminum lap test was the desire to research an easily obtainable lap as hard and as durable as ceramic or cast iron at a fraction of the cost. Total cost of a 6" diameter $3/16$" thick anodized aircraft grade aluminum lap was

$12.37. As anyone familiar with anodizing knows, the anodized surface of the aluminum lap is almost as hard as ceramic.

With all three test laps, I placed 14,000 diamond grit mixed with olive oil. The cast iron lap was set up to run "dry" as diamond cutters say. I spread Elmer's glue and some proprietary glob on the iron surface, mixed in with four carats of 14,000 and then allowed the lap to dry. When running, I merely added olive oil, laced lightly with 14,000 grit. It ran a bit warm, but not too high for corundum or the superglue used as dop adhesive.

The result? Given an efficient pre-form, all three laps were efficient in putting in flat, polished facets. A small stone took only 20-25 minutes to complete, ...not counting dopping time. It ran an extra 10 minutes to dop and transfer. Each stone had four facet rows, two crown and two pavilion.

This system, I realized, could perhaps be dusted off, given a few new wrinkles, and introduced as a viable "new" system for repairing stones, cutting small Montana sapphires, and putting enjoyment into the task of cutting all small, hard valuable stones which heretofore faceters have avoided.

I made absolutely certain that the pre-forms were as close to the final dimensions as possible (I also preformed one crystal on a 220 silicon carbide wheel then touched it up on a used 600 grit belt). This careful operation assured me that material removal on the 14,000 lap would be minimal. Because the crystals were mostly blocky shaped sapphires, I managed to cut most of the stones at 42° pavilion 36° crown angles. I'm sure that when cutting flattish Montana sapphires, the culet angles on all the stones would be only between 30° and 34° with the crown mains down as low as the rough will permit...sometimes down to 22°...in an effort to compensate.

Not too surprisingly, my finished sapphires were quite beautiful—and, in my opinion, commercially acceptable. The finish on all six stones was easily top grade—and matching the preform's angles with a jamb peg proved a cinch. The nice thing about a jamb peg is that you can innovate as you proceed...a convenience that makes hand

Master Gem Polishing

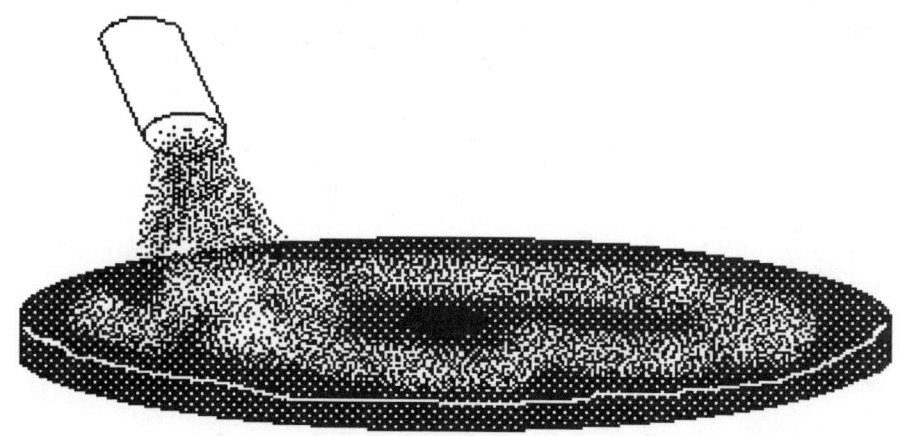

Using an inexpensive anodized aluminum lap, a faceter can add commercial 14,000 diamond paste (or make up some 14,000 + olive oil) and proceed immediately to single lap production. This technique, remember is best for smallish stones—or larger ones that have been VERY CAREFULLY preformed.

holding so useful in the orient. To change angles you merely insert the tailstock of the peg into another angle notch on the jamb...and you've changed angles. If you need to return to a previous angle you merely slip the tailstock back into the old slot. With a jamb peg, you move the jamb up and down on the mast very infrequently: the various slots already cut into the jamb accommodate your need to change to other angles. Repeatability is obviously much easier with a jamb peg than it is with a milling type faceting machine.

Obviously, a protractor type machine requires constant machine setup changes, particularly the facet head's position on the mast. This obligation can and will materially reduce the production time per stone.

Make Your Own Sander-Polisher Lap...

If you're not interested in converting your cast iron or ceramic lap into a sander/polisher lap, consider having an anodized aluminum

Master Gem Polishing

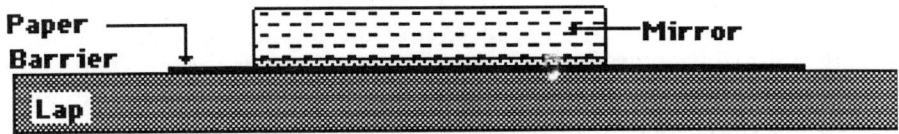

For repair work, a 14,000 lap and a mirror make perfect companions, but don't forget to keep a paper barrier between the bottom of the mirror and the diamond laden lap surface lest you ruin the bottom of the mirror quickly.

lap made. A $1/8$" thick aluminum lap is plenty thick and if you have reservations you can always place it over a thicker master lap. Why is it so important to have the aluminum anodized? The answer lies, understandably enough, in hardness. Aluminum is too soft to maintain the rolling diamond grit on its surface. A hard anodized surface will withstand the pressure of the diamond on its surface so the grit particles can continue to free roll or serve as base for a thin copper film.

You don't want a soft metal lap such as tin or aluminum because the diamond will eventually bury itself in the metal. To get the double sanding/polishing action, you want the diamond particles free on the surface to roll and scratch. Free rolling particles give you aggressive cutting action and speed which you won't get either from a coated or bonded lap of the same grit.

So plan on having the aluminum disk anodized. A machine shop will generally be willing to turn out a couple of 6"or 8" disks with arbor holes for a few dollars each. The shop operator usually knows where to obtain anodizing services and will provide it to you for a slight extra charge. I feel it's best to ask for a black finish. This way, you'll be able to continuously evaluate the surface condition of the lap and know when the diamond grit eventually wears its way through the hard surface. When that happens, it's time to get the lap anodized again...or replace it with a new one.

Don't be too quick about throwing the exhausted anodized aluminum disk away, regardless of the condition of the anodized coating. It just doesn't cost that much to have it re-anodized. Also, be wary of having your disks stamped out rather than sawed or turned. The punch press blade tends to curve down the edges a bit so you're not always certain the final disk is lap flat.

One final thing, if you do decide to try your hand at this old but updated technology, try it first on a small sapphire or other hard stone. Hopefully, you'll use a flattish crystal the first few times so you'll know where the table is going. The table is the first and last facet.

Select the flat section as the table and preform first the girdle so you get the plan shape immediately. Once the plan shape has been established you'll enjoy greater confidence that you've achieved as much advantage of existing thickness as possible. Then work in the pavilion, using up to $3/4_{th}$ of stone depth. Especially with the flat Yogo sapphires, the pavilion will almost certainly finish out below traditional angles for culet facets so, fortunately, you'll be left with a thin crown. I say "fortunately" because a thin crown will help greatly to compensate for the shallow culet shortcoming.

Don't be too quick about throwing away an exhausted anodized aluminum disk, regardless of the condition of the anodized coating. It just doesn't cost that much to have it re-anodized.

For round shapes, don't try to shortcut by attempting to cut in flats facet in while preforming. Let the faceting operation take care of that. In preforming, concentrate strictly on getting the shape as close to the final dimensions as possible. The less material you must remove with the 14,000 diamond grit the easier and faster—and better—will be your faceting performance. Preform what a diamond cutter calls "in

Master Gem Polishing

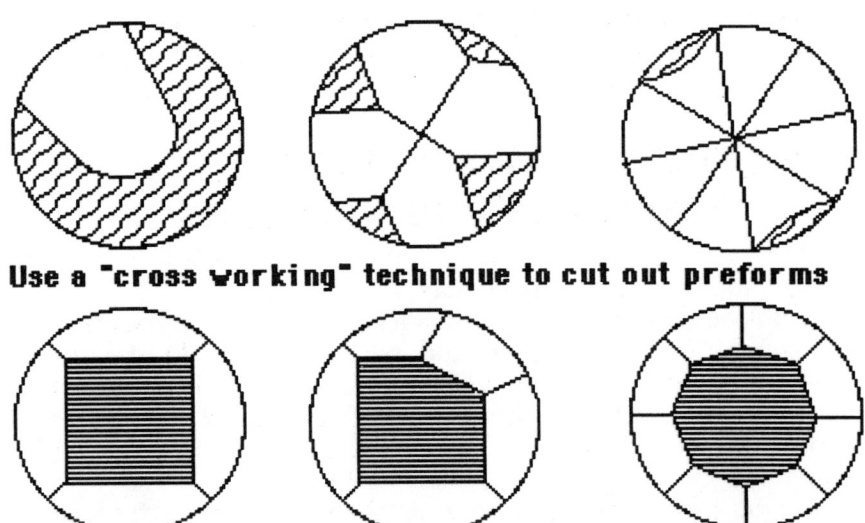

Use a "cross working" technique to cut out preforms

When preforming, esepcially for one-lap production, use the diamond cutter preforming technique...preform by hand and use "cross working."

round" for round cuts. For step cuts, drop in only the main pavilion and crown facets from girdle to culet or table edge respectively.

In the faceting operation, cut in any necessary extra tiers and rows and then dress them up. That's the easy part...and the fun part.

As a final comment on this interesting and useful approach to faceting, it's usually good practice to leave the table polishing until the last step. When you first select as the table a flat section...or grind one in if it's not readily available in the original crystal shape...you might want to pre-polish it. That's all, though. Attach the dop stick onto this roughened flat. Only after you've completed the star facets and determined the final shape and parameters of the table, have you arrived at an opportune time to polish.

If you polish the table at the outset, it's very easy to chip the smooth surface during subsequent cutting operations. Since you'll not have a lot of cushion on the crown dimensions, such an event could be near disastrous. As small as the tables in melee are, you're probably better off hand polishing last on a metal lapping plate.

If using a jamb peg, you don't have much choice but to hand polish if you wait until the end to polish the table. Jamb peg's don't involve 45° adaptors and such. Therefore you'll probably want to polish the crown immediately, dop to it—and take your chances.

Phonograph Records Make Effective Polishing Laps ...

Finding an effective polishing combination for soft stones whether faceted, cabbed or carved is not easy.

One option that many gemcutters have found effective consists of using an old vinyl long playing record, particularly the 45 rpm oldies. I have an old Columbia 45 rpm record of "Unwanted Heart" which features Eileen Rodgers with the Ray Coniff Orchestra...and this lap is my favorite with a colloidal silica or a colloidal chemical oxide polishing paste.

I've used this lap with excellent results on everything from quartz (although I must admit that NOTHING is superior for scratchless quartz polishing than a colloidal silica on one of Moyco's Spectralaps) to stones as soft as gypsum and sulphur.

What makes these phonograph disks so adaptable to lapidary is the recording grooves. They work just like the finest scoring and carry away the debris and swarf with enormous efficiency. This leaves the polish free for direct application on the clean gem surface which hastens the polish and produces uniform action.

Before using a phonograph record, you'll need to modify it for your arbor. The center hole on a recording disk is $1\frac{1}{2}$" diameter. I've found that gluing on a 2" diameter plastic disk directly over the record hole represents about the easiest conversion. Later, you can hot knife or saw out a center hole which will fit your arbor.

Place Over Pre-Polish Disk...

Incidentally, a 45 rpm disk is only slightly more than 1mm thick. This thinness represents a minimum mast height cheating challenge. Consequently, it can be very convenient to drop such a polishing disk permanently over an 8" prepolishing disk and then work back and forth between prepolishing and polishing. Recording disks can be easily loaded up with virtually any polishing substance and they polish beautifully almost all soft and medium hard stones. The old warning that they are effective only for the softest stones is another example of outright fiction or guesswork by so called experts—most of whom have never bothered to test out their admonitions.

If you have a 6-inch machine or pad, the 6³/₄" diameter 45 rpm recording disk can be easily cut down. Just lock it down to a master lap, turn the motor on moderate speed and gently press a sharp razor or knife edge...and in no time at all you can reduce it to a 4" diameter.

The 3¹/₂" diameter label can be peeled away with a fingernail—and then gently—use the sharp blade to score the smooth surface that remains.

You Can Make Your Own Mirror As a Polishing/Facet Locating Aid...

Using a mirror as a device to check on polishing coverage—as well as for locating the height-index-angle setup for existing facets—is an old machinist's trick. It's also been suggested that the mirror is valuable for checking a facet's flatness. Except in very rare instances, buying a mirror to check for facet flatness is rather silly when you think about it. Why would you need to check a facet's flatness if your

Master Gem Polishing

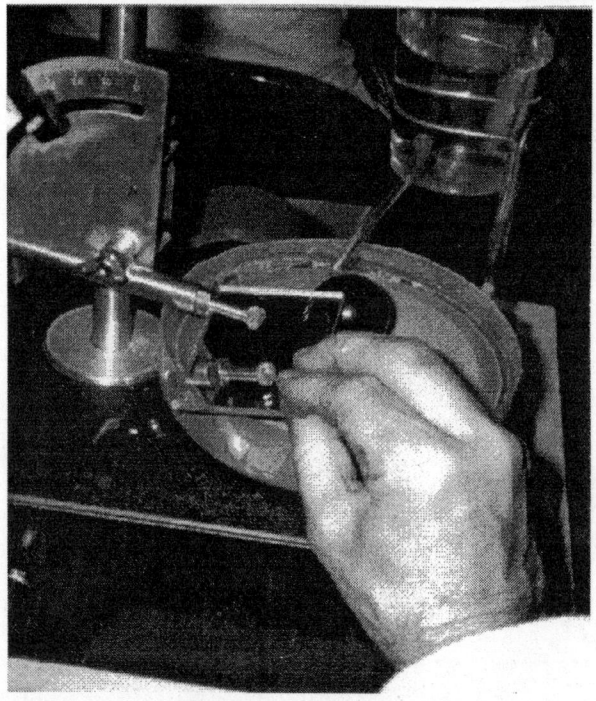

faceting machine and platen are accurate to begin with? And if your laps are causing rounding, it's time for new laps.

By placing down over a mirror a facet or flat surface upon which has been smeared a portion of liquid or paste separation film, a quick view into the mirror will disclose whether or not a true flat-to-flat orientation has been achieved. In this manner—and after this machine set-up adjustment—you can check on polishing progress. That portion of the facet or flat that is not flat to the flat mirror will simply not become as visually outlined as the rest of the facet.

As I'm sure you already know, there are two other simpler techniques for checking polish progress (and neither requires a machine adjustment):

1) look at the facet under progress in reflected light—with a magnifier— and 99 times out 100 you can visually access the condition accurately , or

2) paint the facet with soluble ink and check the wear-away progress caused by the polishing action.

Mirror's Best Use...

That leaves mirror use for its best purpose—identifying a machine's repeat setup on existing facets. When you're repairing a faceted stone, it's nice to have a tool that will quickly, easily and accurately show you the height-index-angle arrangement to work on a particular facet. Without a mirror to help, this task can be a vexing one.

Master Gem Polishing

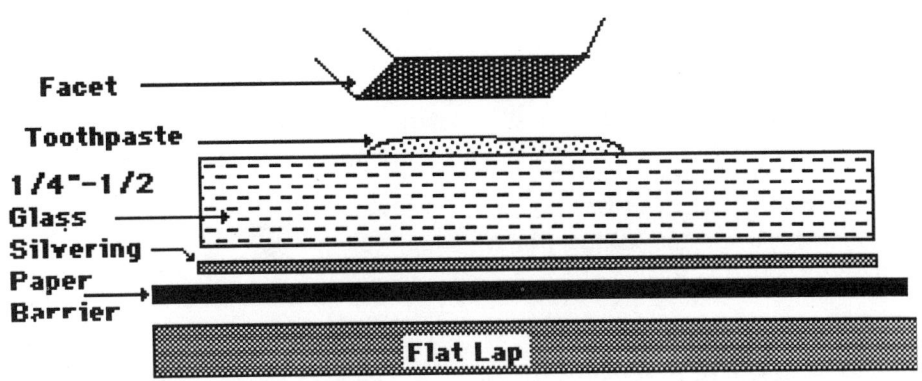

Having available a lapidary mirror to check polishing progress, flatness accuracy or for finding the machine setup on an existing facet involves very little investment in time or money. The application technique is as simple as looking into a mirror and viewing the results

Buying or making your own mirror represents a worthwhile investment for any gemcutter. This holds true for faceters or cabbers and particularly for any gemcutter who takes in repair work.

Jack Christiansen of Green Bay, WI, and Don Merkley of Calgary, Canada, for years have made and sold mirrors to the gemcutting community. *American Gemcutter Magazine* several times has published instructions on how to make a mirror. As mentioned earlier, the easiest approach is simply to go to the store and buy an inexpensive 2" square mirror and start using it. (You can, if you wish, glue some safety glass over the mirrored top surface to keep the latter from becoming scratched during use with hard gem crystals. The added thickness of the safety glass makes viewing the mirror image much easier, too, because the reflected image of the facet seen well from the point where the facet makes actual contact with the glass' top surface.

Following is how Don Merkley makes and uses a lapidary mirror (this is essentially the same approach used by Christiansen).

The concept (using a mirror to find facet setups and check facet

Master Gem Polishing

progress) was first shown to Merkley years ago. It requires no special or expensive equipment and is easy to use.

One viewing will suffice to locate any facet on any stone, the primary application being for repair. However, it may also be used to see if a facet is flat and/or if polishing action is taking place across the entire flat.

Equipment Needed...

The equipment needed to make your own mirror consists of:

- ☐ 1 piece of plate glass mirror 3/4" to 1" thick, and of any area size that will lay flat on the flattest lap you have (use a polishing, prepolishing or flat master lap).
- ☐ 1 Tube of no grit white toothpaste ((Colgate Regular makes a fine toothpaste to use)
- ☐ sheet of newsprint (paper) the size of your mirror. The newsprint enables you to protect the bottom of the mirror from scratches which would occur should you put it directly on a lap containing abrasives.

Mirror Technique For Facet Location...

1. dop your stone, center it carefully, and insert it in the quill, snugging but not tightening

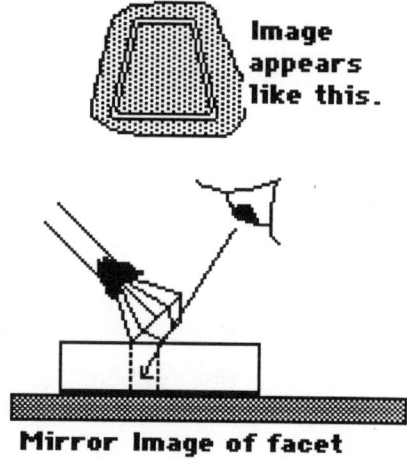

Mirror Image of facet seen through tooth paste

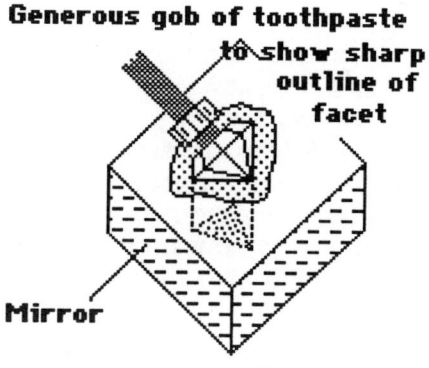

Generous gob of toothpaste to show sharp outline of facet

Mirror

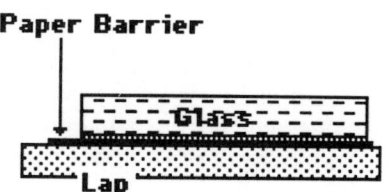

Paper Barrier
Glass
Lap

Master Gem Polishing

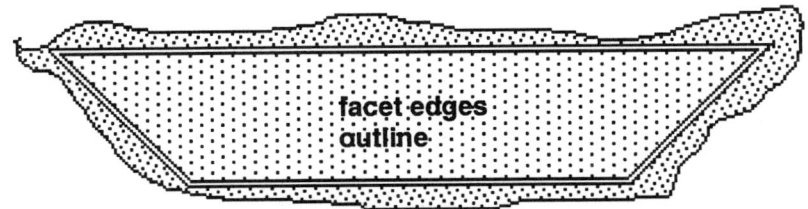

Press the facet with some pressure into the paste (ink, toothpaste, water, etc.) so it squeegees out...leaving an emphatic outline of the facet. All edges will be plainly visible when the facet is flat to the mirror.

To check on polish progress or to find a facet, just look at the image in the mirror. After squeezing out most of the liquid a clear outline of the facet or the flat will appear for easy, accurate viewing.

---

the dop completely
    2.   set the machine for the approximate angle of facet
    3.   set the cheater to zero
    4.   set the index gear for zero reading *i.e.,* 96 setting on a 96 index gear.
    5.   eyeball the facet to be repaired with a zero reading
    6.   place newsprint paper on your selected base lap and place the mirror directly over the newsprint.
    7.   raise the stone up or down with height adjustment till you clear the mirror by about $1/16$" clearance.
    8.   put a layer of toothpaste on the facet so the facet is completely covered (see above). Lower the stone until it touches the mirror. At this point, the toothpaste will squeeze out from between the facet and the mirror—or that part of the facet that is touching the lap. When the facet goes flat-to-flat on the mirror, lock the dopstick in the quill.

    By looking down past the stone at the bottom of the mirror you will see part or all of the facet. Based on the image you see, you might have to raise or lower the mast or cheat right or left until you get the whole outline of the facet showing at the bottom of the mirror. The im-

Master Gem Polishing

age should be very sharp and clear (no toothpaste between the facet and the mirror).

(Note: *The view you will get is the complete outline of the facet shape (provided the facet is flat-to-flat) against the mirror).*

After you are satisfied with your sharp clear picture outline of the facet, remove and carefully clean and put away the mirror. By carrying out this minimum amount of maintenance and care you will inhibit scratching the back surface of the mirror surface and maintain a clear top surface for future viewing ease. Now lower the facet to the lap and resume the finishing work.

Cause of Discrepancies...

The difference in faceting machines and individual workmanship will cause discrepancies in the placement of facets in a gemstone. In a typical repair job, if the stone was not cut on your faceting machine, you will undoubtedly find that it may be necessary to use the mirror to locate each facet individually.

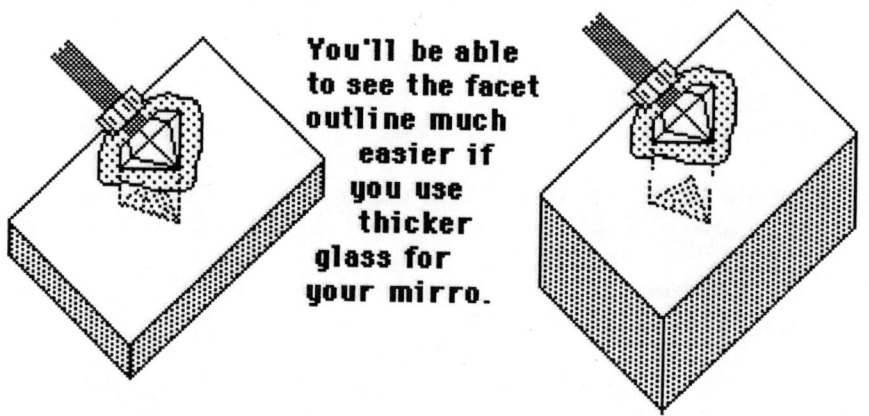

You'll be able to see the facet outline much easier if you use thicker glass for your mirro.

The glass thickness lowers the apparent image in the mirror, making it easier to see—and also provides for protection of the reflective foil.

If it is indeed necessary to recut a facet, proceed as if you are cutting a stone...being most careful to repeat and make it match the rest of the facets in the row so that the overall appearance and profile is maintained. Should the repair be a tiny one, you may be able to get away with polishing a single, defective facet. Often, though, the fault involves a number of facets, perhaps a whole tier.

(**Note:** *It is worth emphasizing the importance of a fine grit lap for this kind of work. Finding the facet is easy with a mirror, but overcutting is an ever present danger. That's why a faceter doing repair work, can load almost any type of polishing carrier with 14,000 diamond paste to perform the whole job. A 14,000 paste provides not only cutting action but will also impart a commercial polish.)*

Polishing...

Set the stone to the polishing lap, which should be in strict parallel alignment with the mirror in the previous operation. Blacken the facet with a felt tip pen and hand stoke lightly on the polishing lap. A quick check will indicate whether further cheating and adjustment is required to lay the facet completely accurate. Once you have proper orientation for flat-to-flat, go ahead with your regular polishing technique.

Again, due to machine and operator discrepancies, you will want to repeat the above procedure for each facet. Depending on the severity of the repair, you may find that an entire tier of facets must be repaired to maintain symmetry and uniform facet size and position.

Techniques on Using Thin Polishing Films...

Thin polishing films—whether plastic or metal—can save a lot of machine manipulation, frustration and time. Mounted atop the prepolishing disk, a quick, easy two-step prepolishing/polishing operation becomes readily available with a few clicks up or down on the vertical cheater. This way, you can prepolish a facet (or tier of facets), quickly click up to polish, and then click back down again for the next series of facets.

To achieve this polishing nirvana, some gemcutters are using film thickness metal disks, copper, bronze, tin and steel and charging them with 14,000 to 50,000 diamond polishing grit . Others are scissoring out their own 3 and 4 mil thick Mylar and/or acetate film disks

Master Gem Polishing

When handling thin film disks, handle them with care, using the fleshy portions of your fingers. Fingernails—or a sharp stone edge— cause destructive creases which usually also lead to irreparable irreparable kinks and folds.

or precoated diamond and metallic oxide films upon which diamond and metallic oxide polishes can be applied. It's much less expensive if you make your own thin film disks. Given their easy sensitivity to ruin and their relatively high cost, commercial diamond films are better left to the video business for which they were originally intended.

Even if you do choose to use a commercial precoated film, the trend is to "boost" the surfaces of these thin laps to give them faster loose grit polishing action. The disk is then usually mounted—with the film disk's diameter slightly reduced to form a "slip disk"—directly onto the larger prepolishing lap. This allows a faceter to prepolish on the outer periphery of the prepolishing lap, make a couple of up clicks for height adjustment—and go to a fast, finished polish before proceeding with other facets and/or tiers. When the polishing is finished, a couple of down clicks will have the machine ready for the next assignment.

The metal films, of course, are made just as thin as the 3- and 4-

Master Gem Polishing

mil plastic films and are much sturdier. For do-it-yourselfers, sheets of thin bronze, copper, tin and steel are readily available from suppliers. Plus the metal film disks offer superior resistence to ruinous accidents as well as superior holding ability for diamond pastes, diamond + olive oil mixes and for metallic oxide polishes as well.

Thin plastic films have been going directly onto the prepolishing laps for decades. I originally wrote in my book, *Master Faceting*, about using 14,000 paste to boost a $1/2$-micron diamond coated thin disk and then keeping it atop the prepolish lap for speed and convenience. I got the idea from a New York state faceter, John Schneider, who probably picked it up from Hap Harris of Freeland, WA who in 1973 suggested cutting out small, 3 and 4 mil thick plastic disks , charging them with diamond polish, and then mounting them directly to the prepolishing lap so the polishing film would be readily available after a quick, minimal cheater adjustment.

A few years ago, along came Oregon's Rick Ford who tested the "boost" conduct of colloidal silica and other various metallic oxide polishes in colloidal form on thin, coated Mylar Ultralaps™—and the

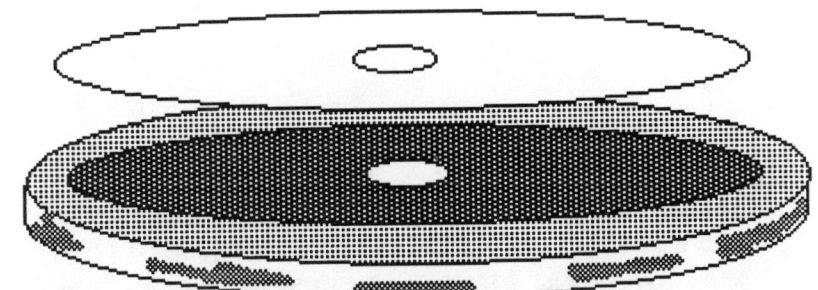

Notice that a thin metal film lap will attach to a base lap as easily as will the conventional plastic films.

A thin tin, copper , bronze or steel disk, made slightly smaller than the prepolishing disk, gives the same, quick, handy polishing convenience of thin plastic films—with much less danger of disastrous kinking, folding or creasing.

results were spectacular. What Ford ultimately discovered was what other gemcutters had found earlier from "boosting" coated diamond and oxide films: the "booster" polishing particles rolling and moving freely on the lap's polishing surface enormously accelerate the abrasive/polishing action, more so than the slower polishing action of embedded particles. This phenomenon can be explained by the new pulverization theory on scratching and polishing, a theory developed and refined at the mineral research department at the University of Arizona, Tucson, AZ.

There, researchers found that abrasive particles don't just plow a tiny ravine through a mineral's surface but rather press down on the crystal's surface and pulverize it, creating internal stresses which must be relieved by fracturing *i.e.*, produce microscopic chipping. Free particles from the "boost" application respond with random occurrence of friction between crystal and lap surface and lap speed, rolling and

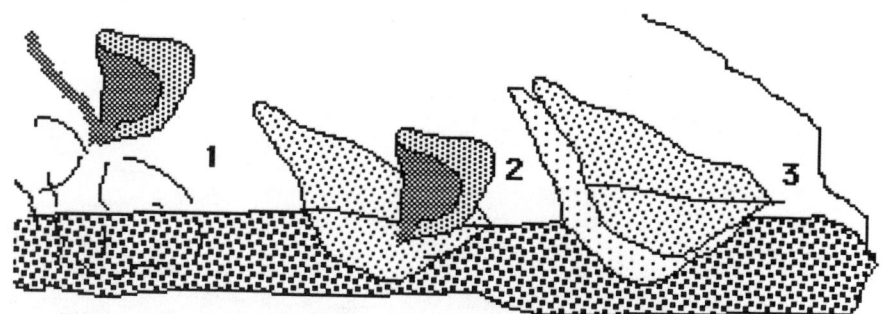

The abrasive particle causes stress (1) which penetrates the stone (2) causing cracks, and a chip (3) pops out when the stress develops.

The latest scientific scratch theory shows that an abrasive particle presses down on a crystal surface, creating stresses which relieve themselves by popping out "chips" of material beneath the abrasive. This is why "free" grit particles cut better than embedded ones *e.g.*, they are free to roll and cause multiple chips whereas embedded particles "chip" only in their ring.

gouging into the crystal, causing multiple tiny chips. That's also why hard laps work best with hard stones and soft laps work best with soft stones. The carrier lap possesses the appropriate hardness to "push back" and cause the particle to pulverize the crystal's surface. On the other hand, an embedded particle is somewhat disciplined in its locked in depth and also chips only in the narrow ring where the turning lap brings it into contact with the crystal.

The polish producing efficiency of tin, tin-lead and copper is established. These metalsnot only work effectively with diamond but are equally efficient polish producers when metallic oxides are also introduced on their surfaces. For many years, the Linde A on tin-lead pioneered by the late Henry B. Graves of Florida was generally regarded as the closest combination possible to a universal polisher.

Despite their short working life and fragility, commercial diamond and metallic oxide coated thin Mylar films have been around the lapidary industry for years. They were originally introduced in 1973 by the Charles Pfizer Company. The technology was later taken over by Moyco of Philadelphia, PA, whose Ultralap™ —consisting of all sorts of abrasives and backing materials as well as the chemical oxide and diamond coated films—is well known to gemcutters. Yet even today, long after the efficacy of thin plastic films has been established, many gemcutters shy away from their use.

... these metals—tin, tin-lead and copper— not only work effectively with diamond but they are equally efficient polish producers when metallic oxide polishes are also introduced on their surfaces.

Thin coated plastic polishing films hardly enjoy universal acceptance by lapidaries. Phil Bean of Seattle, WA, a first rate lapidary inventor who has written extensively on polishing developments, has such a low opinion of thin, polish plastic laps that he simply refuses to discuss them. Glenn Vargas once wrote that they were useful only for softer stones but this notion conflicts with the many faceters who routinely polish hard stones on them. A dozen other writers denigrated them for their fragility, slowness in bringing minerals to a final polish, etc., etc. Many other gemcutters continue to rail against their use, contending they create edge rounding (a charge long ago dispelled by some of the finest faceters in North America) and complain that they have little application among cabbers and carvers (also not true).

Others claim—and this accusation does indeed have merit—that they are too easy to kink, crease or fold. Although available as a disk with an adhesive back, commercial Mylar laps are usually attached to the base or holding lap with water suction (the idea of using olive oil as suction on a ceramic lap is quite recent). If you wet a smooth base lap sufficiently, the water will hold a thin metal or plastic film in place. Given such an unreliable adhesive as water, it requires only a bit too much pressure on a stone especially near the disk's outer periphery for the thin film to lose adhesion—and flip up with disastrous results...often damaging the stone. When that happens, a plastic disk almost invariably sustains surface damage which renders it virtually useless. The metal film disks, of course, can usually be repaired.

Available With Adhesive Back...

Gemcutters generally avoid the commercial gum backed plastic films because the adhesive balls up slightly and produces a bumpy ride for the stone. A series of tests showed that although there is some psychological impact, the bumpy ride exerts less impact on the quality of polish than is popularly believed—if the facet is quickly polished.

When it comes to diamond coated Mylar films, there is the issue,

Master Gem Polishing

too, of cost. It doesn't require too many of these kink/fold accidents—an instant's loss of concentration can produce an incident—to render diamond coated films excessively expensive to use. Diamond coated films cost much more than their chemical oxide counterparts. It's one thing to ruin a dollar or two metallic oxide film lap just because you pick it up carelessly, index improperly so a sharp facet edge slices up the soft plastic surface or your fingernail happens to catch the Mylar film: it's something else entirely when the same thing happens to a diamond coated film that costs at least $20 or more apiece.

Must be Handled Cautiously...

Fingernail creasing is a serious, ever present danger. Anyone familiar with these film laps will tell you to pick them up carefully with the padded portions of your fingers. The rule is: keep your fingernails away from them. Despite the list of complaints I've just listed, I believe that a gemcutter can live with these shortcoming if s/he will rec-

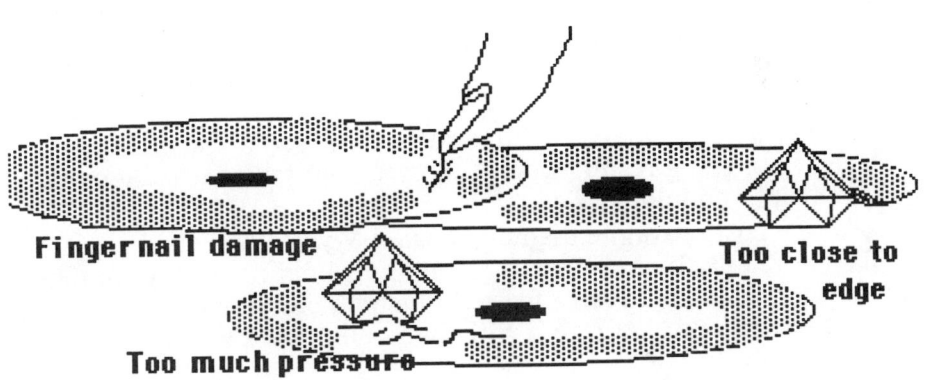

Uneven pressure, working too close to the periphery or careless handling can cause kinks, folds or creases—damaging to metal and destructive to thin plastic polishing films...so keep your concentration focused when using film disks.

Master Gem Polishing

ognize that some of the better technologies such as "boosting" make their lapidary polishing contributions acceptable.

In considering the use of thin, plastic and/or the preferred metal films for gem polishing, most of which you can make yourself, here are a few facts you should keep in mind:

- ✔ when "boosted" with diamond or colloidal polishing pastes, these thin polishing films produce swifter, high quality results
- ✔ if used properly *i.e.*, scratch free prepolish and light pressure without extended polishing periods, thin plastic films won't round off edges any more than harder polish carriers like metal films.
- ✔ for faceters, boosted thin film laps are extremely convenient for placement atop the prepolishing lap so the faceter can swing back and forth between sanding and polishing with only minimal height changes
- ✔ commercial thin, precoated Mylar film stock is available from Ultralap™ in sheets so a gemcutter may scissor out any shape or configuration wanted
- ✔ most thin metal films can accommodate both diamond and metallic oxide films and kinks, folds and creases can be repaired
- ✔ thin metal films—often used as shim material by machinists— can be purchased in large, flat sheets from any machine shop supplier
- ✔ some of oxide Mylar films such as Moyco's Spectralap give spectacular polishing results when "boosted" with the colloidal oxide pastes polish or colloidal silica
- ✔ the cost of fragile diamond coated Mylar films can be reduced significantly by buying your own thin Mylar or acetate (preferably the type which features a frosted finish on one side as used in blueprint shops) and charging it with diamond paste à la Hap Harris' 20-year old idea.
- ✔ thin metal and plastics films are useful and practical for cabochon and carving use: it's not difficult to make a thin plastic or metal film belt or mount a disk to a rubber cushioned carrier for quick cab polishing—especially flats.
- ✔ tests show that the prejudice against gum backed film disks is more psychological than anything and often no serious damage is inflicted on a crystal's surface unless polishing becomes lengthy
- ✔ water is normally used to achieve adhesion between the

Master Gem Polishing

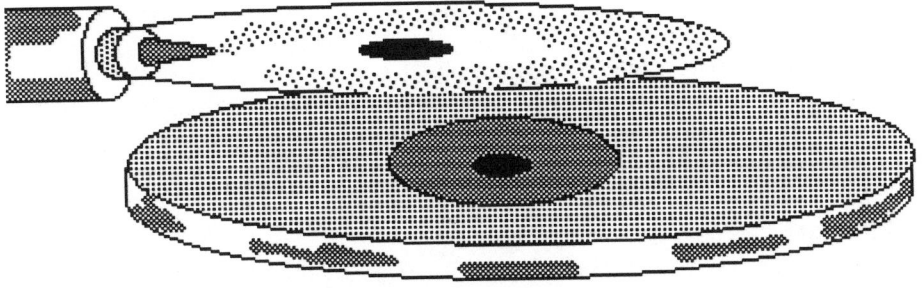

For fast, easy polishing results, put diamond paste or metallic oxide on a thin metal or plastic film and mount the disk directly onto the prepolishing lap.

thin films and the base lap, but now olive oil has been found to do an even better holding job. Read the following section carefully.

Make Your Own Thin Film Laps...

If you're one of those gemcutters who likes the easy convenience of thin plastic and/or metal film polishing laps discussed earlier but balks at their high ruin rate and cost penalties, there are alternatives.

As most readers know, Mylar is the DuPont trademarked name for a thin, strong polyester film and acetate is a cellulose derivative. Both are often sold in rolls with one polished side and one matt side, the latter to make the material easier to unroll. Both are also strong and equally capable of retaining or gripping polishes for various lapidary uses. This gripping quality is an important contribution.

There are a few other significant problems with thin plastic films, especially the diamond coated plastic films. The major difficulty is not their fragility. It's the need to use water or olive oil for adhesion. Olive oil obviously makes a good adhesive because it doesn't need constant replenishing and it's reasonably compatible with soluble pastes or other mixes. Water is different—you need lots of it. With so much water required to maintain them in place, thin plastic films aren't the best material for soluble diamond pastes which wash away too quickly. A combination of diamond grit or paste and olive oil is slightly better because the olive oil acts as a more retentive coolant. As for the colloidal pastes, they are already wet and can be applied to the films so that additional drip water is unnecessary for cooling.

As with commercial films, though, it takes but a momentary loss of concentration while they're on a base lap for the water or olive oil suction to let go with ruinous results. The laps fold, crease or kink...and when that happens you might just as well throw them away.

Notes on Edge Rounding...

As I've indicated earlier, the ever present problem of facet edge rounding, is greatly over stated. It is entirely possible to round edges, though. When the thin film is mounted on a smooth base or fine grit lap, the hard base combines with the 3 or 4 mil film lap's thickness so that edge rounding is virtually eliminated. That holds true only as long as the gemcutter doesn't press too hard during polishing or if the polishing period isn't excessively extended.

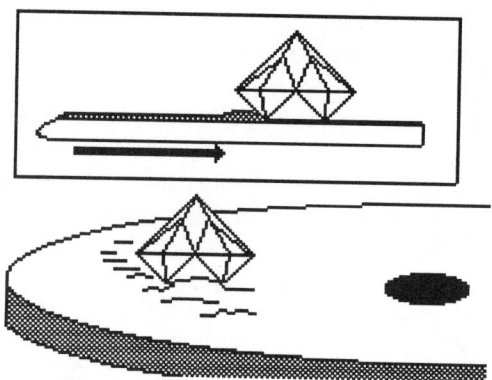

Excessive pressure will often cause a "rollup" in front of a stone's leading edge

The relatively slow polishing speed and short working life of commercially coated diamond and metallic oxide films has led many lapidaries to "boost" their performance with diamond paste or special colloidal polishes. Given these "boosts," the polishing efficiency, speed and finish, plus their longevity is greatly enhanced. Don't ever forget that coated Mylar was developed for the video and magnetic tape business. At a hardness of only slightly more than 1 Mohs, they can't long retain the diamond or oxide polish charge against the enormous battering that rapidly oncoming gemstones with much higher Mohs hardness inflict. The "boosting" extends the working life of the disk. It accentuates the disk's polishing capabilities. Finally, it encourages the easy mounting of these disks directly onto the prepolishing lap so the prepolishing and polishing can be done almost in the same operation.

If you would like to test the use of thin metal or plastic polishing films without making a particularly large investment, you have a couple of viable options. They both call for making your own laps. Keep in mind that the discussion that follows addresses itself to working with thin metal and Mylar and acetate films.

Options on Using Thin Film Polishers...

Making your own thin polishing films is not at all difficult or complicated...and some of these ideas produce polishing films that are superior in lapidary use to coated films because of strategies to keep fine particles on the polishing surface.

One simple approach is to apply a wax film over the thin plastic or metal as a holder for the diamond or metallic oxide.

As an alternative approach, use the Hap Harris idea mentioned a few pages ago *e.g.,* obtain some 3 or 4 mil thick acetate or Mylar, scissor out an appropriate sized disk, load it up with diamond or metallic oxide polishing paste, and mount the thin film polishing disk directly onto the prepolishing lap. Many gemcutters still approach thin film polishing with this latter strategy. The idea is as good today as it was when Harris first proposed it. He intended it for faceting use, but the application works equally well for cabbers—and also with the thin metal laps.

An Adhesion Factor..

Some gemcutters shy away from thin film technology solely because of the water adhesion factor. Since the introduction of thin films, water has filled the role of providing suction or adhesion. Because strong suction is so vital, it's nearly impossible to use coarse grit laps as the base or holding lap. The large particles interfere with the vacuum created by water suction with the result that the adhesion doesn't hold well. There are two ways of holding these thin laps to the base lap...adhesives or an alternative suction liquid. You can't attach them with rubber cement. Commercial laps are available as PSA laps, with gummed backing. Alternatively, you dispense with water in favor of olive oil to create a vacuum suction between the thin film and the base lap. Despite reservations to the contrary, olive oil is usually very dependable for keeping the film attached.

The heavy need for water causes difficulty in "boosting" with water soluble diamond pastes or metallic oxide powders—but there's an easy way around this shortcoming: use olive oil—or a formal adhesive—instead.

Faceters generally have avoided adhesive backed polishing films. Given a choice of two undesirables, in the past they've opted for water. There's an easy way around this shortcoming, too.

The colloidal polishing pastes sold by mAgi of Beavercreek, OR, nicely eliminates the need for a continuous water drenching because the colloidal materials don't need or want top surface water: they're already permanently wetted. As long as you have water (or olive oil) between the film and the base lap the suction will hold.

As for diamond pastes, there is a nice alternative around this difficulty, too. It was published in the NMFG Newsletter, written by Merrill O. Murphy. Murphy came up with the idea of applying carnauba wax over the thin Mylar or acetate film and then embedding diamond grit—and oxide powders— into the wax. This way, you will not only have a permanent diamond coated thin film polishing disk, but it can be run with a slow water flow over the polishing surface without too much fear of washing away the polish particles. Keep in mind during the discussion which follows that Murphy's wax application procedure works equally well with thin metal disks. Of course the wax coated thin disks will still need to be attached to the holding lap with water or olive oil but the easy on-off flexibility of water attachment is now a virtue.

Master Gem Polishing

By applying a thin coating of wax on the thin plastic or metal, you have available a holding coat for diamond particles, in effect, a permanent thin film diamond lap.

Applying Wax to Film...

Here is a summary of the trials that Murphy undertook. He purchased a can of TREWAX brand carnauba paste wax for hardwood floors at a lumber and hardware company. The product is a carnauba wax-based product combined with other waxes and a solvent, but it contains no abrasives or contaminants.

His first test consisted of rubbing some of the wax on an unmounted 3-mil disc of drafting Mylar. (**Author's Note:** *Murphy says he used Mylar drafting plastic, but it's more likely that acetate was the plastic type because this is what's mostly used for drafting purposes.).* Using the waxing technique that would be employed to hand-wax a piece of furniture, he rubbed the wax on with a clean cloth. After a minute or two wait, he then buffed it lightly with a second cloth. The proof step consisted of attempts to polish stones in the 3 to 6 Mohs hardness range using water slurries of alumina as the polishing agent.

This approach was unsuccessful. For one thing, the wax layer wasn't smooth so the stones bounced and peel the wax off. What was worse, the polishing action was only fair. The wax coat had been applied too unevenly.

Murphy realized that he'd applied the wax with the wrong method. In a second test, he again used 3-mil Mylar with the frosted side up, this time over a 1/4-inch thick Plexiglass base lap. Placing some wax on a soft, clean cloth and with the lap turning, he gently rubbed the wax laden cloth across the surface for about a half minute.

Thin Film Polishing Disks

The preparation and use of 3- or 4-mil thin non-porous metal (tin, steel, Titanium) film or thin Mylar or acetate as polishing disks can be accomplished by:

- ✔ **First,** apply a thin, smooth carnauba wax coat (on plastic frosted side) over the film while the lap spins, then buff
- ✔ **Next,** finger rub then light burnish in diamond grit or apply a small amount of a colloidal paste polish on the wax coat once the film has been attached to the holding lap
- ✔ **Or,** cut out a disk with scissors and then apply a diamond paste or metallic oxide polish directly —without the initial wax coat—and mount permanently atop a base lap or a prepolishing lap. Copper or bronze work best when used uncoated.

He was especially careful to apply a thin, smooth wax layer. After a five minute wait to allow the wax to mature, he gently polished the wax film with a clean cloth. That took care of the bumping. It was gone. A thin slurry of alumina in water—not too much but certainly enough to keep the surface wet (a colloidal polishing paste would eliminate this water difficulty!)—on the wax surface improved the polishing action. Still, though, the lap takes a bit of getting used to, Murphy warns. You'll read about this later, but it's a warning that should be sounded a couple of times: don't use spray diamond on a wax coat. The chemicals in the spray tend to melt the wax, destroy its usefulness.

He emphasizes a gentle hand. Use the smallest amount of pressure consistent with good polishing—and don't overload with the polishing agent. Murphy noticed that edge rounding, thanks to the hard base beneath the thin film, was no problem. For experimenters or first time users, he recommends a bit of polishing practice practice first on

Master Gem Polishing

fluorite, apatite, etc.

A polishing speed of 30 to 150 rpm is best, Murphy suggests. Murphy used aluminum oxide but faceters may wish to use the colloidal alumina paste which has greatly superior polishing qualities.

New Polishing Theory?

The science of nanotribology involves friction. Friction largely accounts for the action of gem polishing. Therein lies perhaps an answer to a question that has puzzled lapidaries for a long time.

With the so-called Beilby Layer Theory and the Diamond Scratch Theory pretty well debunked by modern science as explanations for polishing action, nanotribologists may have come up with a partial answer on why gemstones polish. They have recently been investigating the mutual attraction of minerals and metals for each other with the new tunneling microscope supported by high speed computers...and some astonishing discoveries are showing up.

When researchers pressed a gold tip into a nickel surface and then the same thing was done with cerium oxide against quartz, they discovered that atoms from one element exhibited a remarkable attraction for the other. As the gold tip was brought close to the nickel, atoms of nickel and gold leaped across the gap to their opposite, and when the gold tip was pulled back from the nickel, atoms of nickel

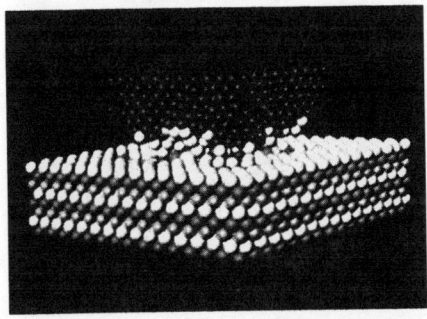 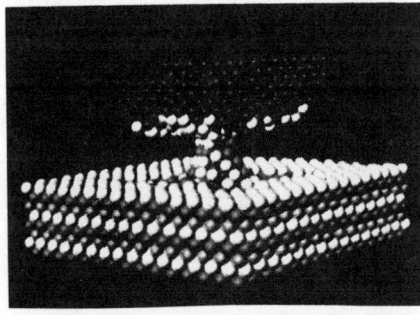

When one metal or mineral was brought close to the other, the atoms from each jumped to the other. This mutual attraction continued, forming a "neck" as the two elements were separated, and the neck snapped only with distance.

Master Gem Polishing

and gold continued to cling to each other forming a "neck." The neck finally separated when the two metals were separated further. The same attraction and "necking" tendency was displayed by cerium oxide and quartz.

Scientists explain the phenomenon as possibly coming from the energy needed by each element to maintain its surface. Gold expends considerable less energy to maintain its surface than does nickel. The same holds true with cerium oxide...

What does this mean to gem polishing? Not too much at this point because much more research remains to be done. But nanotribologists point out that the contemporary thinking about coolants and lubricants may have to change. Perhaps lubricity or viscosity alone isn't the answer to promoting friction-polishing efficiency. It could be that gem polishing takes place because one of the elements removes atoms from another while friction heat accelerates the removal action.

Gemcutters and gemologists have long wondered why some metallic oxide polishes such as alumina oxide or chromic oxide work better with certain types of gem minerals while other polishes fail. The Mohs hardness isn't the answer so maybe it is indeed chemical.

CRYSTALLOGRAPHIC INFORMATION POLISHING COMBINATIONS

NAME	RI	Mohs	Heat	Cleave	Optic	Combination
Actinolite	1.61+	5½	No	Yes	DR	alox on tin
Amber	1.54	2½	Yes	No	A*	tripoli or tin oxide on flannel, felt or flexible leather (work fast to avoid heat)
Amblygonitel	1.61+	5½	Yes	Yes	DR	alox on wax, waxed Mylar w /alox

---

Key to Abbreviations in Polishing Combinations
A*=amorphous   O*=organic   cerox=cerium oxide
alox=aluminum oxide   tinox=tin oxide   chox=chrome oxide

Master Gem Polishing

NAME	RI	Mohs	Heat	Cleave	Optic	Combination
Analcime	1.49	5	No	No	DR	alox on tin, ceox on Lucite
Andalusite	1.63	7	No	Yes	DR	alox on tin
Anglesite	1.88	3	Yes	No	DR	alox on wax
Anhydrite	1.58+	3½	Yes	Yes	DR	alox on wax
Apatite	1.64	5	Yes	Yes	DR	alox, cerox or tinox on wax
Apophyllite	1.53	5	Yes	Yes	DR	alox on leather, cerox on felt (watch undercutting)
Aragonite	1.67	3½	Yes	Yes	DR	tinox on leather, cerox on felt
Augelite	1.58	5	No	Perf.	DR	alox on wax
Axinite	1.68	6½	No	Yes	DR	alox on tin
Azurite	1.73+	4	No	No	DR	alox on wax (responds well to acid addition)
Barite	1.65	3	Yes	Yes	DR	tinox or alox on tin
Benitoite	1.76	6½	No	No	DR	cerox on Spectralap or Lucite, cerox on tin with alox
Beryl	1.56	7	No	No	DR	tinox or alox on tin

   Emerald—green   Morganite—pink
   Aquamarine—blue   Green Beryl—yellowish-green
   Goshenite—colorless

| Beryllonite | 1.55 | 5½ | Yes | Yes | DR | cerox on Lucite |

Master Gem Polishing

NAME	RI	Mohs	Heat	Cleave	Optic	Combination
Boracite	1.66	7	No	No	DR	alox on tin
Bornite	1.66	3	No	No	SR	finish cabs with 1200 on leather, rouge or alox on leather. Flats are best polished on wax or Pellon with watery alox.
Brazilianite	1.60	$5^1/_2$	No	Perf.	DR	alox on tin
Breithauptite	1.61	$5^1/_2$	Yes	No	DR	alox on leather
Calcite	1.50+	3	Yes	Yes	DR	tinox or alox on wood or wax (extremely cleavage sensitive so use low rpm and/or pressure)
Cancrinite	1.50+	$5^1/_2$	No	No	DR	cerox on felt or Lucite
Cassiterite	1.99	$6^1/_2$	No	No	DR	alox (thick) on tin
Celestite	1.62	$3^1/_2$	Yes	Yes	DR	alox on wax
Cerussite	1.80+	$3^1/_2$	Yes	No	DR	tinox on wood or wax
Chondrodite	1.59+	$6^1/_2$	No	No	DR	alox on wax or wood
Chrysoberyl	1.74	$8^1/_2$	No	No	DR	diamond on hard lap, $1/_2$-micron Ultralap with 14,000 boost
Cinnabar	2.91+	$2^1/_2$	Yes	Yes	DR	alox on wax
Clinozoisite	1.72	6	Yes	Yes	DR	(much more sensitive to shock than epidote)cerox on tin, alox on Lucite

Master Gem Polishing

NAME	RI	Mohs	Heat	Cleave	Optic	Combination
Colemanite	1.61	4½	Yes	No	DR	colloidal cerox on SpectraLap, cerox on Lucite
Coral	1.48	3-4	Yes	No	O*	tripoli followed by tinox on cloth or Pellon (some feel that black coral should be polished with jeweler's rouge
Corundum	1.76	9	No	No	DR	diamond grit on copper, ceramic, bronze, tin or cast iron (many professional star corundum cutters like copper lap pre-polishing and polishing with copper lap, too) cabs can be polished on wood or leather with diamond grit.
Covellite	2.02	2	No	No	DR	alox on leather
Crocoite	2.53	2½	No	No	DR	alox on wax
Cuprite	2.85	3½	Yes	Yes	S	alox on wax
Danburite	1.63	7	No	No	DR	alox on tin
Datolite	1.65+	5½	No	No	DR	tinox on Lucite
Diopside	1.67	6	No	Yes	DR	tinox or alox on wood or wax
Dioptase	1.70	5	No	Yes	DR	cerox on SpectraLap or Lucite

Master Gem Polishing

NAME	RI	Mohs	Heat	Cleave	Optic	Combination
Diamond	2.41	10	No	Perf.	SR	diamond polish
Enstatite	1.67	6½	No	No	DR	alox on tin
Epidote	1.74	6	No	Perf.	DR	cerox on Ultralap, alox on tin
Euclase	1.65	7½	No	Perf.	DR	alox on tin
Feldspar Sunstone Moonstone Labradorite Spectrolite	1.52	5-7	No	Perf	DR	cerox on Spectralap or (for cabs) on felt, alox on tin or damp leather colloidal silica on Ultra lap, alox on tin
Fibrolite	1.66	7½	N	Yes	DR	alox on tin
Fluorite	1.43	4	No	Perf.	SR	cerox on wood or wax or Ultralap
Gadolinite	2.02	6½	No	No	DR	tinox or alox on tin or typemetal
Garnet						chox on chrome Ultralap, alox or chox on leather, alox on tin
Almandine	1.78	7	Yes	No	SR	
Spessartite	1.79	7	Yes	No	SR	
Pyrope	1.73	7	Yes	No	SR	
Grossular	1.73	7	Yes	No	SR	
Demantoid	1.88	6½	Yes	No	SR	
Uvarovite	1.87	7½	Yes	No	SR	
Glass	1.45+	5	No	No	A*	cerox on cerox Ultralap
Goethite	2.26	5½	No	No	DR	alox on leather

Master Gem Polishing

NAME	RI	Mohs	Heat	Cleave	Optic	Combination
Gypsum	1.52	2	Yes	No	DR	cerox on damp leather (best to polish by hand because of softness and sensitivity)
Hambergite	1.55+	7½	No	Yes	DR	alox or tinox on Lucite or Ultralap
Hematite	3.22	5½	No	No	DR	cabs best polished with alox or cerox on cloth buffs, leather or wood: faceted gems use alox on tin
Hodgkinsonite	1.76+	5	No	Yes	DR	tinox on Ultralap
Howlite	1.58+	3½	Yes	No	DR	tinox on felt (if undercutting occurs switch to alox on leather
Iolite	1.55	7	No	No	DR	alox or tinox on tin, cabs use alox or chox on leather
Jadeite	1.65+	6½	No	No	DR	diamond polishing best: alox on leather
Jet	1.64+	2½	Yes	No	O**	alox or tinox on leather or cloth or Pellon
Kornerupine	1.67	6½	No	Ye	DR	alox on tin
Kyanite	1.71	4-7	No	Perf.	DR	alox on tin
Lapis Lazuli	1.50	5½	Yes	No	DR	chox on chox Ultralap, alox or chox on leather

Master Gem Polishing

NAME	RI	Mohs	Heat	Cleave	Optic	Combination
Lazulite	1.61+	6.6	Yes	No	DR	alox or chox on leather or wax
Leucite	1.51	6	No	No	DR	cerox on Lucite
Magnesite	1.51+	4	Yes	Yes	DR	alox on wax
Malachite	1.65+	3.5	Yes	Perf.	DR	chox on chox Ultralap, alox or chox on leather (responds well to addition of acid to polish)
Microlite	1.98	6	No	No	DR	alox on tin
Moldavite	1.48	(See obsidian)				
Natrolite	1.48	6.6	Yes	Yes	DR	cerox on Lucite
Nephrite	1.61+	6	No	No	DR	(see jadeite also) alox or chox on leather
Obsidian	1.48	5	Yes	No	A*	cerox on felt
Opal	1.45	5	Yes	No	A*	cerox on felt for cabs: faceted stones best use cerox on Spectralap or Lucite
Peridot	1.67	6.5	No	No	DR	alux + acid on tin or wax
Petalite	1.51	6	No	Yes	DR	cerox on Lucite or alox on tin
Phenacite	1.65	7.5	No	No	DR	alox on tin, almost dry, diamond polish good

Master Gem Polishing

NAME	RI	Mohs	Heat	Cleave	Optic	Combination
Phospho-phyllite	1.61	3	Yes	Yes	DR	alox on tin or wax
Pollucite	1.52	6.5	No	No	DR	cerox on Lucite
Prehnite	1.61	6	No	Yes	DR	alox on tin or leather
Proustite	2.79	2.5	Yes	No	DR	alox on wax
Pyrite	1.81	6	Yes	No	DR	alox on wood or wax (extremely shock sensitive and tends to crumble or break up easily)
Quartz	1.55	7	No	No	DR	colloidal silica on SpectraLap
Rhodo-chrosite	1.60+	3	Yes	Perf.	DR	cab alox on leather, facet prepolish alox on tin, finish with alox on wax
Rhodonite	1.73	5	No	Perf.	DR	alox on leather
Rutile	2.60+	6.5	No	No	DR	watery alox on tin (change directions when polishing)
Scapolite	1.66	5	No	Perf.	DR	cerox on felt or Lucite
Scheelite	1.92	4.5	No	Perf.	DR	alox on tin, finish on wax lap
Serpentine	1.49+	3	No	No	DR	alox on almost dry leather
Sinhalite	1.69	6.5	No	No	DR	alox on tin, cerox on Lucite

Master Gem Polishing

NAME	RI	Mohs	Heat	Cleave	Optic	Combination
Smithsonite	1.62+	4.5	No	Yes	DR	thick tinox or alox on tin
Sodalite	1.48	5.5	No	No	DR	cerox on felt
Sphalerite	2.37	3.5	No	Perf.	SR	alox on leather
Sphene	1.88	5	No	No	DR	alox on tin
Spinel	1.72	8	No	No	SR	alox on tin
Spodumene	1.65	6	Yes	Perf	DR	cabs respond to alox on leather: faceted stones best with alox on tin
Stibiotantalite	2.37+	5.5	Yes	No	DR	alox on tin
Strontium Titanate**	2.40+	6.5	Yes	No	DR	alox on tin
Tektite	1.48	6.5	Yes	No	DR	cerox on felt or Lucite
Topaz	1.62	8	No	Perf.	DR	alox on tin or tin-lead (scored laps produce best results)
Tourmaline	1.61	7	Yes	No	DR	chox on chox Ultralap, alox on tin
Tremolite	1.62	6	No	Yes	DR	tinox or cerox on tin (very sensitive to shock)
Turquois	1.61+	6	Yes	No	DR	alox on leather, chox works well, too
Ulexite	1.49+	2.5	Yes	Perf.	DR	tinox or alox on felt or leather

Master Gem Polishing

NAME	RI	Mohs	Heat	Cleave	Optic	Combination
Variscite	1.55	5	Yes	No	DR	alox on leather, cerox or tinox on felt
Willemite	1.69	5.5	No	No	DR	alox on tin
Witherite	1.53	3	No	No	DR	alox on tin
Wulfenite	2.30	3	Yes	No	DR	tinox on wax
Zincite	2.01	4	No	Yes	DR	alox on tin
Zircon	1.99	7	No	No	DR	alox on tin
Zoisite	(see Epidote)					

SYNTHETICS

NAME	RI	Mohs	Heat	Cleave	Optic	Combination
Alexandrite	Identical with natural					
Diamond	Identical with natural					
Corundum	Identical with natural					
Corundum (star)	Identical with natural					
CZ (Cubic Zirconium)	2.17	$8^1/_2$	No	No	SR	diamond on ceramic, cast iron or copper, alox on tin-lead
Spinel	Identical with natural					
YAG (Yttrium Aluminium Garnet)	1.83	8+	No	No	SR	alox on tin-lead

Master Gem Polishing

NAME	RI	Mohs	Heat	Cleave	Optic	Combination
Beryl		Identical with natural				
Quartz		Identical with natural				
GGG Gadolinium Gallium Garnet	2.02	6½	No	No	SR	alox on tin-lead
Rutile	2.61	6	No	Yes	DR	alox on tin-lead, Ultra-lap
Strontium Titanate	2.41	5½	Yes	No	SR	cerox on tin, tin-lead or Ultralap
Turquoise	1.60	6½+	No	No		Identical with natural except it is harder...alox on felt, leather, muslin

When using alloy laps made of such metals as zinc, type metal and tin-lead, periodically check your hands and fingers for the telltale dark stain that signifies you've picked up dangerous amounts of lead. Wash your hands before touching any food or liquids. Lead and cadmium are dangerous substances.

Master Gem Polishing

NAME	RI	Mohs	Heat	Cleave	Optic	Combination
Synthetic Opal						Identical with natural when silica gel is the agent used to impregnate
						Plastic imitations are polished with plastic polish
Lapis Lazuli	1.50	4½	Yes	No	SR	Synthetic product has higher content of sodalite...polishes with alox on leather, felt
Laser Glasses						Characteristics vary ...most polish well with alox, ceox or chox on Ultralaps or tin, tin-lead

A Matter of Safety...

Mentioning safety around a group of gemcutters compares favorably with trying to stimulate an excited discussion on car insurance. It's a subject that everyone is involved with, but it's often better left out of sight, sound and mind—until needed. Then there's nothing more important.

Some things must be said, though. Then you can forget the subject was brought up—but, hopefully, the little rattles will remain in your mind bothering you each time you fail to consider safety for yourself and others.

For example, many faceters have an old tin-lead lap in their inventory. The lap is a marvelous polishing instrument. It's also deadly. Take the old type metal lap as an example. It is composed principally of lead. Truth is, a type metal lap doesn't scream lead at you but with minor variations most type metal laps are 82.7% lead, 5.1% tin and 11.2% antimony. There are also a few traces of arsenic, bismuth and copper in the mixture, but the principal bad actor is lead.

Rub your fingers across a type metal or tin-lead lap. What you'll quickly notice is a dark stain on the flesh. This stain is mostly lead and is millions of times more concentrated than the 15 parts per billion allowable in tap water. Are you getting the message about lead? The word of warning is: wash that stain off immediately and don't get it near your mouth. The last thing you want to do is handle food or liq-

Master Gem Polishing

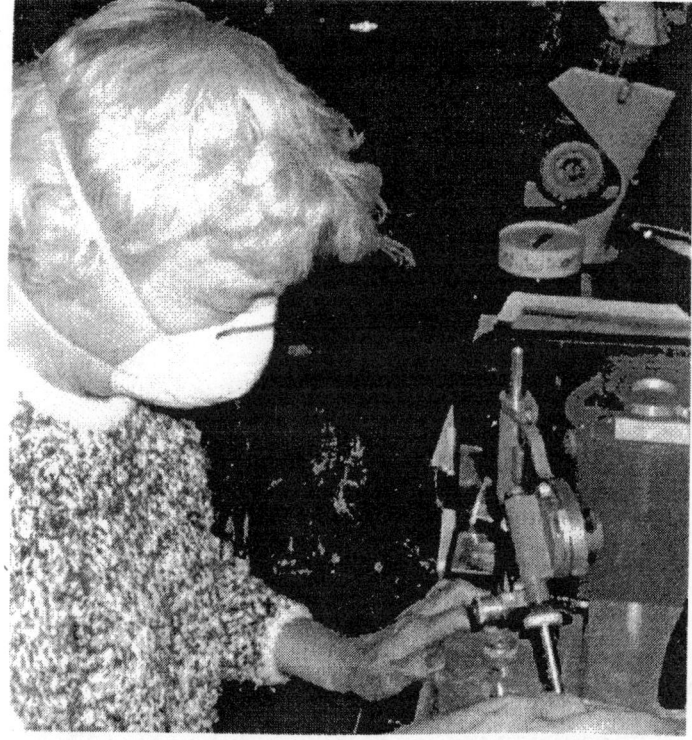

Perhaps it is cumbersome and a bit of a nuisance to wear safety equipment, but do it: it's worth the bother.

uids while you have "gemcutter's hands" *i.e.*, fingers stained with lead from your polishing lap. The absorption of lead compounds is greater in an acidic environment and, of course, our stomachs provide just such an environment.

Lead is truly very dangerous stuff! The average person already has collected a significant amount of the metal just from everyday living... breathing in car safety exhaust fumes, soldered joints in our plumbing systems, etc. When thousands of children throughout the world died in the 1930's and 1940's from lead poisoning, it brought on the ban against lead paints. The tin-type metal lap generally rated by gemcutters as the top polishing lap has a weight content of 50%-60% nontoxic tin and this high ratio helps reduce the amount of lead. The wise word is: always wash your hands regularly while polishing with any lap that contains lead.

Cadmium is a Problem, Too...

Now that I've been dutifully threatening about lead in your laps, I can turn to an even more dangerous chemical element—cadmium. This pernicious metal is always present in trace amounts in lead and zinc compounds and alloys.

Far more poisonous than lead, cadmium is absorbed into the body

Master Gem Polishing

and there is no way of eliminating it. The biggest source of cadmium will be found in all alloys and compounds containing zinc and this include zinc oxide (used for polishing some cabochons). I would pause before recommending the use of zinc oxide for any lapidary use. Besides, there are better polishes available anyway.

The rule of safety when it comes to lead and cadmium is this: if you wouldn't eat it, wash your hands before you eat.

Safety Using Acids...

It goes without saying that the addition of acid to a polishing mix, particularly a metallic oxide polish, greatly accelerates the polishing action for most gemstones. The acid improves the pH content of the lap and polish and this higher alkaline situation makes a decided contribution to a good, fast polish. This is true in cabochon cutting, carving and faceting.

Many gemcutters routinely give their polishes a quick spritz with some vinegar...and this easy, relaxed approach to acid addition is about all that is required. If, though, you intend to use a diluted muriatic acid to get a bigger acid kick, just remember that this acid bears a little more caution than ordinary vinegar. The rule when handling acids is the Three A Rule:

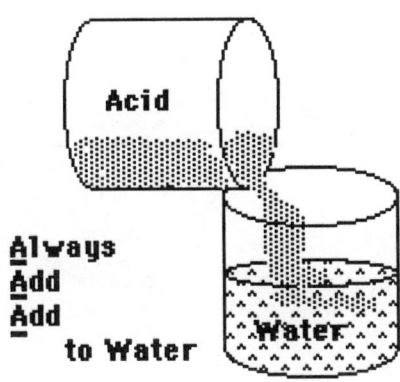

Always Add Acid to water...not the other way around because the results can sometimes be a shade greater than spectacular. I've been preaching this rule for years because it's a simple little thing that can save gemcutters from serious harm. Remember: AAA=Always Add the Acid to the water.

When mixing acid and water, remember to apply the AAA Acid Safety Rule. This rule is a reminder that you should Always Add the Acid to the water...not the other way around

Advanced Tips on Ceramic Lap Use...

In faceting, the ceramic lap remains controversial at best. Some faceters swear by the hard aluminum oxide lap and others swear at it. The latter just can't make the tool work.

When it comes to polishing corundum, chrysoberyl and spinel, though, the benefits of a ceramic lap—as well as a cast iron or an anodized aluminum lap—are considerable. That's why these three lap types are so popular with the truly hard stones...they do a good polishing job. They don't do all that well on stones softer than $7^1/_2$ Mohs, though, and better alternatives exist. It's that or fight scratches.

Here are some methods used on ceramic laps by some advanced cutters with a long history of sapphire polishing.

First, the lap must be prepped properly if you expect it to produce a polish. Ceramic laps glaze over rather swiftly. To correct, go over the surface with a wet or dry 260 sanding cloth while the lap is turning on the spindle. Some faceters hand lap their ceramic laps on a plate of glass upon which has been placed some 250 silicon carbide or Boron

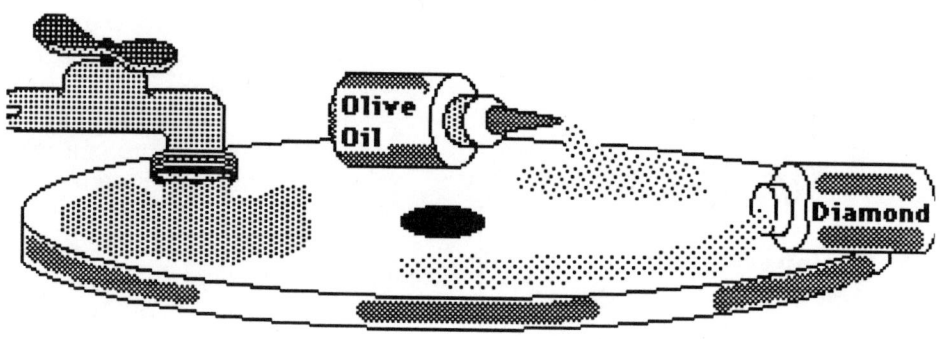

To prepare a ceramic lap for use, clean it thoroughly with soap and water then smear a light film of olive oil over the surface, finally applying a tiny amount of diamond. Wipe the diamond off before using: contrary to popular feeling, excessive diamond grit will not improve polishing action...it will tend to scratch.

Carbide grit.

Either way, after the sanding operation you'll want a white ceramic surface, free of all debris from previous operations.

One of GIA's faceting instructors recently came up with this prep formula for ceramic laps. Mix up a compound consisting of $1/3$ RV anti-freeze, $1/3$ mineral oil and $1/3$ isopropyl alcohol, then mix in some diamond polish and smear on the ceramic lap. Don't add any coolant-lubricant, extender, etc.

Opinions on Coolant-Lubricant Liquids...

The coolant-lubricant can be commercial extender, WD-40, machining oil or olive oil. There's some controversy over the type of extender. Some faceters swear by the toughness and efficiency of a WD-40 film on a ceramic lap. France's Alex Wolkonsky urges faceters to avoid petroleum based substances because, like vegetable oil, they break down too easily (car owners will be thrilled with this tip). Allowing facets to worry through onto the bare ceramic surface where the facet touches the dry, bare ceramic surface is an open invitation to scratching. Diamond cutters and lapidaries, incidentally, have been using olive oil for years without excessive film deterioration.

A coolant-lubricant on a ceramic lap must control heat and encourage smoothness—but it's main function is to provide a tough film to keep the facet off the bare polishing surface.

Wolkonsky still uses a graphite pencil to build a polishing film. Before applying diamond to the lap, he lightly coats the entire surface from arbor nut to lap edge with graphite, giving the surface an even grey coat. For corundum, he applies a somewhat thicker graphite coat.

You can use graphite if you wish but don't overlook the obvious: when it mixes with any liquid from a diamond spray or extender you have one exceptionally messy polishing operation to contend with.

Yes, a coolant-lubricant is intended to control heat buildup while encouraging a smooth passage of facet over the abrasive surface. It's primary function, though, is to maintain a film on the lap surface so the facet doesn't ride on the bare lap material.

Most faceters simply spray the diamond grit on the surface in quick, 2-second bursts. After a wipe-off to remove surplus grit, some extender is added and the polishing operation can commence.

As for speed, set the rpm about 75/100. For a long time, the word of wisdom held that facets should be hand lapped on a motionless ceramic lap or at least with a lap run at a maximum of 25-50 rpm. Low speeds and graphite on ceramic laps are pretty much passé.

It was Wolkonsky who developed a nice technique for getting the most out of each diamond charging of a ceramic lap. Once the entire surface has been charged, he claims excellent results can be obtained by polishing in rings, starting the first ring at the extreme outer edge of the lap. Polish and inspect the facet, he explains, and each time it becomes necessary to return the facet to the same ring he suggests touching it first gently and quickly in the inside area adjacent to the ring. This way, the facet will pick up a fresh charge of diamond before it's moved into the polishing ring again.

By following this procedure, Wolkonsky says you will gradually expand the film protected polishing ring halfway across the lap before exhausting the diamond/oil/graphite mix supply.

Is Finer Prepolishing Helpful..

For those of you who indeed find difficulty in getting a ceramic lap to cooperate, will a finer prepolishing help?

Can you prepolish a corundum at 1200 or 3000 and then expect the diamond polish to "take?"

Don't bet on it!

Corundum's hardness does vary by direction and the mineral surface is characterized by intermittent hard spots. At the finer abrasives, the surface tends to slake off or pit. You might get away with a 1200 prepolish but certainly at 3000 you'll find the corundum surface being ripped away. Most of the time a 600 diamond grit polish is really all that's necessary to polish corundum.

Polishing With Wood Wheels...

Cabbers, especially opal workers, like wood for polishing.

A number of suppliers over the years have found a ready market for powered maple wheel sets upon which a range of diamond grits can be applied. Not only are the small wood polishing machines effec-

Master Gem Polishing

tive for soft stones, but they are inexpensive and offer a clean operation. Slow in performance and somewhat limited in what they can do, wood wheel sets are still fine for prepolishing and polishing.

There's a good reason for wood's continuing popularity. If it is sufficiently hard and thoroughly soaked in paraffin (so water won't cause warpage later), the grinding and polishing action is predictably acceptable. Wood with the help of wax readily accepts diamond pastes or diamond-olive oil mixes, retaining them enough that they create the necessary "drag" on a mineral surface that causes removal.

Only lately have faceters, too, found that wood makes a fine polishing lap. An increasing number of faceters buy plywood which is made with hard maple or boxwood facing. It takes only a short time to saw out a 6" or 8" lap disk, give it a good paraffin soak and then put it on the machine for polishing.

It's important to use the most desirable type of wood for lapidary polishing purposes. The wood types you want include:

Apple	Beech	Birch
Boxwood	Cherry	Cocobolo
Ebony	Holly	Hornbeam
Lignum vitae	Mahogany	Maple
Olive	Pearl	Plum
Rosewood	Sandalwood	Teak
Willow		

Woods that are only marginally acceptable for lapidary are:

Alder	Aspen	Basswood
Cottonwood	Gum	Horse chestnut
Lime	Poplars	Sour gum
Walnut	Whitewood	Redwood

Making Special Polishing Tools...

Even for the gemcutter fortunate to have drawer after drawer filled with lapidary tools and equipment, there still comes a time when a special polishing task requires a new tool.

Whether you facet, cab or carve you are bound to run into

those one-time situations that demand a bit of innovation on your part. That would include a spot or area on a table facet that simply will not respond to advanced swearing or polishing technique, a blemish on a fine cabochon which is already in a mounting, or a complex configuration on a new carving.

Summary of Polishing Problems...

Here are some responses to various problems that gemcutters encounter when polishing:

❑ *What causes fine, parallel streaking in corundum when polishing on cast iron with diamond?*
Possibilities: The first things that comes to mind are an unburnished cast iron lap and/or ferric streaking. Before using a cast iron lap, you should burnish it vigorously with a chunk of corundum to remove the jaggies. If you don't, the slips of iron will cause streaking.

Ferric streaking happens often with some corundum or chrysoberyl on a cast iron lap, especially if you are polishing with 14,000 diamond grit.. The condition is visible as closely packed parallel grooves, bearing a strong resemblance to numerous cat whiskers that run completely across a flat surface. The edge-to-edge streaking can be removed by touching the facets with 50,000 diamond—and sometimes a bit of alumina powder right on the diamond lap. This extra step improves any final polish imparted with 14,000 diamond.

Fortunately, you don't get ferric streaking with every corundum or chrysoberyl specimen.

❑ *Why doesn't malachite come to a fine polish every time when using the same polishing combination that has worked successfully before?*
Possibilities: First of all, chrome oxide works best on malachite. Try adding soap to the polish mix (to make it wetter) as well as some vinegar or diluted muriatic or oxalic acid. Malachite owes its variability to a copper carbonate personality so a bit of hand

rubbing—plus a clear water rinse if acid is used—will bring up a good polish almost every time.

❑ *Peridot drives me crazy. It's so variable in polishing response and I keep shifting around...still with no luck.*
Possibilities: Peridot is another of those pesky magnesium (its pH is near the isoelectric point) gem types. The pH factor contributes to a poor polish response so always add some acid to lower pH...or polish peridot with colloidal silica. Peridot often responds to alumina on a wax lap...it's slow but it gets there.

❑ *I can't get some fine amethyst to take a good polish on my cast iron lap? What gives?*
Possibilities: Quartz and cast iron just aren't a good match up for polishing. Use a cast iron lap strictly for hard stones (seldom less than $7^1/_2$ Mohs). Polish quartz on a soft lap such as tin, tin-lead, Lucite...and you'll avoid all the scratching.

❑ *What is the fundamental difference between polishing cabochons on felt or leather? I seem to have good luck with both materials—although it's been my experience that some leathers don't work as well as others, do they?*
Possibilities: Felt undercuts and leather doesn't. That's the the major difference. It's best to avoid felt with stones that are notorious for undercutting *i.e.*, malachite, rhodonite, etc.
As for different results with different leather types, keep this rule in mind: the rough side retains coarser abrasives and powders while the smooth side offers more with finer abrasives and polishing agents. Here is a rundown on the various kinds of leather:
Buffalo (water buffalo, not American bison)—good for small thick buffing wheels
Calfskin—not particularly useful in lapidary
Camelskin—good for small thick buffing wheels
Chamois—natural or synthetic...not particularly useful in lapidary
Cowhide—most used in lapidary for small thick wheels,

Master Gem Polishing

buffs, covers.

Deerskin—not particularly useful in lapidary
Goatskin—good in lapidary, but too expensive
Horsehide—excellent for fine sanding and polishing buffs
Kidskin—not particularly useful in lapidary
Lambskin—not particularly useful in lapidary
Pigskin—useful in lapidary with any type of polish...tough and durable
Sheepskin—not particularly useful in lapidary

❑ *Is it true that real fine diamond grit is best used on softer stones?*

Possibilities: Yes. You'll invariably get best results with 200,000 diamond grit when polishing soft and/or very brittle stones. The same holds true with 100,000 and even 50,000 (medium hard to soft stones).

As for 14,000 grit, realize that this grade represents the average commercial polish. The grit size works best on hard stones and is seldom used—or especially effective in polishing—on stones under 8 Mohs. Here is a suggested list for using various diamond polishing grits:

Grit	Use
200,000	Extremely fine polish, particularly on soft or very brittle materials
100,000	Very fine polish on very soft or brittle materials
50,000	fine polish on soft to medium hard materials
14,000	Polish most hard minerals, with significant material removal
8,000	Very fine prepolish, gives acceptable polish on hard stones
3,000	Fine prepolish

Master Gem Polishing

1,200	Moderate material removal, good for most prepolishing
600	Rather fast material removal, acceptable prepolish on some minerals
325	Rapid material removal, good for preforming and shaping, rough cutting
200-	Extremely rapid material removal, leaves significant subsurface fracturing

❑ *I hear dealers talk about selling "4 kilos" or "5 kilos" and wonder what they're talking about. What is a kilo?*

Possibilities: Kilo is short for the metric term kilogram. A kilogram is 1,000 grams which, as you already know, would be 5,000 metric carats (1 gram = 5 carats).

A kilo also often refers to 643.01 pennyweights (dwt.) which works out to (20 dwts. = 1 ounce) 32.15 ounces or roughly 2 pounds.

❑ *Is there any standard for the amount of diamond used in various sanding or polishing laps? I read about some manufacturers claim of "heavy charge" and that sort of thing? Also, some gemcutters warn against using extenders because they're petroleum based?*

Possibilities: Let's talk about extenders first. They are either a slow-evaporating fluid like a glycol (any of several dihydric alcohols) for use with water-soluble pastes, or light petroleum oils for use with oil-based compounds. They're both fine for lapidary use.

As for the amount of diamond per gram of compound, manufacturers understandably keep this as a proprietary secret. The actual amount is calculated on the basis of a monolayer of diamond particles when a spot of paste is properly flattened upon the lap. According to Diamond Boart, S.A., of Brussels, when one gram of their compound is properly spread it will cover one square meter of lap surface.

Keep in mind that there is an upper limit of the amount of diamond particles that can be used in a monolayer. When this upper limit is exceeded, the lap will not perform as well. When it comes to diamond content claims, it's probably best to look at price—and go with the cheaper item on the grounds that content isn't all that important. When two laps or polishing disks of essentially the same construction vary significantly in price, chances are you're paying for something other than the diamond content.

❑ *Is there really a good polishing combination for tourmaline?*

Possibilities: Yes, try chrome oxide on a chrome oxide Ultralap™ or the same company's Spectralap™. mAgi's colloidal chrome oxide paste works wonders on these coated Mylar materials. These combinations work well for both faceting and cabbing.

The traditional approach for faceted tourmaline is alumina on a tin lap. For cabbers: it's the same oxide polish on leather.

❑ *What is the benefit of colloidal polishes other than they've been premixed with water? I mix my powders with water without difficulty.*

Possibilities: The important thing is that you do what works for you. Colloidal polishes contain more than just water and oxide powders. To the basic mix have been added surfactants, thickeners, etc. so the polishing powder will remain permanently suspended in solution. What benefits a colloidal polishing paste really offers is convenience, ease of application, lack of messiness and consistency. When you get used to using a paste, you tend to standardize your polishing techniques—and this leads to fewer problems.

❑ *Speaking of oxide polishing powders, what's the shorthand for these polishes?*

Possibilities: I'm not sure what you mean by shorthand so I'll put the chemical formula, the abbreviated spelling form and some other vital data about metallic oxides:

Master Gem Polishing

Polish	Abbrev.	Formula	MP	Mohs
Aluminum oxide[1]	AlOx	Al_2O_3	2,040° C.	$6\frac{1}{2}$
Tin oxide[2]	TinOx	SnO_2	2,061° C.	$9\frac{1}{3}$
Chrome oxide[3]	ChOx	Cr_2O_3	2,435° C.	$5\frac{1}{2}$
Magnesium oxide[4]	MagOx	ZrO_2	2,715° C.	$6\frac{1}{2}$
Diamond[5]	Dia.	C	3,550° C.	10
Zirconium dioxide[6]	ZrDi	ZrO_2	2,715 °C.	$6\frac{1}{2}$
Colloidal Silica[7]	ColSil	SiO_3	1,200° C.	7
Chalk[8]	Chalk	$CaCo_3$		3

1. Useful for most minerals of medium to high Mohs
2. Excellent all around polish
3. Efficient with copper sulphate minerals, jade and tourmaline
4. polishes nickel and aluminum, also used by German lapidaries for polishing pyrite and hematite
5. Universal polisher, owing to its hardness and fine grit size
6. Good for polishing metals and ores
7. Efficient on most minerals
8. Good for bone, ivory and low Mohs substances

❑ *What is the word on Linde A? Is it still manufactured or what? I get a fine alumina polish when I still order Linde A from my suppliers.*

Possibilities: As you'll read elsewhere in this book, Linde A is a proprietary trademarked name owned by the Union Carbide Company for its chemically produced micronized (particle size: c. 0.3 micron) hexagonal shaped alumina particle. As a polish, it is equally efficient on minerals, metals and metallographic specimens as well as other materials.

The same company also produced Linde B, a smaller particle but gamma *i.e.*, cubic, shaped in crystallization and while it is a highly efficient polishing agent for metallographic work, it is not nearly as good or as fast in lapidary as Linde A.

At last report, Union Carbide no longer manufactures Linde A or B. There is a plentiful supply, though, of hexagonal

Master Gem Polishing

shaped 0.3 micron sized alumina on the market so there should be no shortage of this fine lapidary polish.

❏ *Is graphite coating on ceramic laps no longer an accepted tactic in polishing?*
Possibilities: Probably. Graphite gave way to various extenders because the former material is so dirty to work with. Some faceters still use graphite on their ceramic lap because it still functions as a lubricant-coolant but it doesn't seem to have magical values.

❏ *Is most polishing theory a lot of overtalked, unproven nonsense? I had an old faceter once tell me that 90% of polishing theory is pure hokum...that you can polish a gemstone with some cigarette ashes and spit on the lap?*
Possibilities: Which probably explains why you described your mentor as "...an old faceter..." He's probably still waiting for the polish to come up. Yes, cigarette ashes, being carbon, will eventually polish a gemstone. So will rubbing an agate in your fingers over time. Every hear of a "worry stone."
Most gemcutters, though, would like to get the polish on their stones before the century is out.

❏ *Is their a less messy way than a brush to apply metallic oxide polishes onto leather or felt?*
Possibilities: Yes. Obtain one of several plastic "accordion" bottles in which spray-type deodorants are sold. A few squeezes on the side of the bottle will send a nice, controlled stream of polishing agent to the buff.
It wouldn't be a bad idea to dedicate each bottle to a specific polish. Of course, you'll need to premix the powders with water to get maximum service out of your bottles.

❏ *What is the real secret to a good polish?*
Possibilities: Prepolish...prepolish...prepolish!
If you properly prepolish a gem mineral—that is, get all the

scratches and subsurface fractures removed—then the polishing step is really easy. Often, almost any polish will do the trick if the prepolishing surface is prepared properly.

When you are experiencing difficulty polishing a gem stone, go back and review the prepolish. Often the answer will lie there.

❑ *Is there a reliable polish for jade? I have all kinds of trouble getting a bright finish.*
Possibilities: In China, where they take jade seriously, many craftsmen use chromium oxide—with a dash of alumina mixed in. Try mixing on an 8:1 ratio and you may find this polish on either felt, leather or canvas will work wonders.

Also, you might want to try wool carpet with this polish mix sometimes. Some jade cutters like the combination.

❑ *Just what is rottenstone? I've heard that the German masters of Idar Oberstein still use it a lot?*
Possibilities: Rottenstone is also called Tripoli, an extremely fine silica derived from decomposed limestone. Tripoli is still used extensively for polishing precious metals, but it's lapidary importance—even with the German masters—is greatly diminished. The "air floated tripoli," regarded as the best, is made by stirring up a cloud of its dust and capturing the airborne particles, hence the name.

❑ *What is meant by the technique of "swipe polishing?"*
Possibilities: To "swipe polish" means to sweep the stone across the buffing surface with moderate pressure in short, disciplined motions that are opposed to the wheel's direction. The stone is pressed against the polishing surface, usually in the lower quadrant of the wheel, brought up to mid-wheel quickly and then released.

A series of these swipe motions are made, then the stone is inspected...and returned to swiping if necessary. Swipe polishing, you'll find, works best with a nearly dry wheel: it's not a technique for getting the most out of a wet or saturated polishing surface.

Master Gem Polishing

❑ *What's a good technique for restoring a leather polishing pad that has become glazed over?*

Possibilities: Try using an ordinary pumice block. This material works great on leather and doesn't destroy the integrity of the material either. Press the block vigorously against the running pad.

❑ *Should polishing pads for cabochons have a convex surface to accommodate roundness?*

Possibilities: It isn't absolutely necessary but a convex surface is certainly beneficial. Many cabbers swear by the bowl device where leather is stretched over and then held in place with twine or wire: the cab can "sink" into the flexible leather and receive a nice, even exposure to polishing.

Other materials can be placed against a soft foam or rubber cushion disk so pressure can cause a good polishing action between the stone and the polisher.

❑ *Of what use to lapidary is boron carbide? I understand it has great hardness but brittleness presents a problem?*

Possibilities: That's right! It's very hard and very brittle. So brittle in fact, that it hard minerals break it up in short order.

For that reason, manufacturers have been reluctant to coat or impregnate surfaces that would be used in lapidary. BC is very effective for long fibered materials such as metals but most minerals are short fibered. Such fibered minerals as jade and spodumene respond to BC...but it's best use for gemcutters would be as a loose grit for sanding and prepolishing.

It's pretty hard to get BC particles finer than about 1,500. Also, don't get boron carbide mixed up with boron nitride (CBN=cubic boron nitride), a much harder and blockier synthesized abrasive which is produced in a manner similar to diamond.

❑ *Is a wetting agent useful in lapidary?*

Possibilities: Wetting agents remain controversial. So far, their contribution to better or faster polishing has been anecdotal. There is little solid physical evidence that they do anything beneficial.

Master Gem Polishing

If you wish to conduct your own tests, obtain some wind shield wiper solution and mix it in with the polish. That'll give you the wettest polish you've had in a long time.

❏ *A Chinese craftsman once hinted to me that the Chinese technique of polishing jade includes a mysterious, highly protected extra step that clearly gives them a superior polish. Does this so-called "mysterious step" really exist—and, if so, what is it?*

Possibilities: You may be referring to the ancient Chinese practice of boiling a polished piece of jade in molten wax for more than 48 hours. A buffing follows—and up comes a magnificent jade luster.

This same trick, incidentally, has been known to work with plain agate and reputedly with turquoise and some of the other sulphate based gem types. I know it works well with jade and agate, but you'd be better served by experimenting with other gem types, given the variations that exist even in the same gem family.

❏ *Do I really need to keep rough and cut opal in water to keep it from crazing? I notice dealers, who know opal, do it all the time?*

Possibilities: First, the dealers put rough opal in water because refraction encourages the opal's play of color to show better? As for keeping opal in water to avoid crazing, it doesn't hurt to put the opal in water—and it doesn't help much either. Opal is a hydrated silica, of course, but the water as a savior idea came along before we understood what caused color in opal *e.g.*, small spheres, not water.

❏ *I hear how thin metal and plastic film disks can be used by cabbers but I'm not certain what you mean. How do I set up for using these films?*

Possibilities: You can attach thin metal or plastic films directly to a hard disk made of wood, plywood, composition wood, etc. You can also attach a piece of canvas, medium hard rubber or leather (smooth side out) to these hard surfaces and then use adhesive to attach the thin metal or plastic films to these softer intermediary surfaces. I prefer an intermediary material so I can press the stone slightly into the thin films (NEVER use heavy pressure, though).

Master Gem Polishing

Knowledge of Mixing Powders Vital To Keep Gem Polish Consistent

Why does a gemcutter puzzle when s/he mixes up a batch of cerium oxide and water only to discover that the polish doesn't work too well at first and then improves as the polish supply gets closer to the bottom? Why are all the larger polishing particles on top all the time? Why does most scratching occur with new powders?

Well, after years of experimentation, University of Chicago physicists have come up with an answer. They have developed new insights on why the large things tend to rise to the top of collections of small objects of different sizes...even when the items have been carefully graded.

These new insights may prove highly valuable to numerous industrial processes, from the mixing of cement to preparing pharmaceutical pills and powders and mixing seeds with fertilizers. But they mean a great deal right now to a gemcutter trying to come up with a good, workable polishing paste.

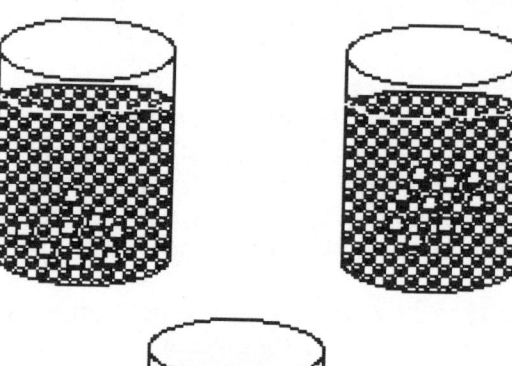

Large particles (1) move up the center (2) but remain, ulnable to move down the sides (3).

Knowledge of Mixing...

"It's important to understand the underlying processes of mixing," says Sidney Nagel, a University of Chicago physicist. "The hope is that once you understand that, you can get to the point where you can tell people how to improve the mixing process."

What Nagel and three of his colleagues, Heinrich Jaeger, James Knight and Chu-Heng Liu, found is this: if you shake a cylinder full of small beads the action will create convection currents similar to what happens when you boil a pot of water.

The beads, large and small, in the cylinder's center rise slowly to the top while those along the edge fall to the bottom.

Unless there is a mechanism for keeping polishing particles suspended individually—such as a surfactant—the same thing happens with powders. The larger particles find their way to the top and the smaller ones to the bottom.

Nagel and his colleagues reached this conclusion after long hours studying small glass beads of different sizes and colors shaken

> *Advice: Before using polishing powders taken from a container, shake and turn the container upside down a few times to assure even distribution of the polishing particles.*

in tall cylinders. They watched how the beads moved and made videotapes.

The process was tedious enough because the scientists couldn't see what happening in the cylinder's center. They had to stop the experiment and remove the beads to note how they had arranged themselves. This had to be done over and over at different times in the shaking process.

Several Secrets Unveiled...

Several secrets of mixing solid materials still have to be uncovered through more experiments, Nagel admits, but the researchers found that the container's shape played a prominent role in the outcome.

"The slope of the container's wall is important," Nagel says. "If you use a cone instead of a cylinder, the process reverses itself. The beads go up the walls and fall down the center so the big ones settle on the bottom instead of rising to the top."

Another discovery is that surface texture also makes a difference. Cylinders with rough walls produce far more convention flow than those with smooth walls, he said.

Nagel and his colleagues have been studying various properties of granular material such as sand and grains for four years, studying how sound waves travel through grains and the dynamics of avalanches as well as mixing powders. Their finds were published in a recent issue of Physical Review Letters.

Thin Metal Polishing Films Can Improve Repeatability, Ease

For decades, faceters have been using thin plastic polishing films atop the prepolishing lap as an aid in solving repeatability and machine adjustment problems associated with polishing.

The whole idea behind the thin polishing film approach has been to gain the advantage of small height adjustments needed to go to polish. As a result, a growing trend finds faceters utilizing a "slip lap" *i.e.*, a thin lap of smaller diameter than the prepolishing lap. These laps make it possible to avoid major machine setup adjustments in order to finish individual facets or rows which can be polished immediately after the prepolish step. It's a simple matter to slip on a small, thin disk coated with either diamond particles or metallic oxide paste and get conveniently to the polish easily and cleanly with only an up click or two.

When commercially coated plastic films were introduced to the lapidary industry in the early 1970s, polishing became a bit easier...first with Ultralap™ metallic oxide films and then Ultralap™ diamond films. The big problem with commercial diamond films became quickly obvious. This involved the excessive cost when you consider how rapidly such fragile films lose their abrasive charge, or fold, wrinkle or kink under normal lapidary use. Pick up a commercial coated plastic film improperly and it may kink—and that is ruinous for further polishing use. Press down a bit too much or allow the disk to become slightly dry and you wipe away the diamond charge from the soft plastic. When you're paying more than $20 or more for a single diamond coated plastic film, the search for more economical options becomes critical.

Master Gem Polishing

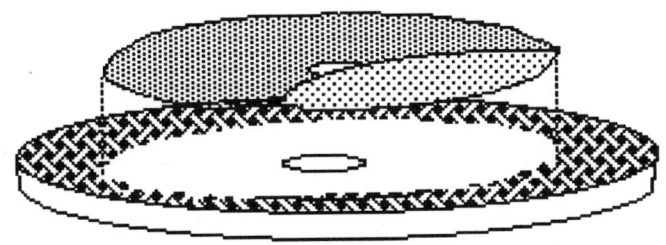

Slip Laps provide good results, convenience

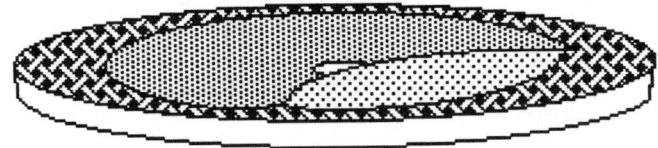

The excessive costs of commercially coated diamond plastic films can be overcome by charging your own thin metal films such as copper with diamond and using them directly as "slip laps" directly atop the prepolishing lap. Metal films are cheaper, stronger, longer lasting...and can be repaired.

Thin plastic films with metallic oxides, of course, have the same fragility problem, but they cost much, much less so the cost per disk issue isn't a serious economic problem.

Turning to Metal...

Now, increasingly, faceters are turning to equally thin but much hardier metal films such as copper, bronze, tin and even steel for the same task—and the ruin rate on these laps plummets. Why? Well, metal films are cheaper, stronger, longer lasting and if they fold, kink or crease you repair them by ironing out the kinks with your fingers, the family steam iron...or close the damaged disk up in a thick, heavy book for a spell. You can't do that with plastic film. Further, metal is much harder so it more easily handles hard stones.

With these advantages, it's easy to see why the cost of polishing on thin metal polishing disks is so much less than plastic. You can scissor out as many as twenty 3"-6" slip disks from a 6"x54" section of 3-mil to 5-mil thick tin, bronze, copper, aluminum or even stainless steel (or incredibly hard Titanium). A sheet costs only

Master Gem Polishing

about $10-$25. Squirt on a couple of pea-sized mounds of your own diamond charge, attach to a prepolish lap with olive oil—or spray adhesive—and you're into thin films in a big way. If you prefer the convenience of thin polishing films but balk at plastic's high ruin rate and prohibitive cost, metal is truly a viable alternatives.

Obviously, copper makes the best polishing disk. Don't overlook the porosity benefits of phosphor bronze, though. When you charge bronze with diamond grit, the metal's natural porosity makes available tiny reservoirs the particles—as well as metallic oxide powder particles—can "seat" and go to work...just like Mehanite cast iron. You'll find that polishing particles roll around free on tin, steel or Titanium surfaces—unless, of course, you don't want the aggressive cutting of free particles and apply a thin wax coating. Aluminum, unless anodized, isn't of much value: too soft.

Obviously, copper makes the best polishing disk for diamond use....don't overlook the porosity benefits of phosphor bronze, though...it provides reservoirs for the polishing particles.

By putting a diamond charge on your own cutout metal slip laps you reduce costs to under $2 per disk. If edge rounding has you worried (most top performing faceters say this is a false fear even with plastic) you will find that thin—but hard— metal film polishing laps can end that fear and, in the case of copper, retain the diamond charge. That's a lot of benefit over the $20-$30 each for commercial plastic films... particularly when you are free to put any grade of diamond grit you want on the metal laps.

If you are just starting out in faceting and wish to keep your costs down you might even be well served to buy some thin film metal stock and make yourself a series of changeable disks running from sanding to prepolishing to polishing. All you need are metal sheets, a pair of snippers or scissors and some diamond powder.

As was pointed out earlier, commercial pre-coated plastic polishing film was originally developed for use in the video and magnetic tape industry and found its way into the lapidary industry as an after thought. It is still natural for gemcutters to reach for such thin

Master Gem Polishing

diamond and oxide coated films as are manufactured by Moyco of Philadelphia, PA, under the Ultralap™ name.

Even after more than two decades, there remain serious reservations about the efficacy of most thin plastic films as polishing agents. Prejudice against them is considerable. Phil Bean, facet machine inventor and a long time thinker about faceting problems, simply refuses to discuss them. Many lapidary suppliers won't stock them. Cabochon cutters can't use them and faceters avoid them because they dislike the excessive dependence on water to wet the polishing surface and keep the film attached to the underlying base lap.

Easy to Ruin...

Plastic's major difficulty, of course, lies with fragility. At 1.6 Mohs, any plastic film can be rendered useless for gem polishing by simply running a fingernail over the surface. A momentary loss of concentration while in the middle of a difficult polishing chore can

A radius cutter or a razor blade is all you need to cut out a slip disk in thin metal. If the edges are slightly deformed, just place the disk on a flat surface and burnish down flat with your fingers...the same as kink repair.

What Makes Thin Copper Films Superior to Plastic....

How is it that a thin film copper polishing disk is so superior to thin Mylar or acetate?

Keep in mind that commercially coated diamond films were not developed for lapidary use: they were intended for use in video and magnetic tape manufacturing. Copper has a long history of lapidary efficiency. It's proven its worth over decades of use...and is still used.

A number of other factors make copper film disks preferable to plastic. For one thing, copper at 3.0 Mohs is twice as hard as the 1.6 Mohs rating of both Mylar (which commercial companies and most gemcutters use) and Acetate. Also, copper—unlike any plastic— has an enormous affinity for diamond and works hardens swiftly and securely around each particle. That means you can polish any stone on a copper film, up to and including corundum.

The biggest advantage of a thin copper lap, though, lies is the ease with which copper can be charged with diamond grit. You can use your fingertips to rub diamond grit of 260 or finer into the copper surface where it will only need an occasional "boost" now and then to maintain its high cutting efficiency. Because the copper will grip the diamond particles, using water or olive oil to hold the copper film to the base lap causes no wash away problem. You can run all the water you like because it won't have any effect on the diamond charge (it will with metallic oxide powders, though—so use olive oil for suction and minimal water on the top surface).

Yes, you can finger charge and then also use a fine oxide or diamond paste "boost" on the copper. You REALLY get polishing action then. Brass, aluminum and steel films work well, too, but you can't finger charge these hard metals. Use a diamond or oxide paste—and keep the water flow on top to a minimum..or, alternately, first use a basic wax coating technique (see page 233) and then finger charge the wax coating.

Master Gem Polishing

be ruinous because the disk might run dry momentarily or water suction lets go. The disks fold, crease or kink...and when that happens you might just as well throw them away. Furthermore they can lose their diamond charge...wear out quickly.

Also, the relatively slow polishing speed of both the coated diamond and metallic oxide plastic films has encouraged many lapidaries to "boost" their performance with diamond paste or special colloidal polishes. Given these "boosts," the polishing efficiency— speed and finish— is greatly enhanced.

The other great danger is the ever present problem of facet edge rounding. As already indicated, this isn't as big a problem as many gemcutters contend, especially with metal films. If mounted on a smooth base or fine grit lap, the hard base combines with the 3 or 4 mil film's thickness so that edge rounding is virtually eliminated—if the gemcutter doesn't press too hard during polishing or if the polishing period isn't excessively extended.

Fear of edge rounding is simply unjustified using standard technique with the harder, flatter thin metal disks.

Options With Metal Films...

If you'd like to test the use of thin metal polishing disks without making a particularly large investment, you have a couple of excellent options.

First—and the easiest—calls for making your own disks...and most of the following suggestions can produce abrasive and polishing benefits that are even superior to most commercially coated products.

A good strategy calls for applying a wax coat over the metal— this can also be done on plastic film disks—as a holder for the diamond on metallic oxide. Or, you can use an idea proposed originally by Hap Harris of Freeland, WA. Back in 1973, Harris published an article on how you can simply obtain some used 3 or 4 mil thick acetate or Mylar from a blueprint shop, scissor out an appropriately sized disk, load it up with diamond polishing paste, and mount the thin film lap directly onto the prepolishing lap.

Many gemcutters still approach thin film polishing by mounting slip disks atop the prepolishing lap as a ploy to avoid repeatability problems. The idea is as good today as it was when Harris first proposed it. As a matter of fact, in my book book, *Master Faceting*,

Master Gem Polishing

To apply an even wax coating on a thin metal disk, wet a rag or towel with furniture wax and apply it while the lap is turning about 150 rpm.

I describe how you can take a $1/2$-micron diamond coated thin film, "boost" it with 14,000 diamond paste, and then mount it permanently on the prepolishing lap for easy sanding plus polishing-finishing work. Besides a faster polish, the "boost" offers an additional benefit in that it will enable a faceter to touch up meet points while simultaneously proceeding toward the final polish.

Use Olive Oil for Suction...

Some gemcutters have shied away from the Harris and Wykoff idea because of the water factor in thin film use. Water has long been been the accepted primary suction or adhesion agent when thin Mylar or acetate film laps are attached to a base lap or a fine grit lap. Because of water it's difficult to use coarse grit laps as the base or holding lap because the large particles interfere with water suction with the result that the adhesion doesn't hold well.

If this is your complaint, don't use water. Use a thin film of olive oil instead. Olive oil does a much better holding job—and doesn't complicate polishing paste retention. Furthermore, olive oil's higher viscosity enables it to function much better than water when coarse surfaced laps are used as the base.

There are only three ways of holding thin film laps to a base

Master Gem Polishing

lap: adhesive, water or oil suction and lock down nut. First, you can attach them with spray adhesive. Commercial laps are available as PSA laps, with one side covered by a gummed adhesive. Second, you can use water or a thin film of olive oil to create a vacuum suction between the film and the base lap. Don't depend on a lock down nut to hold a film: the edges will spring up on you too easily.

If you question the application of thin polishing films, remember that the thin metal disks do avoid many problems of plastic films such as short working life, excessive cost, fragility and adhesion difficulties.

Gemcutters generally avoid adhesive backed films, contending with considerable justification that the adhesive contributes to a bumpy surface condition that promotes plowing *i.e.*, edge rounding, and can even dislodge a dopped stone.

That leaves the suction method. The need for copious amounts of water has always complicated the application of diamond pastes (which are usually water soluble) or metallic oxide powder slurries. For example, the colloidal polishing pastes sold by mAgi of Beavercreek, OR, don't want or need a continuous water drenching: they're already permanently wet. Ford tells users to avoid the drip on top: you don't need it for a positive polishing condition. As long as you have water—or preferably olive oil—underneath, between the film and the base lap the suction will hold. You can, of course, use colloidal pastes over a wax coat on metal or plastic laps...and that suggestion brings up a technology that has a long lapidary history.

Wax Coating...

The value of wax polishing laps for soft stones is well known. What isn't so well known or applied is the addition of a thin wax coat over a polishing surface so the polishing particles will have an agent into which they can embed. It's a proven strategy for improving polishing action.

Gemcutters who use Mehanite cast iron or Corian (plastic) polishing laps generally apply a carnauba wax coat. A thin wax coat has

Master Gem Polishing

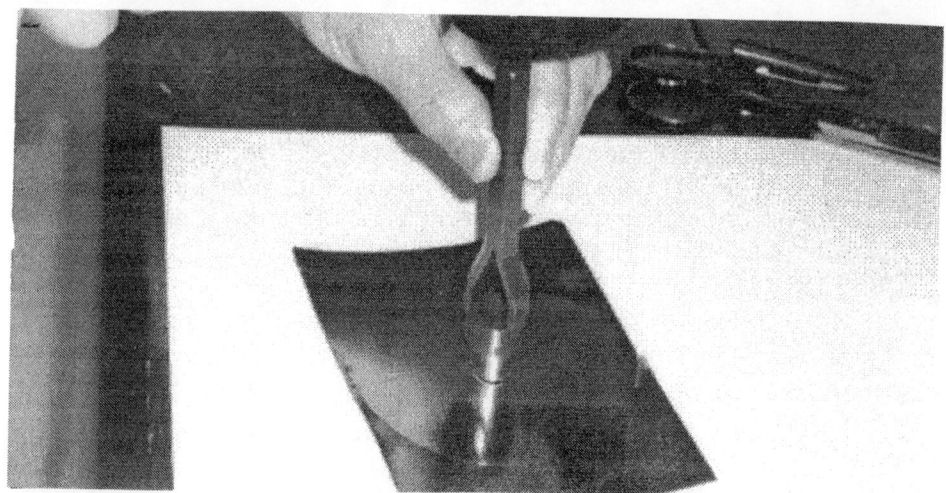

By careful measurement, a series of slip disks can be cut from a single section of thin metal. Sold by machine shop suppliers as shim material, thin metal sheets are generally sold in rolls.

even proven beneficial on tin or other metal type polishing laps.

Applying Wax to Corian...

From previous information you should already be familiar with the wipe-on technique for applying a thin carnauba wax coating to thin metal and plastic films.

Here's another technique for applying wax on polishing laps made of Corian plastic and which are sold by the Jarvi Manufacturing Company.

A Corian lap offers textures on each side, a grooved side and a smooth side. You can do either side but it's good procedure to charge the slightly grooved side with 14,000 diamond (when you wants to remove material, too) and the other side with either 14,000 or 50,000. Because a Corian lap is relatively soft, a polish even with 14,000 can be quite impressive.

Before using the Corian lap, though, its surface must be prepared with a thin layer of wax. **Note:** *Waxing a Corian lap isn't a must: the wax is helpful is all. Without wax the lap deteriorates rapidly.* There are all kinds of waxes, but the best is an ordinary non-cleaning type paste car wax (avoid the the cleaning type which has unwanted abra-

Master Gem Polishing

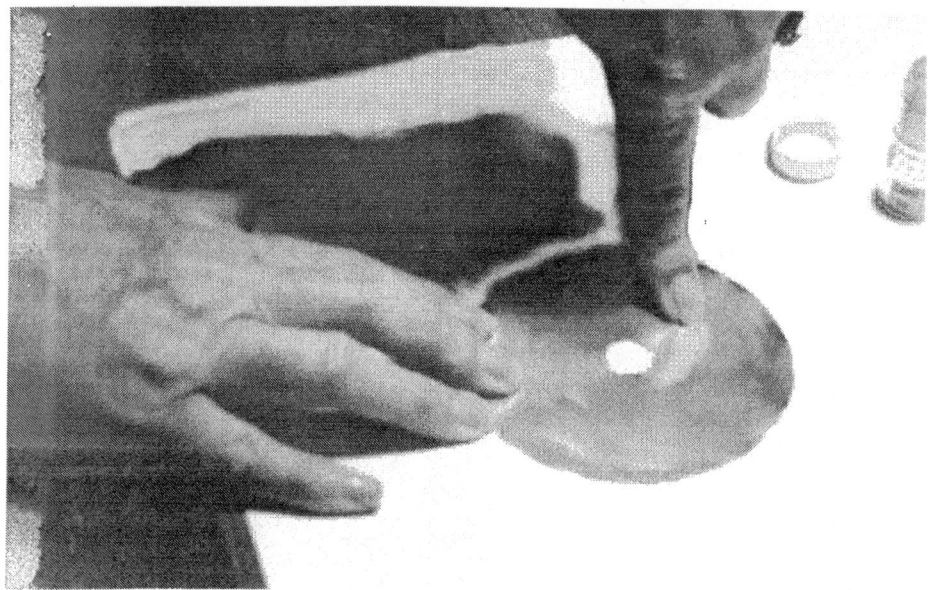

The advantage of a finger charged copper polishing film—or a wax coated hard metal film—lies in the lack of need for heavy water flow on the polishing surface. With copper and wax coated laps, use coolant water sparingly.

sives) works just fine. The method of charging is critical and a turning lap—similar to the Murphy method on film—is the key.

Clean the lap without scrubbing it (no scratches), then apply with a wax saturated clean rag, applying in a light coat as the lap turning slowly and constantly. Allow it to dry and then lightly buff it. Let it sit awhile to mature and then apply another coat. Again, buff the coat. Don't work at the buffing too hard, just enough to get the bulk of the wax off. After the first charge, wax can later be added to the lap and buffed off without cleaning off the old diamond.

As with any wax application, if you get it on too thick, it encourages the diamond particles to ball up and produce scratches.

At this juncture, with the lap mounted on the machine, apply 5 to 10 pinheads of diamond powder around the lap along with a very few drops of water. Don't make the mistake of thinking that more diamond produces greater polishing action. It doesn't. Too much diamond will produce scratches so keep your charge to a minimum amount. **Note:** *Also, do not use spray diamond on a wax sur-*

face. The chemicals in the spray tend to melt wax.

As with copper films, finger spread the diamond dust into a more or less uniform layer. At least for the first charge (only) with diamond, run the lap at slow speed and lightly burnish in the diamond particles with a smooth stone.

Diamond particles work their way into the lap's grooves while other dust rides on the lap surface...so keep the water flow MINIMUM. Try spraying water on rather than use the drip. Some cautions about using a wax coated Corian—and other—polishing laps:

- ✔ don't run the lap dry (it'll ruin the wax coating rapidly!)
- ✔ keep the stone moving (wax wears out quickly otherwise)
- ✔ slow rpm is probably best...but use your own speed
- ✔ be wary of pressure (Corian AND wax are soft) especially when introducing sharp edges or non flat-to-flat situations
- ✔ don't expect a fast polish: it often takes minutes to finish

Diamond Powders Effective...

As a way of summarizing here all the previous information on thin metal and thin plastic and Corian laps, for gemcutters preferring to fine polish with diamond, you can use 50,000 or finer powdered grits on a wax-filmed lap. As already indicated, for a standard commercial finish on your stones, you get a faster and an equally good quality polish with 14,000 particles. As always when finger charging diamond powder, the recommended technique is to massage in the diamond with a CLEAN finger tip. Don't press hard: it isn't necessary. Just gently massage the diamond particles into the wax...the same as if you would if you were charging bare copper. Burnish LIGHTLY a diamond charge on wax with a smooth stone.

Now you have a permanently coated thin metal or thin plastic or Corian lap (all will occasionally need a bit of a "boost") and which can accept a water drip without dire effects.

Most gemcutters apply the oxide and diamond polish to the frosted side of plastic film, realizing that the smooth side will work just as well. As earlier indicated, plastic films are often sold in rolls and one side is left rough so the rolls can more easily be unrolled. Thin metal can be purchased in rolls or in flat sheets.

Following the advice that in polishing, hard laps work best

Master Gem Polishing

with hard stones and soft laps work best with soft stones, here is a list of the various polishing materials used for making polishing laps. This compiled list comes from a variety of sources:

LAP MATERIALS

Lap Material	Mohs	Components
Ceramic	9.0	Aluminum oxide
Anodized alum.	6.5	electrolytic coat
Mehanite* Iron	5.0	porous cast iron
Corian*	4.0	methyl methacrylate plastic
Phenolic	3.5	benzene derived plastic
Copper	3.0	pure rolled copper
Zinc	2.5	pure zinc
Plexiglas*(Lucite*)	2.0	acrylic plastic
Type metal	2.0	lead, tin, antimony/copper
Tin/lead	2.0	lead & tin 50%-50%
Pewter	2.0	lead, tin, other variables
Metallized Resin	1.9	metal pellets/plastic
Tin/type metal	1.8	variable percentages
Tin	1.7	pure tin
Mylar*	1.6	polyester plastic
Acetate*	1.6	cellulose derived
Lead	1.5	pure lead
Polyurethane	1.5	high porosity plastic
Vinyl	1.0	ethylene derived plastic
Beeswax/carnauba	0.3	90% beeswax, carnauba
Beeswax	0.2	pure beeswax

   * trademark owned by General Electric
  ** a cast plastic of about 78 Durometer hardness which is useful in lapidary because of its porosity. Fumes are toxic.
 *** various ceramic compositions are possible, but for lapidary use the surface porosity is important.

Master Gem Polishing

The 14,000 Lap: Sanding and Polishing at the Same Time...

So your work bench looks messy at times, does it? Especially when you are into production polishing of small cabs as well as perhaps finishing the tables on several round brilliants.

As usual with polishing, things don't always go that well. In addition, maybe a few words described as sulfurous, do escape your lips from time to time. When faced with a production run, sanding and then polishing individual stones in separate steps often isn't the most prudent course to follow.

The cabochon cutter can manage this operation rather well. S/he is usually hand holding the dopped stone and can move quickly and easily from the prepolishing wheel to the polishing pad. Most cabochon machines anyway are set up to allow the gemcutter an easy sequence from sanding to polishing. It's just a matter of moving over to another wheel.

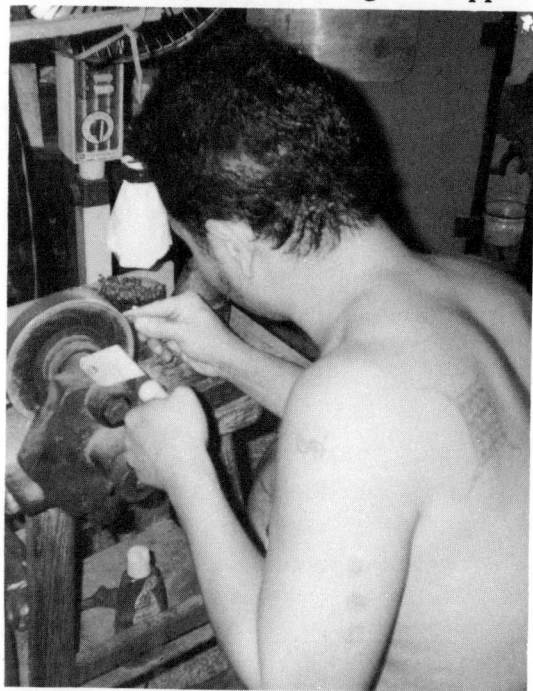

In the Far East, the gem is preformed by hand exactly and then 14,000 diamond grit is used to trim up facets and apply polish simulitaneously.

It's not that easy in faceting, largely because of the need to change wheels. Hence a serious repeatability problem often exists. Too many faceters will carefully prepolish the table on each stone in a 45 degree dop. Then they'll remove each dopped stone from the dop and proceed to the next stone. Next, often as not, they'll change the lap set up and commence polishing each stone sequentially...after adjusting the machine for any thickness differential. Ten stones represent 30 or more repeatability challenges since there'll inevitably be minute differences in each stone or setup.

The Taiwan polishing factories don't look at it this way. All tables are prepolished in a single operation and are then polished one after the other in a separate operation. The traditional resolution of this challenge rested with an adjustable collet wherein each dop stick's extension from the quill could be adjusted. That ploy takes care of slight height differences, not perfectly but effectively.

In the paragraphs that immediately follow, you'll see a considerable emphasis on 14,000 diamond grit. Don't be upset about this obvious bias. Throughout most of the world, 14,000 grit is considered the polish of choice. It will by itself impart a commercially acceptable polish on virtually any gemstone. When added as a complement to other polishes, it allows a gemcutter to "touch up" the stone, refine meet points and generally improve the appearance of the cut while polishing at the same time. You've already read how the small sapphire faceters in Bangkok use 14,000 grit to produce upwards of 200 finished stones per day per cutter.

Better Options Exist...

There are equally efficient ways to achieve polishing production. For example, if you're faced with the task of polishing a number of fractional sized quartz or beryl or topaz stones it's not all that hard to set up an operation. For a one-at-a-time procedure, a simple piece of 3- or 4-mil thick copper polishing film impregnated with 14,000 diamond grit or coated with an oxide powder or colloidal paste, is perfect to accommodate this kind of situation. For an interesting polishing experiment, try charging a copper film disk with 50,000 diamond grit and then adding a pinch or two of 14,000 diamond. This is the same principle that I reported on earlier in my book, *Master Faceting*—except that here you're substituting a copper disk for a commercially charged film— and the copper alternatives works exceptionally well for polishing and light touchups. If you want faster polishing action or don't wish to take the time to buy the thin metal film and scissor out a series of slip or full-sized disks, use one of the pre-coated diamond or oxide Ultralaps™.

If using an 8-inch prepolishing lap on the machine, you can slip a 6-inch thin film disk treated with 14,000 diamond or chemical

Master Gem Polishing

oxide—making certain there's olive oil or water between the thin film and the prepolishing lap. That will leave a nice 2-inch wide working ring on the outer perimeter of the prepolishing lap which frees up plenty of room to work on a table facet.

Using diamond impregnated thin, metal laps poses little if any edge rounding problems for stones regardless of their relative hardness.

This procedure represents a good production method to finish each stone in order. When you've completed the prepolishing in each tier of facets, click up a few steps to achieve a flat-to-flat match on the polishing film. The stone should lay flat on the polishing disk without any further machine adjustment. Doing it this way won't require that you remove the dopstick or make serious mast height changes each time you face an operational change. When you've polished the facet(s), click back down and finish up the next stone. With the minimal thickness of the metal film disk, you know you're about 2-3 clicks up on the vertical cheat from the 1200 prepolishing lap. Also, applying a few pea-sized dots of 14,000 paste on a $1/2$-micron diamond coated Ultralap™ will accelerate the polishing action. Indeed, many faceters use this technique for the entire stone, polishing individual facets or finishing up rows before proceeding to the next cutting step. **Note:** *Remember to wipe and/or clean off a facet before moving from a prepolishing grit to the polishing lap to avoid contamination.*

The method is simple enough and it's used by many gemcutters—both in faceting and in cabochon cutting. When you're working with tricky polished girdles you want to be able to get a polish on them with minimum searching. By drifting in the cuts on a fine lap and then using a tiny vertical cheat to accommodate the polishing lap, you take a lot of the guesswork out of repeating the setups.

The only limits on this kind of technique is how far do you want to move the vertical hold to get a polishing flat-to-flat position for the inside lap. It's not all that difficult to do even with a thin film coated with chemical polish and also "boosted" with a shot or two of 14,000 paste. You don't have to "boost," of course, but it makes for faster production. Plus the 14,000 gives abrasive assis-

Master Gem Polishing

tance for drifting in meet points. For harder stones, 50,000 or even 100,000 diamond grit works for the primary coating on the film ...although 14,000 accelerates an embedded 50,000 grit action

If faceting fractional sized stones or well done preforms, try an 1/8" or 3/16" thick anodized aluminum with 14,000 diamond grit for truly rapid finishing of even hard stones.

Truth is, you don't need to restrict yourself to thin metal or plastic film disks. You can put just about any 6-inch lap over an 8-inch lap—or a 3-inch or 4-inch film over a 6-inch wheel—and obtain the same potential. It's just that with other lap materials the thickness may be a bit greater so you'll have repeatability problems.

Following are some lap combination experiments with your laps. Some will work fine for you and a few may perhaps leave something to be desired...but here they are for your consideration:

Experiment #1—put a 1/16" or 1/8" thick anodized aluminum slip disk lap smeared lightly with 14,000 diamond paste atop a standard 260 lap. The aluminum lap may be a bit thicker than thin films but it doesn't need water or olive oil to hold it to the base lap. With loose diamond grit on the hard anodized surface, you have a whiz of a one-step lap for grinding and finishing with 14,000 diamond grit.

Experiment #2—for cabbing, place a Pellon disk (the harder plastic-like Pellon, not the soft type used by clothiers: the softer type

Master Gem Polishing

is useless in lapidary) atop the prepolishing lap. You must shift up only a bit higher here. Because of the thicker Pellon but as long as you can predict the difference and don't need to make fundamental changes you could be ahead on time and accuracy. If you use colloidal silica as a "booster" on Pellon lap, you have a promising polishing combination. Try it: it works. Incidentally, even hard Pellon is a relatively soft, thick material so you definitely have an edge rounding danger : I suggest using Pellon on cabs or table facets only.

Experiment #3—for something new in a sanding-polishing lap setup, place a thin copper slip disk finger charged with 1200 grit atop a standard 260 grit lap and finish up all your coarse grinding and prepolish sanding in a single operation. You rough grind with the 260 on the outside rim and then, with a couple of clicks up of cheat, pre-polish on the 1200 grit lap. When it's time to polish, you switch slip disks,

Now many gemcutters may say this is a poor man's variation on Crystallite's DMD™ two-grit faceting lap. That's true...and it's considerably less expensive, too. Of course, if you can afford it, the fine Crystalite lap is the way to go. Still, with thin metal laps, if you do perchance get one contaminated you can inexpensively replace it. That's why making an on-the-spot two-tone lap setup is more convenient and flexible...and it finishes up your sanding and polishing chores with little fuss.

Avoid Contamination With Overlay Laps...

The one-lap setups—intended to perform two cutting functions without a significant machine change—using the thin copper or plastic slip disks suggested earlier significantly minimizes contamination problems. Perhaps it is because the finer copper lap surface always remains 2-3 clicks above the coarse base lap. Regardless, before proceeding to a finer lap wipe the stone carefully. If faceting, just cut the main facets in, wipe them off, move the stone up the required distance and finish off quickly on the finger lap. Keep repeating this back and forth sequence for the other rows or tiers.

One thing you'll find out: with a little judicious and original thinking, a lot of the lap changing and setting duplications can be very effectively eliminated...with no appreciable loss in the quality of the cutting or polishing. It's a proven fact, that using two-mesh laps in your gemcutting can reduce repeatability problems. The danger of contamination is minimal, too, so long as you wipe off the stone between steps.

Proper Illumination Vital For Best Polishing Results

The gemologist's microscope can be a critical instrument for gemcutters, too. There are few better ways to evaluate the progress of a delicate polishing task than to review the work through lens that will reveal a stone's secrets. As helpful as a good microscope can be, though, just turning on the lamp and looking at a stone's partially completed surface or a finished gemstone isn't all there is to it.

Depending on what information you seek from the illuminated view, you could be using the wrong type of lighting. When that happens, chances are you don't stand a chance of gaining a good view. Magnification is helpful: properly illuminated magnification is vital.

As any experienced gemcutter or gemologist knows, the principle obstacle encountered when attempting to illuminate any gemstone lies in the significant proportion of the light that reflects back from the stone's surface.

Incident light isn't enough. Such light can be very useful in some circumstances, particularly when assisted by a pair of eyes capable of challenging the prowess of a hungry, young hawk. In the absence of such a remarkable physical attribute as gifted vision, most gemcutters must fall back on old owl tactics.

Use Proper Lighting...

In the face of imposing difficulty, it goes without saying that knowing the type of lighting setup to get the best viewing results is of paramount importance. This realistic approach is infinitely superior to attempting feats requiring superhuman vision. All the squinting in the world probably won't detect striae in colored glass or flame fusion corundum. But an application of *diffused transillumination* will do the trick just about every time. All you need is a light source such as a flashlight or strong penlight, a frosted piece of glass or

Master Gem Polishing

plastic and a 5x or more magnifier.

What is *diffused transillumination*? Well, it's nothing more than holding your specimen over a frosted piece of glass or plastic and shining a strong flashlight or penlight up through the glass so the light goes through the glass, through the specimen and into your eyes (hopefully, you'll have a magnifier of some power to get a better view of the innards of that specimen).

Every gemcutter should develop some knowledge of different lighting techniques. They'll come in handy

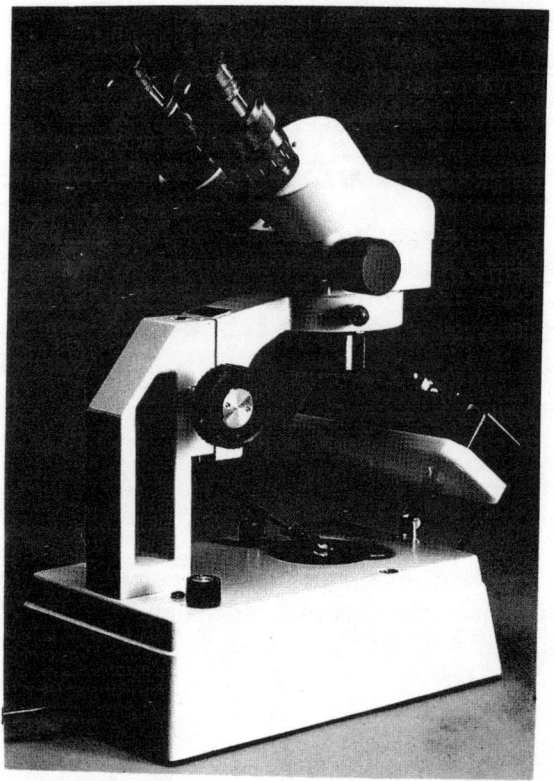

when viewing a piece of rough or to check progress on cutting. The challenge is to ferret out as many potentially troublesome secrets— or optical qualities with the potential to enhance— as the specimen has to offer.

When you view a piece of mineral or polished gem crystal with appropriate lighting techniques you open up your inspection to many of the gemological quirks of the specimen. Most of these quirks wouldn't even come to your attention with improper viewing *i.e.*, illumination.

For example, let's say you want to view carefully the emerging

Master Gem Polishing

polish on some turquoise and tourmaline. It's important to know if there are any flaws or imperfections or crystallographic conditions that would involve your polishing decisions.

When you have two different kinds of stones, such as tourmaline or turquoise, would you illuminate both specimens in the same way? Of course, not. To properly view the polished surface of opaque turquoise you would want to use incident lighting possibly assisted with fiber optic illumination...with magnification. For a transparent stone, you might need to utilize a whole series of lighting illumination techniques such as dark field, light field, crossed polars, diffusion, diffusion with immersion, etc.

The Microscope...

Most microscopes feature built-in means of illuminating a specimen on the stage. It can be as basic as a lamp under the stage and a diffuser plate, sometimes with an iris mechanism that allows variation of the illuminated area.

More expensive models provide for selectivity of lighting types. These would include incident, light field and dark-field illumination. The latter two types are contained beneath the stage. As most gemologists know, *light-field illumination* consists in transmitting light up through the specimen and into the microscope's objective. For *dark-field illumination,* a dark (usually black) baffle plate pivots over the lamp (incandescent), blocking the direct light path to the specimen and the objective. Light instead is directed into the sides of the specimen through the use of substage mirrors. *Incident illumination* is provided by a separate lamp (often a color-corrected fluorescent lamp which can simulate "northern light) which is fitted with a reflector or lens to provide focus.

In recent years, gemcutters have opted for the pin-point lighting benefits that fiber-optics offer. In normal large-area incident illumination, a great deal of the light is reflected back from the stone's surface. This abundance of backscattered light can often confuse and disguise conditions that a viewer is looking for.

By attaching a fiber-optic light-guide probe to a lamp source, a gemcutter can inject a small-diameter high-intensity beam into the stone with minimum backscatter of light.

From the foregoing, it becomes obvious that proper microscope use and illumination involves five major areas. These are:

Master Gem Polishing

    1. *Focus*—is the microscope focused properly on the proper area?
    2. *Magnification*—is magnification appropriate for viewing the desired condition?
    3. *Orientation*—depending on the direction from which light will strike it, is the stone situated properly so the desired viewing objective can be realized?
    4. *Control of light source*—for best viewing, is the light coming from the proper direction so as to illuminate the specimen properly?
    5. *Character of illumination*—is an incandescent or fluorescent lighting source best for the viewing objective and will the light be diffused, reflected or direct?

Using "Shadow Technique...

To increase the contrast between a host crystal and inclu-

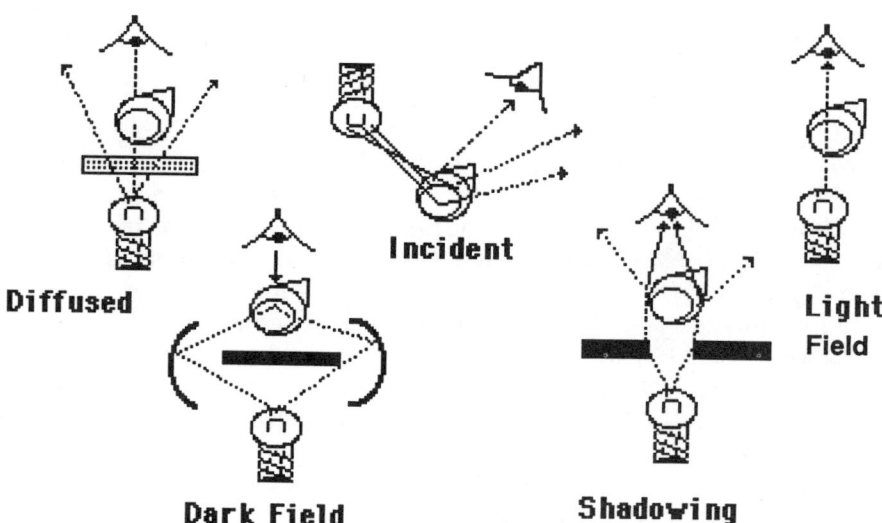

Subtle strategies in light control differentiate shadowing techniques from dark-field and light-field illumination. It's helpful to know the difference between the basic lighting types—some of which can be improved with new fiber-optic attachments.

sions, a technique known as "shadowing" is often employed. The shadowing technique calls for the use of an opaque black light shield introduced between the light source and the specimen. An iris control restricts the area of illumination.

Should inclusions, though, have a different RI than the host crystal, the diffraction *i.e.*, scattering of light rays on the edges of an object, can be used to enhance the contrast. When scattered light rays run through a specimen, some of the rays are reflected when they strike an inclusion having a different optical density. These rays cause a darkening of that area while the light that is reflected into the microscope lens appears light. The overall effect is to enhance the contrast of the inclusion, making it easier to see and evaluate. This same tendency holds true when viewing polished and unpolished areas *e.g.*, optical density produces a visible contrast.

It may appear that dark-field illumination and shadowing are identical. This is not true. Both techniques do utilize a plate between the lamp source and the specimen but the difference appears in how the light is handled. With dark-field illumination, the light is diverted from its source to side mirrors so that it will be reflected into the sides of the specimen. In shadowing effect, light diffraction on the edges of the baffle plate send scattered light through the specimen. Thus it will reflect off inclusions and crystal so that the contrast becomes highly visible when viewed through a microscope. Mirrors aren't needed to direct light in shadowing.

Dark-field illumination is a major requirement for gem-

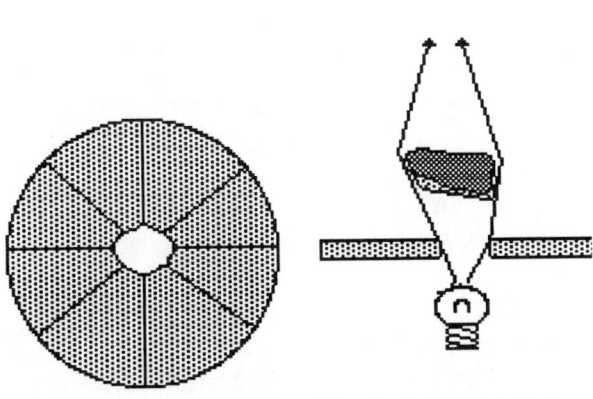

Iris controls light for "shadowing" ∀ mirror reflections in dark field (r.)

The iris controls the aperture size and thus the area of illumination for the "shadowing" effect produced as light rays scatter on the object's edges.

ological and gem cutting work because it makes a gemstone stone's internal features (inclusions plus stress flaws, etc.) more clearly visible against the darker background of the baffle plate under the stone specimen.

Shadowing technique is useful for developing higher contrast for inclusions as they appear in the microscope. Unlike dark-field illumination where the crystal is merely held in place over the baffle plate, shadowing is achieved by using transmitted light and inserting an opaque shield of appropriate shape and dimensions between the light source and the specimen.

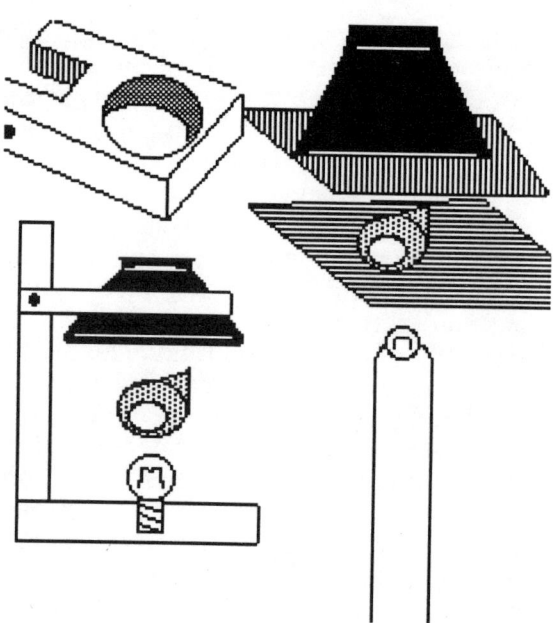

To make a simple polariscope, insert a pair of crossed polarizers between the penlight and a magnifier. At left, is a self-made viewing stand for holding an ordinary loupe.

The shield is slowly moved across the field of view until shadowing begins to take place and the inclusions under inspection appears to stand out in sharp contrast to the background of the stone.

Light-Field Illumination...

When a gemcutter wishes to inspect polish and color variations in a gem crystal, it's best to use diffused light-field illumination. In this instance, light is transmitted from the source up through a light diffuser and then through the specimen and into the microscope's objective. What's important in light-field viewing is having the entire specimen bathed in diffused, even light.

The disappearance act that occurs when a transparent crystal is immersed in a heavy liquid whose refractive index is close to or the same as the crystal is nothing new to most gemcutters. For years,

Master Gem Polishing

it's been an accepted technique for inspecting gem rough for inclusions. The light rays will pass through the liquid and the same RI crystal without interference—until they do strike something—an included crystal, fracture, veil, imperfection, etc.— with a different RI. When this happens, the stranger stands out in the clear liquid as if X-rayed. This same phenomenon can be put to good use in an illuminated dispersion cell.

As indicated earlier, the major problem encountered when illuminating a gemstone is that a significant proportion of the light is reflected or scattered back from the surface. All the scattered light often makes it particularly difficult, if not impossible, to light and inspect the interior of a faceted stone. One effective technique to prevent the scattered light being reflected back is to immerse the stone in a heavy RI liquid. Instead of back reflections, the light rays enter the stone and illuminate its interior.

Because a gemcutter is usually more interested in immersion functions of a microscope, it might prove preferable to obtain the special microscopes that are built primarily for immersion work. These instruments are designed so that the light path into the objective is horizontal. Such a configuration allows the stone holder to be inserted vertically from the top into the immersion cell. With conventional upright microscopes, the height of the cell is limited to allow for the introduction of tweezers to hold stones.

Of what value is an immersion cell and microscope? Of course, the combination represents the best technique there is for locating and evaluating defects in a finished or a rough gemstone specimen. Anything that interferes with the uninterrupted flow of light waves—such as polish—will become evident to the viewer.

Not only does this technique unveil inclusions and blemishes, but it also represents the best way to determine if any enhancement work has been performed on a stone. Laser drilling tunnels jump out quickly, and filling of gletzes becomes highly evident. Even diffused sapphires and rubies give up their true identity when an immersion cell filled with heavy RI liquid becomes filled with transmitted light.

Many microscopes are manufactured with a design that lends itself to modular construction. That is, various optical heads, stands, sources of illumination and accessories may be added or used interchangeably. This enables microscopes to be set up so as to meet the needs of various applications.

Among the numerous accessories that can be added to a contemporary microscope are polarizing filters, color and neutral density filters, cameras and video attachments, tracing attachments and projection screens.

Crossed filters on a microscope offers all the benefits of a regular polariscope—plus more controllable lighting and magnification. A microscope can be converted for polariscope analysis by inserting one filter (as a polarizer) between the light source and the specimen and attaching a second filter (as an analyser) to the objective.

By setting the two filters to the extinction position, the setup will reveal internal stresses (that's another way for saying anomalous birefringence), single or double refraction as well as distinguishing between microcrystalline or polycrystalline structures in a gem.

Incidentally, if the polarizer filter is removed the remaining one on the objective can be used to check for dichroism, or for enhancing the visibility of inclusions.

It should be apparent that a good microscope takes the place of a number of other rather expensive gemological instruments. When a microscope is properly equipped, it can be used to:

1. examine the interior of gemstones for inclusions or growth features which identify the gemstone as natural or synthetic
2. inspect the surface of gemstones to assess the quality of cut and finish
3. detect dichroism (using a polarizer filter on the objective)
4. detect double refraction using two polarizing filters as polarizer and analyser

Using Small Magnifier...

For gemcutters reluctant to spend upwards of $1,000 or more for a serviceable gemological microscope, the small hand loupes offer an effective, inexpensive alternative.

The ideal magnification for a gemcutter remains 10x. Seldom will there be a valid need for much more magnification than this because 10x is sufficiently powerful to reveal the majority of gemstone internal and external secrets...including evidence of diffusion treatments.

Master Gem Polishing

By striving for greater magnification, say 25x, you should realize that a hand loupe this powerful would have a very, very critical focus and a limited field of view. Further, the working distance (the distance between the lens and the specimen) would be very short, limiting your ability to maneuver stones, filters, lights, etc.

A single lens loupe is quite sufficient for checking cutting and polish progress, meet points or edges on a faceted stone as well as on a cab. It will prove particularly useful for inspecting for edge crumbling and abrasions. If you wish to use your loupe for gemstone analysis, too, be sure to obtain a loupe that has been corrected for spherical aberration (image distortion) and chromatic aberration (color fringes). High quality loupes are usually referred to as "triplets" because they consist of a three lens elements.

To avoid eye fatigue if you do a lot of louping, get in the habit of keeping the nonwork-ing eye open while you look with the other eye.

Conventional lenses focus blue light more strongly than red light: this phenomenon is known as chromatic aberration. The strong curves in such lenses also cause the focus of rays passing through the edges to lie in a slightly different plane to those which pass through the central area of the lens. In both cases, multiple lens elements are necessary to correct the aberrations. When a lens system has been corrected for both spherical and chromatic aberration, it is called an "apochromatic" lens.

Initially you may experience some difficulty juggling the gemstone, a hand lens and your head, keeping them all steady and in the correct alignment so as to maintain focus. To avoid eye fatigue if you do a lot of looking with the loupe, get in the habit of keeping the non-working eye open while you look with the other eye. It serves no useful purpose to squint one eye while using a loupe—and such a habit is indicative of the amateur.

For advanced gemological use, get one of the hand lenses that has been combined with a battery-powered light source. Alpha of Bremerton, WA, and Edmund Scientific of Barrington, NJ, both carry these type of instruments. They not only provide you with incident (top-reflected) but also dark-field illumination.

One gemcutter cut a 3/4" hole in a section of wood and

Master Gem Polishing

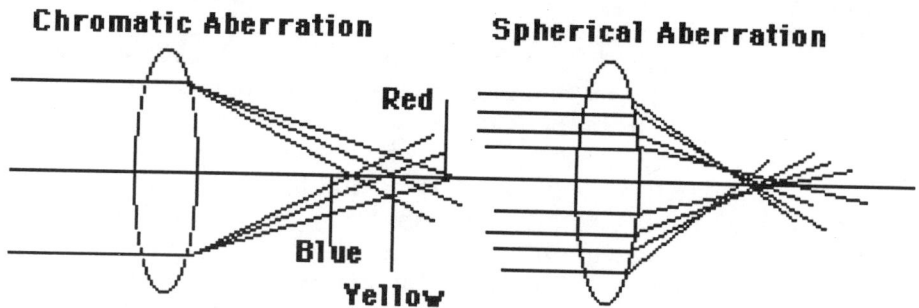

It doesn't cost all that much extra to buy an apochromatic lens for use in louping gemstones. Because accuracy in polishing is vital, chromatic and spherical aberrations can give you false readings.

propped the barrel of his hand loupe in the block. Mounting the loupe to a firm, free standing structure, he was free with both hands to manipulate his accessories.

It's natural to feel that you can hand hold a piece of rough or a gem. The best advice here is to obtain a stone holder. Once the specimen is firmly gripped, the holder can easily be turned and twisted without danger of losing the stone.

Can a hand loupe be rigged to provide a polariscope function? Of course it can. Just attach a piece of polarizing material over the light and another one under the magnifier. Set them to the extinction position and the setup will allow you to perform any test that is normally conducted with a polariscope.

Setting up for a cell immersion is rather difficult with hand loupes. The small magnifiers have a depth of field limitation which makes it difficult to get a good view on a specimen that is inside a cell. It can be done, of course, but you must really hunch down to get a view while keeping the stone holder, the light barrel and the cell itself from interfering.

With all loupes, the correct illumination of the stone specimen under inspection plays a vital role. Adjust the lamp used to illuminate the stone so light angles into the side of the stone, not directly into the eyes. Any internal features of the gem will then appear bright and visible against the darker background of the stone.

Whether you use a formal gemological microscope or innovate with a hand held loupe, proper illumination and magnification can make the vital area of specimen analysis much easier and accu-

TABLE FOR DETERMINATION OF LIGHTING METHODS WHEN VIEWING GEMSTONES

Subject	Lighting Technique
Striae in glass	diffused transillumination
Doublet bubbles	darkfield, diffusion
Color banding	brightfield, diffusion
Colorless included crystals	crossed polars, brightfield
Synthetics	
color banding	diffusion + immersion
incl. xstals	crossed polars
flux filling	darkfield
fingerprints	darkfield
Verneuil	
curved striae	brightfield, diffusion
Soudé emerald (glass)	darkfield, immersion
spinel triple	immersion w/ diffusion through the girdle
Ruby	
inclusions	darkfield
twinning	crossed polars
oiled	fiber optic
surface repair	fiber optic, immersion
Sapphire	
color banding	diffusion w/ immersion
incl. xstals	darkfield
diffusion	immersion cell
colorless xstals	crossed polars
Emerald	
(natural) veils	darkfield
3-phase incl.	darkfield
colorless xstals	crossed polars (stay bright when host is dark)
negative xstals	darkfield
oiled	diffusion (shows yellow dried oil on cracks)
Diamond	
surface features	fiber optic
opaque incl	darkfield, immersion
colorless xstals	immersion
surface repair	fiber optic, immersion
lasering	darkfield

Definitions For Terms Used in Lighting Method Table

Diffused transillumination=viewing a specimen with light that passes through the specimen after it has first passed evenly through a diffusion screen

Incident Light=generally a color-corrected light source which is directed on the surface of a specimen (see also Fiber Optic). Incident illumination is often provided from a lamp (or lamps) fitted with a reflector or lens so as to provide a focusable spot.

darkfield=viewing a specimen against a dark background while it is illuminated by reflected light from a concealed lamp

brightfield=viewing a specimen with unshielded light that is directed from the rear of the specimen and applied evenly through a diffusion system

*immersion**=coating or immersing the specimen in a comparable RI liquid for viewing:

*immersion cell**=placing the specimen in a cell containing high RI liquid and illuminating the specimen with diffused lighting.

crossed polars=viewing a specimen through a polariscope when the instrument's lens are crossed so minimum light is transmitted

fiber optic=a glass-like plastic tube capable of transmitting a strong, concentrated pin pointed incident light from a separate lamp source.

diffusion=light is diffused when it is transmitted through a frosted or translucent lens

reflected light=viewing a specimen when incident light is reflected away from the view.

* common RI immersion liquids include:

Liquid	RI
♣ water	1.33
♣ alcohol	1.36
♣ turpentine	1.47
♣ glycerine	1.47
♣ toluene	1.49
♣ Bromoform	1.59
♣ Carbon Disulfide	1.63
♣ methylene iodide	1.74

rate. It's been said that the actual cutting of the gem represents the least challenging aspect of cabbing and faceting. The real challenge of the mineral itself poses the most exciting challenge...getting the most out any piece of gemstone—whether transparent, translucent or opaque—that arrives in front of you.

THE END

Appendix

Appendix 1

List of Useful Lapidary Suppliers

Following is the contact information for some of the top quality mail order suppliers in lapidary. Please keep in mind that this list is subject to changes (moving, going out of business, name change, etc.)

Polish, Laps, Rough

For an exclusive line of colloidal oxide polishing pastes, thin metal polishing film, colloidal silica, Ultralap™ materials and gem rough

>mAgi
>Attn: Rick Ford
>PO Box 426
>Beavercreek, OR 97004
>1-503-632-3653

Faceting Machines

Also a good source for Mehanite and Corian laps, plus other lapidary tools and implements:

>Jarvi Manufacturing Company
>Attn: Norman Jarvi
>780 Debra Lane
>Anaheim, CA 92805
>1-714-774-9104

(The Jarvi company manufacturers the Facetron faceting machine.)

For top quality faceting machines and equipment:

>Poly Metric Company
>Attn: Douglas Hoffman
>PO Box 400 (Spokane st)
>Clayton, WA 99110
>1-509-276-5565)

(Poly M manufactures the OMF (curved facets) cutting unit, plus the Scintillator 88 Dial, Scintillator 88 Digital and the Xstal-Tek 87 faceing machines)

MDR
Attn: Robert Livingston
PO Box 6951
Kingwood, TX 77325
1-713-358-3027

(MDR has re-introduced the modernized variation of this famous faceting machine.)

Dyna Systems Ltd.
Attn: Peter Dyna
505 E. 46th st.
Boise, ID 83714
1-208-375-8854

(Dyna manufacturers the 6" Simplex 6 faceting machine.)

Rough Gemstone Supplies

This company specializes in fine quality rough for both faceting and cabbing. Ulatowski and his associate, John Garsow, are both experienced gemcutters and extremely knowledgeable about gem materials and appropriate lapidary techniques:

New Era Gems
Attn: Steve Ulatowsky
14923 Rattlesnake rd
Grass Valley, CA 95945

Proprietor Rick Ford specializes in Montana sapphire rough and other fine rough. He's also a good resource for cutting information on these fine stones:

mAgi
Attn: Rick Ford
PO Box 426
Beavercreek, OR 97004
1-503-632-3653

General purpose lapidary supplies

This company offers a fine catalog listing the full range of lapidary and gemological tools and supplies

Alpha Supply Inc.
Attn: Jim Bryant
PO Box 2133
Bremerton, WA 98310

Australian opal

This is a direct-from-the-mine source. The proprietor, Murray Willis, is a true miner. He goes regularly to Lightening Ridge, Andamooka and other famous Australian mines to replenish his supply of fine opals. When you deal with Murray, you deal with a bona fide Australian opal miner.

> Australian Opal Mines
> Attn: Murray Willis
> Box 345
> P/O Magill, 5072
>   South Australia

Cabochon equipment

> Contempo Lapidary
> 9175 San Fernando rd
> Sun Valley, CA 91355
> 1-818-768-2800

Gemcutting Information

For information about the activities of American gemcutters and gemcutting:

> American Society of Gemcutters
> Attn: Gerald Wykoff
> PO Box 1991
> York, PA 17403

Laps, Wheels

For a complete line of quality diamond products

> Crystalite Corporation
> 8400 Green Meadows dr
> Westerville, OH 43081
> 1-800-777-2894

For a complete line of inexpensive resin based diamond impregnated grinding and polishing wheels:

> Dyna Systems Ltd.
> Attn: Peter Dyna

505 E. 46th st.
Boise, ID 83714
1-208-375-8854

The exclusive supplier of Mehanite cast iron laps, Corian (plastic) laps...as well as other lapidary and some jewelery bench supplies

Jarvi Manufacturing Company
Attn: Norman Jarvi
780 Debra Lane
Anaheim, CA 92805
1-714-774-9104

Appendix 2

Descriptions of Materials Used in Polishing Gemstones

ALUMINA, ALUMINUM OXIDE—A pure white crystalline powder, whose hexagonal shaped particles are useful in lapidary. An isometric form is also manufactured but it does not polish minerals well.
MP = 2040° C.
H = $90^1/_2$
Brittle, hard, insoluble in acids, it is prepared chemically from various aluminum compounds or from synthetic corundum. Can be used as abrasive or polishing agent. Natural corundum has largely been superseded by synthetic corundum under trade names LINDE A (hexagonal type) and LINDE B (cubic type).

BORON CARBIDE—A super abrasive consisting of hard, brittle rhombohedral shaped black crystals
H = $9^1/_2$
MP = 2,350° C.
BC's brittleness becomes a problem for polishing short fibered minerals: works best with long fibered materials found in metals. As lapping compound, it is superb with all medium to very hard stones and serves quite well for prepolishing.

BORON NITRIDE—a man-made superabrasive of cubic shape that is made by the same process as synthetic diamond. CBN is nearly as hard as diamond.

BRASS—a useful, harder alloy for lapping with loose grit and for polishing very hard gems (corundum, chrysoberyl, spinel) with diamond. Faceters use it to for standard base laps as well as for slip-laps.

BRONZE—phosphor bronze is often used interchangeably with brass. It's a bit harder metal.

CANVAS—A touch and long lasting tightly woven cotton fabric, canvas is a useful polishing carrier with diamond grit and metallic oxide polishes. It functions best when stretched tight over a hard base lap or a convex bowl-like wooden lap so the material can stretch to accommodate rounded surfaces.

CARBORUNDUM—this is the trade name for silicon carbide, owned by the Carborundum Company.

CARNAUBA WAX—a hard Brazilian palm wax which is quite useful for providing a coating that will hold diamond or alumina on cast iron and plastic laps. Ordinary furniture wax represents a good, inexpensive source of carnauba wax.

CAST IRON—a hard, porous metal—Mehanite is a trade name owned by General Electric Company for its special type of porous cast iron—that can serve as a diamond grit lapping or polishing disk.

CERIC OXIDE (CERIUM OXIDE, CERIA)—A chemically prepared white powder used effectively for polishing quartz, silicate minerals and glass. Colored powders which reflect impurities is equally as effective as more expensive white powder.

CHALK—primarily a calcium carbonate, chalk is white, porous and useful for polishing ivory, bone and equally soft materials.

CHROME OXIDE (CHROMIUM OXIDE, CHROMIC OXIDE—chemically prepared hexagonal particles which produce a greenish powder that is effective for polishing stones of varying hardness (tendency to undercut). It's chief disadvantage is the ability to cause hard-to-remove green stains on porous stones and skin.

COPPER—a popular metal for abrasive and polishing laps, copper has a special affinity for diamond in that it quickly work hardens over diamond particles. Alumina is also used for polishing hard stones on copper.

CORK—not used all that much as a polish carrier because of its relative fragility, cork is nonetheless a fine, soft and granular material that works well with silicon carbide and diamond pastes.

CORUNDUM—natural aluminum oxide or levigated alumina, it has largely been replaced by chemically produced synthetic Al_2O_3.

DIAMOND—cubic carbon which is the hardest substance on earth. Useful as an abrasive and as a polishing agent. Diamond is now synthesized by a number of companies and these particles, consistently blocky and same size, are largely replacing natural diamond. Like all brittle abrasives, though, brittle diamond does break down when bonded or fixed in position and gradually loses its abrasive power.\

EMERY—primarily corundum, emery usually also consists of quartz, hematite and magnetite which makes it a useful prepolishing agent. It's seldom used in lapidary.

FELT—A white, extremely compact and porous material made by interlocking short wood fibers. Favored by cabochon cutters, the rock hard type can still "give" enough so round surfaces can be pressed into its surface. Heat friction builds quickly . Felt undercuts. To form felt over a mold shape, soak it in warm water until it becomes pliable.

GLASS—an amorphous silica, glass plate is very useful for hand working large flats with abrasive grits and metallic oxide polishes. It is quite effective for producing flat surfaces when constructing doublets and triplets

GREASES—the most common substances used for binding polishing agents consist of stearic acid, mutton tallow, vaseline and other past petroleum greases, beeswax, paraffin and some animal and vegetable oils and waxes. Olive oil paste, made from crushed garlic, makes an outstanding binder.

LEAD—identified as a dangerous carcinogen, lead is still an effective soft metal for abrading and polishing soft and sensitive faceted gemstones. It is often used as an alloy with tin and other low temperature metals. When working with lead, remain cautious about dark stains on the fingers (these are lead oxide) and wash them off to avoid ingestion.

LEATHER—extensively used for polishing—as well as some abrasive work—in lapidary, leather is inexpensive, tough, long lasting and accepts heavy pressure without breaking down. The rough side is reserved usually for coarser abrasives and polishes, and the smooth side for fine work. Soaking leather for several hours in water will soften it so it can be stretched over a base lap or a bowl-like holder where it's flexibility accommodates rounded mineral surfaces.

LEVIGATED ALUMINA—When alumina is crushed and graded into uniform size it is referred to as levigated alumina.

MAGNESIUM OXIDE—used mostly for polishing metals and ore specimens, MgO is a white synthetic polishing powder that must be carefully resealed because of the speed with which it alters when exposed to the air. It is used extensively in Germany for polishing (with flannel) pyrite, marcasite and hematite.

PELLON—an excellent man-made material for polishing use with diamond and oxide polishes, including colloidal silica. Use the hard, almost plastic-like Pellon: the soft type used in clothing shops doesn't polish very well. Pellon is more fragile than leather and may tear when wet. It can be highly effective when used with cerium oxide to polish quartz or chalcedony.

PLASTICS—because they are effective with both diamond and metallic oxides, plastic laps are finding increased lapidary use. Lexan, Lucite and Plexiglass are useful as base laps and polishing carriers, especially for cerium oxide. These plastics become worn easily or smear through frictional heat and need to be dressed or repaired. Thin film (3- and 4-mil thickness) plastics such as Mylar and Acetate make excellent polishing laps for faceted stones, especially as convenient slip laps to be fitted over the larger diameter prepolishing lap. A 3- or 4-ply vinyl, sometimes described as engraving stock, works as a polishing lap, but other plastics are superior—except for old 4-ply vinyl phonograph records which make excellent polishing laps for soft stones, thanks to the grooves *i.e.*, scoring.

PLYWOOD—when coated with or soaked in paraffin before use, plywood makes an excellent abrasive or polishing disk. Be sure to use plywood that has been faced with a birch, maple or other hard, suitable wood laminate.

PUMICE—a volcanic obsidian, pumice in the past had been used as a loose grit on buffs for smoothing gems. It's no longer used much. A pumice block, though, is still very useful for removing the glaze on Lexan or Plexiglass laps.

ROTTENSTONE—a derivative of limestone with the calcium removed, it contains enough silica to be once used as a gem polishing agent. Similar to Tripoli so the names are used interchangeably.

RUBY POWDER (RUBY DIX, SAPPHIRE POWDER)—various names for polishing powders made from crushed synthetic corundum.

SLIP LAP (MINI LAP)—a thin polishing disk of either metal or plastic whose diameter is reduced to about 4" so it can be slipped atop the prepolishing lap allowing prepolishing and polishing to be performed quickly and conveniently with minimum machine adjustments. The plastic slip laps of choice are Mylar and Acetate: the metal ones are tin, copper, phospor bronze and, sometimes, stainless steel.

TIN—often alloyed with lead or typemetal, tin is a soft and highly reliable polishing lap material for either diamond or metallic oxides. Tin oxide polish immediately establishes a tough oxide film over a pure tin lap, virtually eliminating the possibility of scratching. A diluted acid strengthens the oxide film while reducing pH, thus comprising a very effective polishing combination.

TIN OXIDE (STANNIC OXIDE)—an insoluble, tetragonal shaped particle which in white powder form remains one of lapidary's most popular, effective polishing agents.

TRIPOLI—uniform quartz particles largely used in polishing precious metals, tripoli's role in gem polishing has largely been replaced by better, less messier (it stains terribly) agents.

ULTRALAP™—a trade marked name, owned by Moyco of Philadelphia, PA, for its line of inexpensive, thin Mylar laps that have been coated with either diamond or one of the metallic oxide polishes. Used mostly by faceters over a wetted base lap or as slip laps, they also work well on cabochons, too, when used over a foam or rubber backed disk.

WAX—most wax laps are self-made by pouring molten wax into a mold, by applying molten wax over a fabric covered disk, by attaching strips of Kerr wax on a disk and trimming, by coating a Mylar or Acetate film with a wax saturated cloth or by cutting a disk out of a sheet of wax. The material obviously deforms quickly but it can be reworked by wetting with Benzene or lighter fluid and then rubbing vigorously with a cloth or a smooth agate. Particularly effective for polishing soft stones because it provides a soft, shock free polishing surface, wax will accept both diamond and metallic oxides.

WOOD—wood laps and wheels have fallen off in lapidary popularity, but the material still provides a fine polishing carrier. Lapidary use requires a hard, end grain wood soaked first in paraffin to make it water proof.

ZIRCONIUM DIOXIDE (ZIRCONIA)—like magnesium oxide, $ZrO2$ is used mostly for polishing metals and ore specimens. It is favored by German lapidaries as a polish for pyrite and hematite.

Appendix 3

Avoirdupois and Troy Weight Chart

AVOIRDUPOIS WEIGHT

1 pound = 16 ounces = 7000 grains
1 ounce = 28.35 grams
1 ounce = 437.5 grains

Quartz = 163 pounds avdp. per cu. ft.
       = .0943 pounds avdp. per cu. in.
       = 1.509 ounces avdp. per cut. in
       = 6601 grains per cu. in.
       = 1 gram = .2859 inch cube
       = 1 carat = .1672 inch cube

TROY WEIGHT

1 pound = 12 ounces = 5760 grains
1 ounce = 20 pennyweights (dwt.) = 480 grains
1 ounce = 31.103 grams

GEMOLOGICAL WEIGHTS

Conversion Tables
Carat—one carat equals 0.200 milligrams by the International Metric Standards. Do not confuse "carat" with the word "karat" which is a statement of gold's fineness.
1 Gram = 5 Carats
1 Carat = 200 Milligrams
1 Kilogram = 1000 Grams
1 Ounce = 141.5 Carats

1 Ounce = 28.3 Grams
1 Pound = 433.6 Grams
2.2 Pounds = 1000.0 Grams
    GRAIN: (1/4 Metric Carat or 0.0500 Metric Grain)
1 Gram = 15.4 Grains (avdp.) 3.858 Carats
3/4 Gram = 11.624 Grains (avdp.) 2.906 Carats
1/2 Gram = 7.716 Grains (avdp.) 1.9295 Carats
1/4 Gram = 3.858 (avdp.) .9645 Carats
1/8 Gram = 1.9029 Grains (avdp.) .482 Carats
1 Pearl Grain = 1/20 of a Gram
1 Carat = 4 Pearl Grains
    Comment: A pearl grain and an avdp. grain are not equal.

GEMOLOGICAL MEASUREMENTS

1 Inch = 25.3 Millimeters
1 Millimeter = 1/25 inch
12 Inches = 1 Foot = 0.3048 Meter
3 Feet = 1 Yard = 0.9144 Meter
5,280 Feet = 1 (Statute) Mile = 1/6093 Kilometers

CLARK STANDARD SIZES FOR ROCKS

1mm or less = particle
1mm to 1/8 inch = fragment
1/8 inch to 2 1/2 inches = pebble
2 1/2 inches to 10 1/2 inches = cobble
over 10 1/2 inches = boulder

Bibliography

Anderson, B. W.—*Gem Testing.*, 6th ed., London: Heywood & Co., Ltd., 1958—Useful and practical treatment of gem identification techniques and theory

Arem, Joel—*Rocks and Minerals*, New York, Bantam Books, 1973—Contains excellent section on crystal structure. Useful mineral information.

Dana, J. D.—*Manual of Mineralogy*, New York, John Wiley & Sons, 1975—Valuable reference for information on various gems

Greenbaum, Walter—*The Gemstone Identifier*, New York, Prentice Hall 1983—Useful gemological information.

Leiper, Hugh—*Gem Cutting Shop Helps*, San Diego, CA, Lapidary Journal, 1964—Dated, but many methods and techniques on lapidary skills are still valid.

Ng, John Y and Root, Edmond—*Jade For You* Los Angeles, CA, Jade N Gem Corp. 1984—Excellent book on jade, with explanation of Chinese method of waxing.

O'Donoghue, Michael—*Encyclopedia of Minerals and Gemstones*, London, Orbis Publishing Ltd, 1976—Outstanding resource for all mineralogical entries

Pough, Frederick H.—*Peterson First Guides: Rocks and Minerals*, Boston, Houghton Mifflin Company 1991—Contains some useful information about minerals.

Read, Peter G.—*Gemmology*, Oxford, England, Butterworth-Heinemann Ltd. 1991—An excellent resource for gemological information

Roberts, W. L. Rapp, G. R. and Weber, J.—*Encyclopaedia of Minerals*, New York and London, Van Nostrand Reinhold Co. 1974— A comprehensive reference for each mineral

Schumann, Walter, *Gemstones of the World*, New York, Sterling Publishing Co. 1977—Best work of its kind.

Shore, Eric—*Lapidary for Pleasure & Profit*, London, John Gifford Ltd. 1978— A good introductory text.

Sinkankas, John—*Gem Cutting: A Lapidary's Manual*, New York: Van Nostrand Reinhold Company, 1962—Contains useful information on polishing.
—*Gemstone & Mineral Data Book*, New York, Van Nostrand Reinhold Company, 1972—Wide ranging collection of data and information on lapidary

Soukop, E. J.—*Facet Cutters Handbook*, Mentone, California: Gemac Corp. 1959—Excellent short treatise on faceting and polishing

Sorrelll, Charles A.—*Rocks and Minerals*, Racine, WI, Golden Press 1973—Good intro to mineralogy and the chemistry of minerals

Sperisen, F. J.—*The Art of the Lapidary*, 2nd Ed., Milwaukee: Bruce Publishing Co., 1961— Contains useful and still valid information on the techniques of polishing gemstones

Vargas, Glenn—*Amateur Faceting*, Palm Desert, California, Desert Printers 1969— Dated, but still contains useful information about faceting and polishing.

Webster, revised by W. W. Anderson—*Gems: Their Sources, Descriptions and Identification*, Oxford, England, Butterworth & Company Ltd. 1990—Good resource for gem data

Willems, J. Daniel, Gem Cutting, Peoria, IL Chas. A. Bennett Co. 1948—Dated, but still contains useful data on polishing gems.

Winchell, A. N. and Winchell, H. J.—*Elements of Optical Mineralogy*, 4th Ed., New York, John Wiley, 195—Good work in a vital area

Wykoff, Gerald—*Master Faceting*, Washington DC, Adamas Publishers, 1985—The best work in the field of faceting and polishing
—*Master Jewelry Design*, Washington DC, Adamas Publishers, 1987—Contains information on polishing and gem enhancement
—*Beyond the Glitter*, Washington DC Adamas Publishers, 1989 —A good beginner's book on gemology with useful information on polishing and treatment of gems.
—*Master Gemcutting Tips*, Washington DC Adamas Publishers, 1992—Numerous techniques on proper polishing techniques

Index

A

AAA rule........................ 200
absorption, water.............. ...5
accordion bottle.....42, 46, 260
acetate film..............7, 29, 277
acetone 19
adamantine...............123, 173
adhesion factor 231
adhesion, olive oil 147
adularescence 175
aggregation 48
air-float tripoli 61
Alpha supply 291
alumina............... 67, 200, 298
aluminum laps..................267
aluminum oxide 53
American Gemcutter
 Magazine...............104, 141
American Society of
 Gemcutters...............11, 297
anistropic 176
anodized aluminized
 lap............................207-8,
 277, 281
apochromatic lens 291
Arizona, University.......13,23,
 80, 86
asterism .... .175
Attack 199
Augsberger, Willard 147
Australian opal.........199, 297
avoirdupois .... .303

B

Bean, Phil 9, 225
beeswax.......................... 277
Beilby 9, 51, 63, 65, 151
biaxial gems 98
bifocals 168
black felt pen................... 221
bleaching.................188, 191
blockers 205
boost......................... 72, 80
boron carbide...........142, 262, 298
brass 267-8, 299
brilliance 172
brillianteerer................... 206
Brinell, Rockwell and
 Vickers 88
bronze.................267-8, 299
Bruce bar 36, 79, 84
Buehler Ltd................24, 81, 105, 109
buffing wheels 19
buffs 52
 canvas..................... 52
 leather..................... 52
 muslin..................... 52
 velvet..................... 52
 felt 52
 wood..................... 52
buttons 75

C

cabochon (polishing).......... 1
cabochon equipment 297
cadmium 248
Calibrated Jamb Peg 208
canvas............................ 299
canvas............................ 71
Carbopol 56

Carborundum......... 153, 299
carnauba wax..........233, 299
carriers for polish 7
 felt 7
 pellon 7
 wood.............................8
 wax..............................8
cast iron.................255, 299
casting resin 160
cat hairs 93
ceramic lap 4, 38, 146, 250
ceric oxide (cerium oxide, ceria)................................ 299
ceramic............................277
cerium oxide 66
chalk 299
Charles Pfizer Company..225
chatoyancy 175
cheek method 70
Childers, Carl 109
Chinese 263
chrome oxide (chromium oxide, chromix oxide)..... 299
chromatic aberration 291

chrome oxide 53
circuit board (copper) 137
circuit board 140
Clark standard 304
Clark, Don 70
cloth 62
coarse texture, gems 120
coated films 22
coffer dam 81
coffer dame 19
Coke 199
Colgate toothpaste 218
colloidal 11
colloidal oxide polishes 23
colloidal paste, gems 121
colloidal silica 13, 23, 80,
 104, 109
contaminant 127
contemporary polishing
 theory 85
Cook, Don 146
coolant 251
copper 267, 270, 277, 299
copper lap 137
copper wire 43
Corian lap 273, 277, 295
cork 199, 299
corundum 149, 300
crossed filters 290
crust 136
crystal pad 9
Crystalite 297
Crystalite Corp 45, 203
Crystalite poly pad 110
Cubic Boron Nitride 262
cubic zirconia 158
curved surface 43
cyanoacrylate 136

D

Damascus powder 67
damp-dry 50, 71, 79, 201
dark-field illumination 286
dedicated pads 129
detergent 69
diamond 300
diamond boart SA 257
diamond paste 34, 146
diamond scratch theory ... 63
diamontine 67
diasterism 175
dichroism 290
difficulty, polishing 15
 cabochon 16
 faceted 16
dislocation 125
double refraction 98
dry sanding 31
dull luster 123
dyeing tigereye 194
Dyna Ltd 45, 198, 296

E

edge rounding 230
Edmund Scientific ... 16-8, 291
Elmer's glue 209
emery 300
epiasterism 175
Exacto blade 18
faceter's hands 248

F

Facetron 27
Fast Lap 5
feldspars 74
felt 62, 70, 300
ferric streaking 254
fiber optics 285
fine grained, gems 118

finger chargng 139
focus 285
Ford, Rick 11
Foredo 2
formica 17
Fresnel 176
Fruitman, Clint 13

G

garlic 37
gelatin 70
gemological measurements
 274
gemological weights 304
gemstone minerals 112
General Electric Co. 144, 164
genus allium. 37
glass 300
glass polishing 151
glasses, safety 135
glastic 100
glazed 262
Goodrich, B. F. 56
graphite 260
Graves & A & tin-
lead 4, 78
Gray, James 32
grease pencil 31
greases 300
greasy 123, 173

H

Halogen 144, 164
hand lapping 141
hard/durable, gems 116
Harris, Hap 271
heat treating 189
heavy chage 257
high fiber mineral 54
high melting point 60
hydrogen 125

Hypnolap 45

I

illumination 283
imperfections, polish 91
immersion cell 289
incident light 283
iridescence 174
iris agate 202
isoelectric 126
isotropic 176
Italian 207

J

Jackson, Cliff 95
jade 52, 55, 90,
169, 195, 261
jamb peggers 207
Jarvi 158, 295

K

Kerr 95
kilo 257
Knoops 88

L

labradorescence 175
lap material hardness 235
lapper 17
Last Lap 5, 149
lead 247, 300, 277
leather 63, 255, 300
leathers types in lapidary ..255
    buffalo 255
    calfskin 255
    camelskin 255
    chamois 255
    cowhide 255
    deerskin 255
    goatskin 256
    horsehide 256

kidskin 256
    lambskin 256
    pigskin 256
    sheepskin 256
Lee, Darrell 45
Leeco company 45
Leiper, Hugh 58
levigated alumina 67, 301
light field 285, 288
ight management 162
lilium tribe 37
Linde A 65, 259
Lindquist, C. Allen 6
looking style 163
lubricant 251
lucite 39, 277
luster 122, 171, 174

M

Maalox 83
mAgi 11, 273, 295
magnesium oxide 301
magnesium, gems 125
magnification 286
magnifier 166
malachite 254
mandrel 76
marks, polishing 126
MasterFaceting 223, 271
Mastermet 81, 105, 109
MDR 27, 50, 296
Mehanite 4, 158,
197, 198, 273
melting points, polish 66
metal 61
metallized resin 277
metallic luster 123
metallic 173
micarta 17
Michelangelo 196
Michelsen, Sofus 207

microscope 290
mini lap 302
mini wheel 75-76, 78
mirror 215-221
Mohs 88
Mohs hardness (scale) 154
Montana sapphire 205, 207
Moyco 135, 225
Munsteiner 135
muriatic acid 188
Murphy, Merrill O. 232
Mylar 5, 229, 277

N

Nagel, Sidne 264
National Bureau of Standards
.... 151
New England Wood Company 75
New Era Gems 296
northern lights 285

O

olive oil 34, 272
olive oil paste 32, 34, 37
OMF machine 44
onyx 197
opal 71
Opti-Visor 91, 164, 166
optic axis 98
orange peel 54
orientation 286
overlay laps 282
oxalic acid 196, 200
oxide polishes 39

P

paint spray 101
pearly 173
pebble finish 94
pelletized lap 3, 5, 47

Pellon.........28, 106, 301, 281
Pepsi 199
pearly................................ 123
petroleum jelly 160
pewter............................... 277
pH...................................... 69
phenolic............................ 277
phonograph record
    lap.............................8, 214
photo-transistor 173
Physical Review Letter ... 266
pie pan polisher 71
pink castingwax 17
plastic deformation............ 89
plastic lap 5
plastics............................. 301
Plexiglas...100, 128, 202, 277
plywood 301
polariscope 96
polarizer 290
polish carriers.................. 185
    cotton velvet.............. 187
    canvas......................... 185
    felt 185
    leather......................... 185
    muslin......................... 187
    pellon 187
    thin films 187
polish difficulties..............119
polish paste 83
polish recommendations. .178
    tin oxide 178
    chrome oxide.............. 178
    aluminum oxide 179
    cerium oxide.............. 179
    diamond 180
    tripoli......................... 180
polishing combinations ...236
polishing combinations....159
polishing problems 254
Poly Metric.................27, 44

polyurethane.....................277
porosity 3
potpourii 196
powder..............................10
powder (mixing)...............264
preformer block................. 76
prepolish.......................... 260
prepolishing..................... 196
prepolishing 201
pressure 72
profit.................................. 31
pulverization theory 224
pumice 301

R

reflectance (list) 176
reflectance, interior 171
reflection 165
reflectivity 171
repeatability.............. 26, 130
resin 38
resinous....................123, 173
rhodonite 169
RI liquid 289
Rocks & Gem Magazine...54
rottenstone................. 61, 301
rouge 156
rough.......................295, 296
ruby powder (ruby dix, sapphire powder)................302

S

sander-polisherlap 210
sapphire cabochons, polishing
   169
Saran wrap 192
scintillator 295
score.................................. 15
scoring 47
scratch theory 151
7-UP..................................199

shadowing........................286
shaping 152
sheen................................174
shiller................................175
shimmying 28
shorthand, polishes..........259
silky 123, 173
Sinkankas, John................ 28
slip....................................89
slip lap.....................302, 267
soluble ink .... .144
Spanish 37
special handling, gems.....116
species, gems 114
Spectralap...............135, 214
sponge.............................. 201
spray diamond................. 235
streaking (See ferric) peridot
   255

stress stone .... .86
subadamantine...........123, 173
suction, water 232
superglue 134
surface............................. 172
swift polishing gems....... 121
swipe polish 261
synthetics 245
safety 247

T

Taiwan.............................279
trifocals 168
theory, gem polishing...... 63
thickness 25
thin polishing films 221
thin metal lap..................266
thin sections.......39, 161, 202
three A rule 249
tigereye............................ 188

tin 277, 302
tin lap 4
tin/lead lap 4, 277
tin oxide (stannic
    oxide) 53, 302
titanium 267
tourmaline 258
transillumination 283
transparent, gems 116
Trewax 233
tripoli 302
troy weight 303
turquoise 73
type metal lap 4, 277

U

U. S. Botanical Gardens 37
Ultralap .. 6, 197, 223, 266, 302
uniaxial gems 98
Union Carbide 196, 259

V

Vale, Stephen 274
Vargas, glen 225
Vaseline 38
vitreous 123, 173
vinegar 69, 200
vinyl 277

W

Watermeyer, Basil 207
wax 302
wax coating 273
wax lap 95
wet sanding 31
wetting water 69
Willems, J. Daniel 108
wood 61, 302
wood types (list) 253
wood wheels 252
wooden points 2

Z

zinc 277
zirconium dioxide 303

Other Outstanding Lapidary Books
by Gerald L. Wykoff CSM GG

Beyond the Glitter *Hardcover 206 pp $17.95*
Hailed by critics as an outstanding introduction to gemology, this book provides a comprehensive review of gem and jewelry knowledge. If you don't have the time to commit to a long, formal study of gemology this book will give you the knowhow you need. ISBN 0-9607892-6-X

The Techniques of Master Faceting *Hardcover 234 pp. $24.50*
Acknowledged as the "Bible" of faceting, this remarkable book is the most comprehensive book ever written on faceting gems. It covers the optical and gemological aspects of various gem species, enabling cutters to retrieve maximum performance in yield. ISBN 0-9607982-2-7

The Techniques of Master Stonesetting *Hardcover 212 pp. $24.50*
Every possible technique and method for setting gemstone sis described and illustrated in this best selling book. Tools, setting methods, gem characteristics, optics and even metal finished are treated. ISBN 0-9607892-3-5

The Techniques of Master Jewelry Design and Creation
Hardcover 276 pp. $24.50
If you can trace a straight line, cut a piece of paper and glue, you can design and create fine jewelry featuring precious metals and gemstones like a pro. Introduces TIM (temporary impression molding). ISBN 0-9607892-5-1

Master Gemcutting Tips *Papercover 170 pp. $14.95*
Here is a comprehensive collection of the best and most advanced tips and techniques on gem cutting ever collected. Also included are instructions for easily making your own tools, equipment. ISBN 0-9607892-7-8

The Master Keys to Profits in Lapidary *Papercover 170pp $19.95*
If you wish to produce income from your lapidary skills, this book contains hundreds of unique ideas to make money either as a hobbyist or as a professional. ISBN 0-9607892-8-6

Send Your Orders (plus $3 s/h) to
Adamas Publishesrs
PO Box 1991
York, PA 17405